1000 FRY'S SIGHT WORDS

1000+ INTERACTIVE ACTIVITIES

LEARN TO READ ACTIVITY BOOK FOR KIDS

This book belongs to

Wonder House

Introduction

Welcome to the wonderful world of high-frequency sight words.

The Fry list contains 1,000 words and includes all parts of speech. They are broken down into groups of 100, focusing on a few words at a time until a student memorize the entire list.

Combining explicit phonics instruction with Fry's list of sight words, this combination helps children quickly build fluency by providing a base of words they recognize on sight and a method for decoding unfamiliar words.

Fry words are often taught as early as kindergarten. You can begin introducing Fry words once children are familiar with the alphabet and letter sounds. Start with only 5 to 10 words. Once the child masters that list, add 5 to 10 more, but continue to review the previously mastered words.

Help your children master the Fry words quickly and easily by making learning fun and keeping them engaged with this workbook packed with 1000 Fry Words. Each word includes a practice section where the child will trace and write the word along with a fun activity.

Through different activities which focus on specific spelling skills, this book will help children to be better readers by exposing them to high-frequency words. The more fluent the child is as a reader, the better he will be in understanding what he reads.

So let the learning and fun begin!

the

Trace the word.

the the the

How many times can you spot the?
Count and write.

if

him

the

the

you

are

the

his

○ times

of

Trace the word.

of of of

Circle each bee with the of board.

of   of   he

me   she

you   of   of

and

Trace the word.

and and and

Spot and 3 times and color it.

a	r	h	o	e
a	n	d	g	n
n	w	t	z	p
d	b	v	x	w
f	e	a	n	d

a

Trace the word.

a   a   a

Color each apple that has an a.

a   of   is   a

it   as   am   a

to

Trace the word.

to   to   to

Help the cat reach its mat. Color the cushions with to.

to	to	his	go
fun	to	to	did
her	pop	has	to	to
the	the	go	am

in

Trace the word.

in   in   in

Color each fish scale red that has in. Color the rest of your choice.

do as in is
if in it he
him is no in
in go to a

is

Trace the word.

is   is   is

Circle each pair of glasses that spell is.

is is   as as

do do   ok ok

is is

you

Trace the word.

you you you

Find the word you. Draw a line to connect the letters.

y s m s u

c d o o l

that

Trace the word.

that that that

Fill in the missing letters to get that.

t	h		t
	h		t
t		a	
t			t

it

Trace the word.

it   it   it

Connect the dots with it to finish the picture.

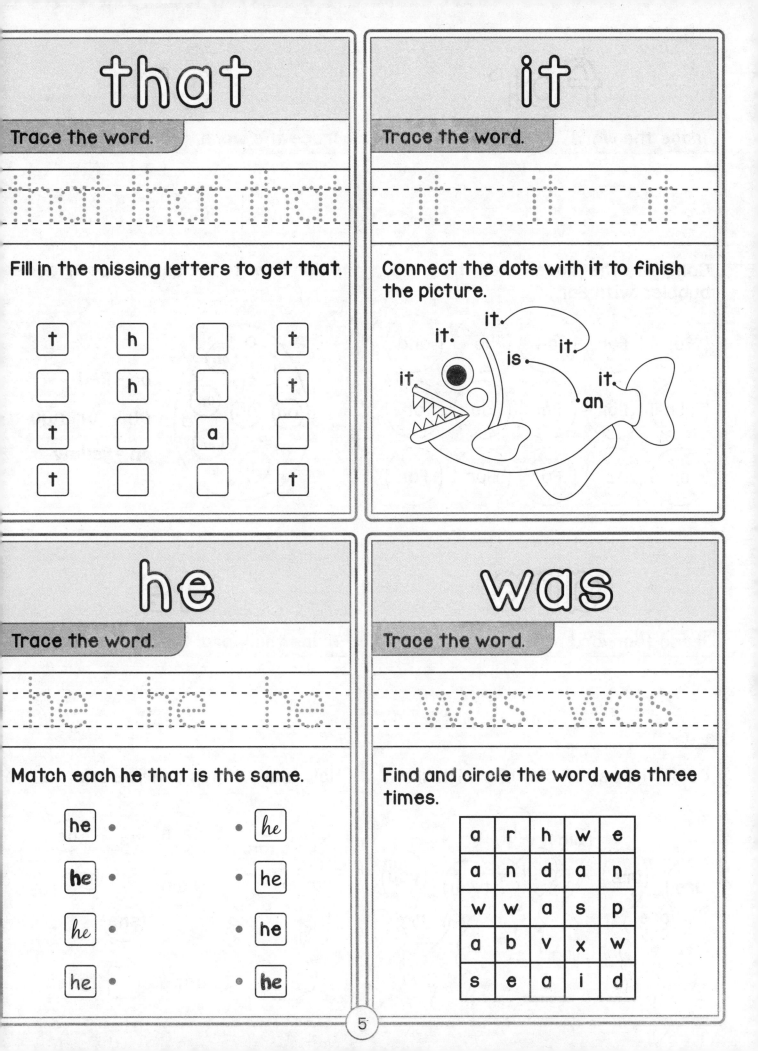

it.
it.
it
is
it.
it.
an

he

Trace the word.

he   he   he

Match each he that is the same.

he •   • he
he •   • he
he •   • he
he •   • he

was

Trace the word.

was   was

Find and circle the word was three times.

a	r	h	w	e
a	n	d	a	n
w	w	a	s	p
a	b	v	x	w
s	e	a	i	d

for

Trace the word.

for for for

Complete the maze. Color the bubbles with **for**.

for	for	an	is	and
run	for	for	do	or
or	it	for	for	for

on

Trace the word.

on on on

Color **on** with the correct color code.

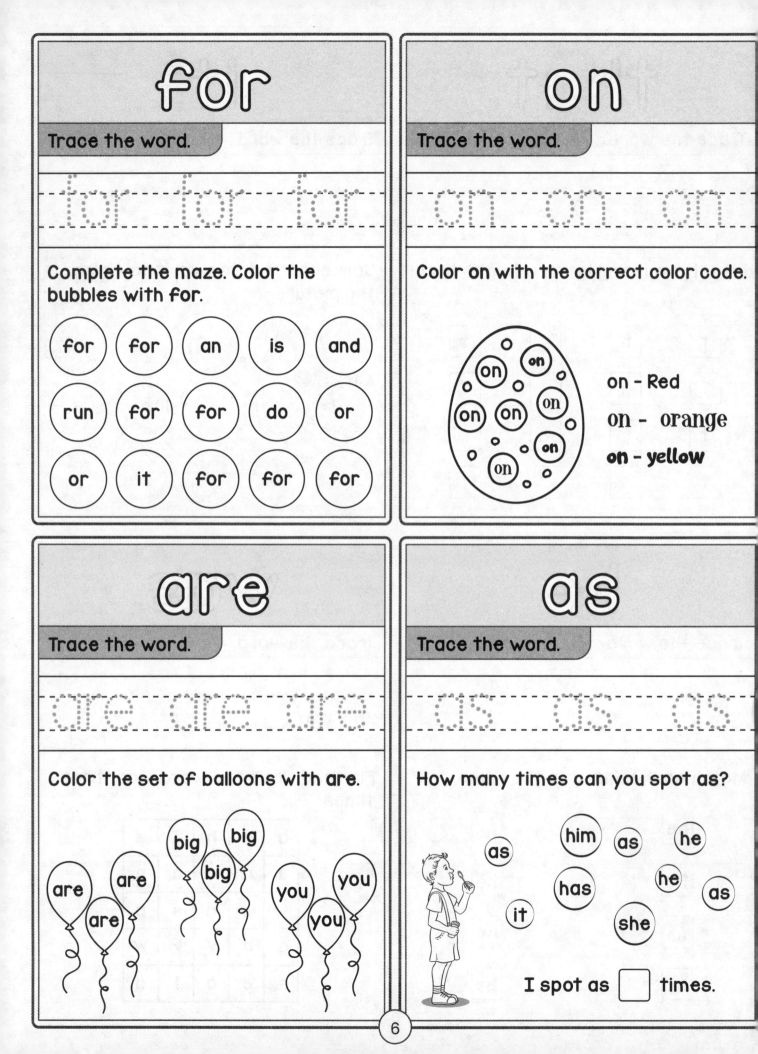

on – Red

on – orange

on – yellow

are

Trace the word.

are are are

Color the set of balloons with **are**.

are are are
big big big
you you you

as

Trace the word.

as as as

How many times can you spot **as**?

as   him   as   he
has   he
it   as
she

I spot as ☐ times.

with

Trace the word.

with   with

Color the letters to find with.

a	v	c	e	v	w	t
d	e	p	a	d	f	b	i	j	h
	j	w	i	t	j	e	b	a	g	a
p	a	g	a	h	a	t	a	p	g	i
c							w	h

his

Trace the word.

his his his

Circle the word his.

- Matt left his tie in school.
- Joy and his brother are off to the zoo.
- She praised him for his honesty.
- Rendel bought his son a camera.
- Matt rode his bike to school.

they

Trace the word.

they they

Help the calf reach its mama. Color the path with letters that spell they.

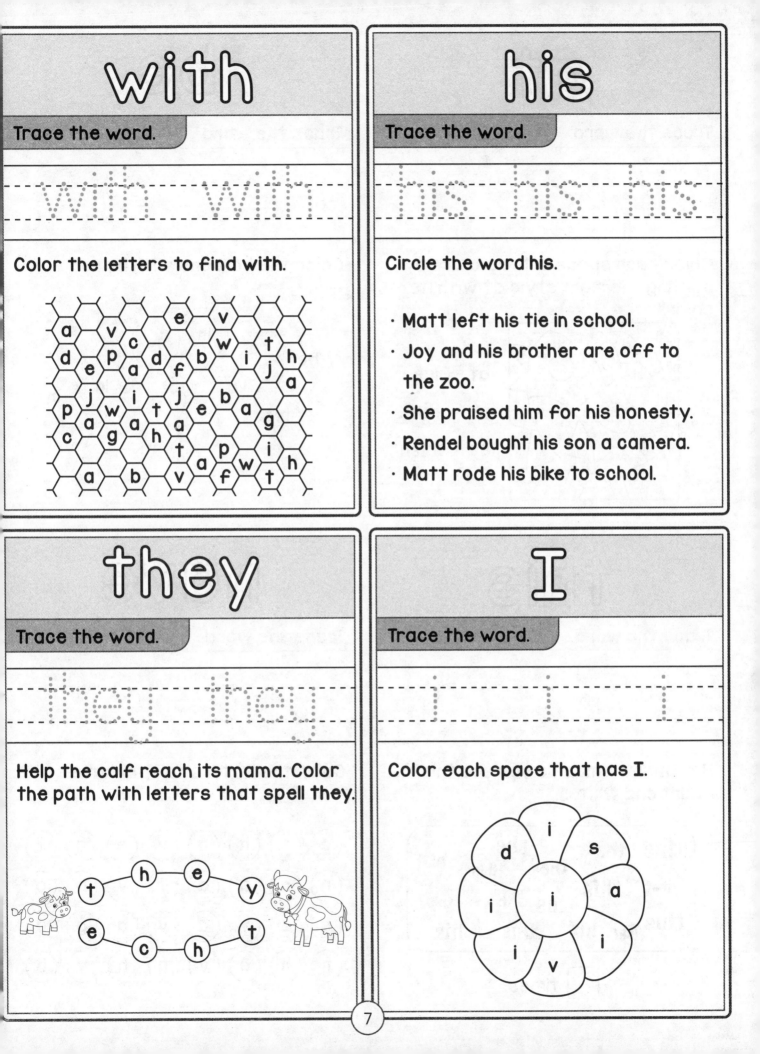

I

Trace the word.

i   i   i

Color each space that has I.

at

Trace the word.

at at at

Color each space in the picture by sorting the right style at with its color.

at - Blue

at - Pink

at - Green

be

Trace the word.

be be be

Color the balloons with **be** red.

this

Trace the word.

this this this

How many times do you see this? Count and write.

this the the
that this the this her
this his that this
this her his this his

□ times.

have

Trace the word.

have have

Color the letters to spell **have**.

a s h a v e g l
r n a d t v b o
a z v a v a g p
r h e v a h y h

from

Trace the word.

from from

Connect the dots to spell from.
Find the word two times.

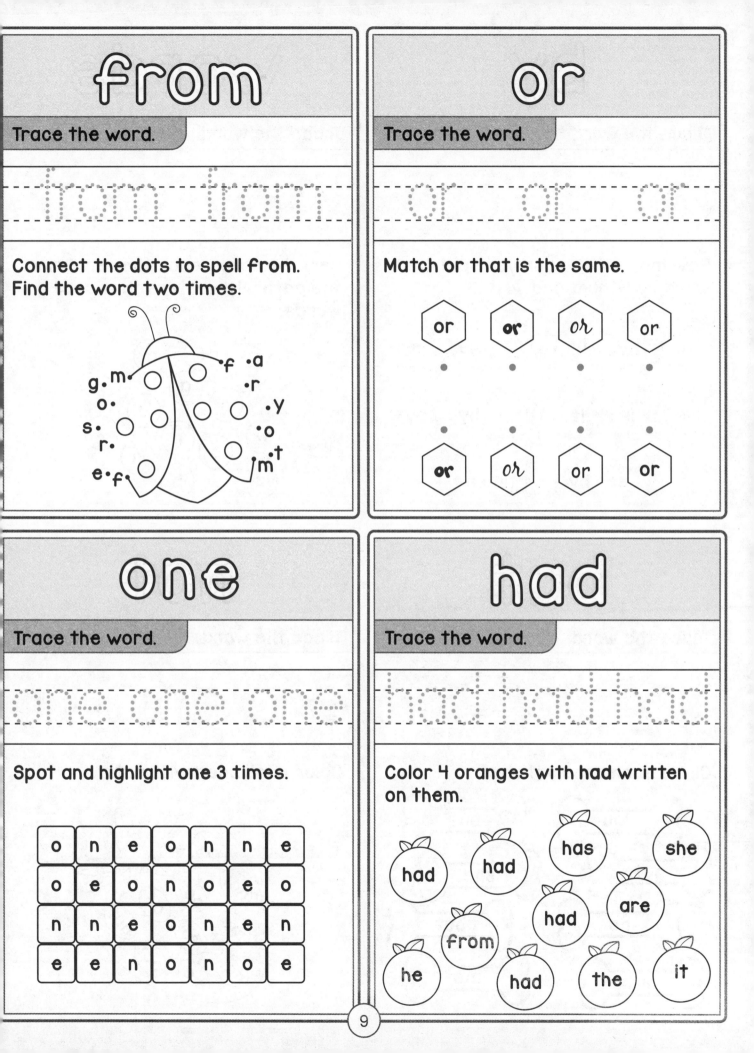

g. m f •a
o. •r
s. •y
r. •o
e•f m• t

or

Trace the word.

or   or   or

Match or that is the same.

or   or   or   or

or   or   or   or

one

Trace the word.

one one one

Spot and highlight one 3 times.

o	n	e	o	n	n	e
o	e	o	n	o	e	o
n	n	e	o	n	e	n
e	e	n	o	n	o	e

had

Trace the word.

had had had

Color 4 oranges with had written on them.

had   had   has   she

had   are

from

he   had   the   it

by

Trace the word.

by by by

How many times can you spot the word by? Count and write.

by □ by
he □ he
he □ he
is □ is
it □ it
by □ by

I see by □ times.

words

Trace the word.

words words

Help the chick reach the hen. Color the path with letters that spell words.

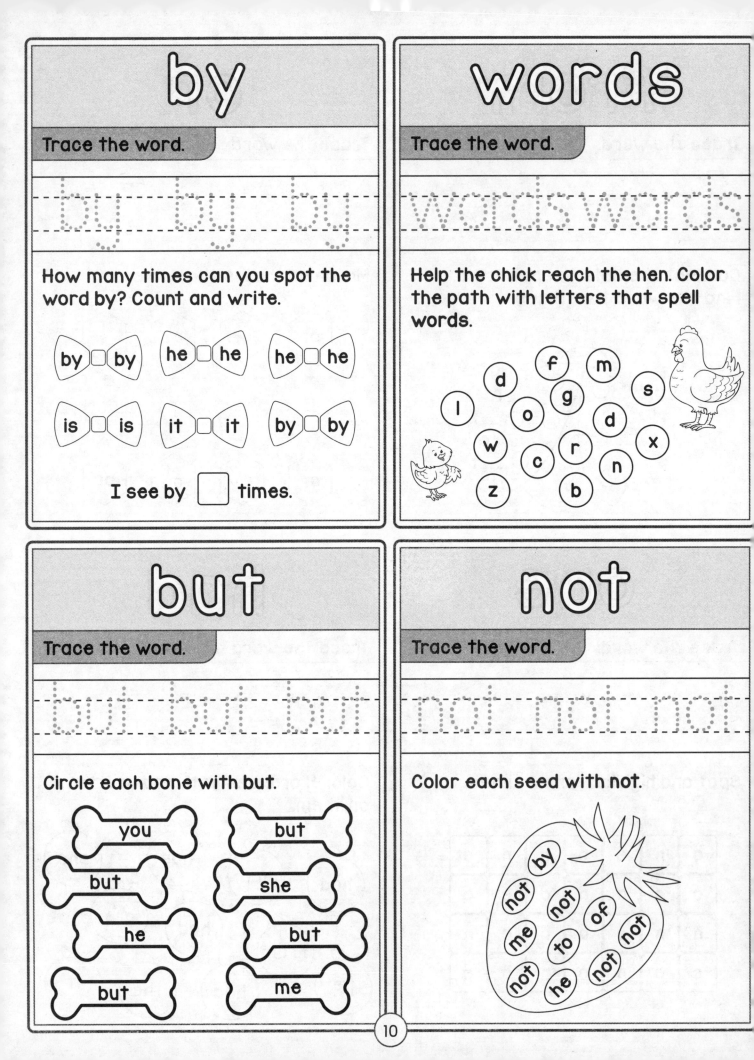

but

Trace the word.

but but but

Circle each bone with but.

you
but
but
she
he
but
but
me

not

Trace the word.

not not not

Color each seed with not.

what

Trace the word.

what what

Spot and highlight what 4 times.

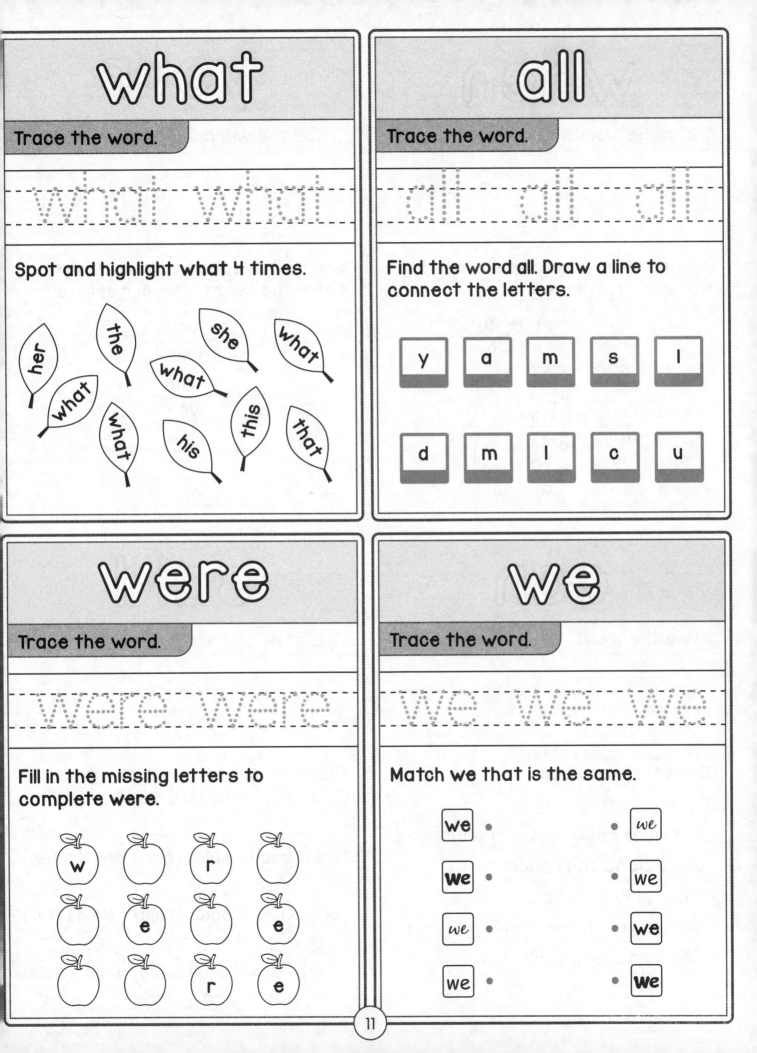

her

the

she

what

what

what

what

this

his

that

all

Trace the word.

all all all

Find the word all. Draw a line to connect the letters.

| y | a | m | s | l |

| d | m | l | c | u |

were

Trace the word.

were were

Fill in the missing letters to complete were.

w   r

e   e

r   e

we

Trace the word.

we we we

Match we that is the same.

we •   • we

we •   • we

we •   • we

we •   • we

when

Trace the word.

when when

Connect the dots to spell when. Find the word two times.

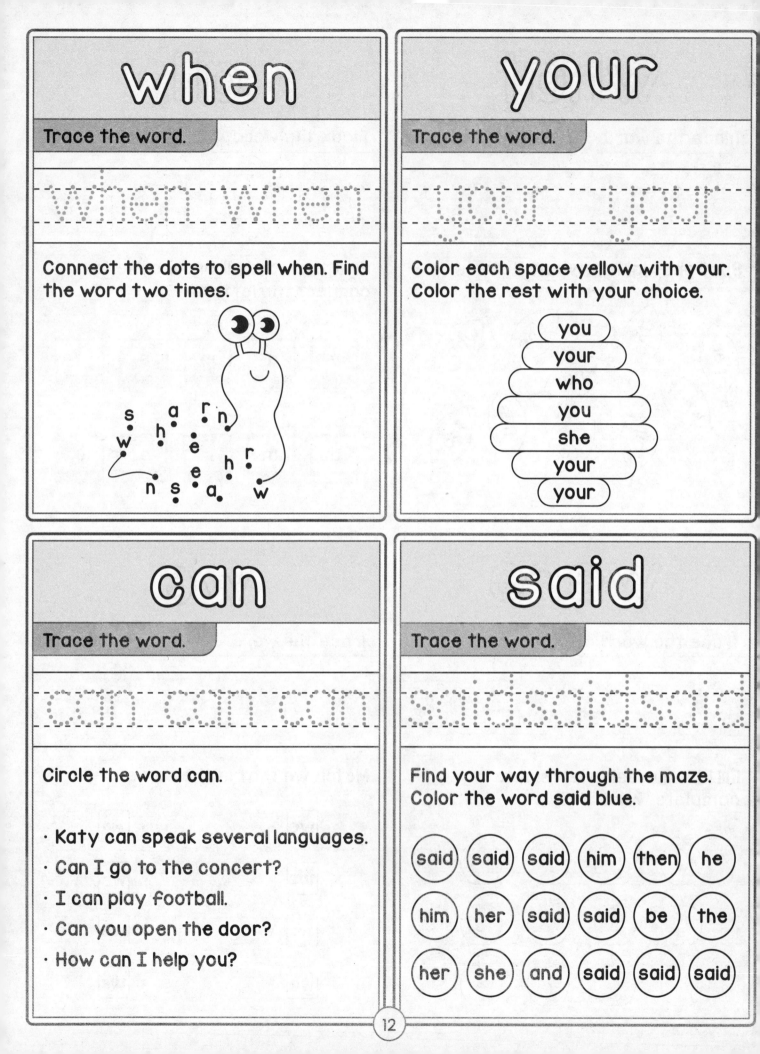

your

Trace the word.

your your

Color each space yellow with your. Color the rest with your choice.

you
your
who
you
she
your
your

can

Trace the word.

can can can

Circle the word can.

· Katy can speak several languages.
· Can I go to the concert?
· I can play football.
· Can you open the door?
· How can I help you?

said

Trace the word.

said said said

Find your way through the maze. Color the word said blue.

said said said him then he
him her said said be the
her she and said said said

there

there there there

Write the first letter of each picture to get there.

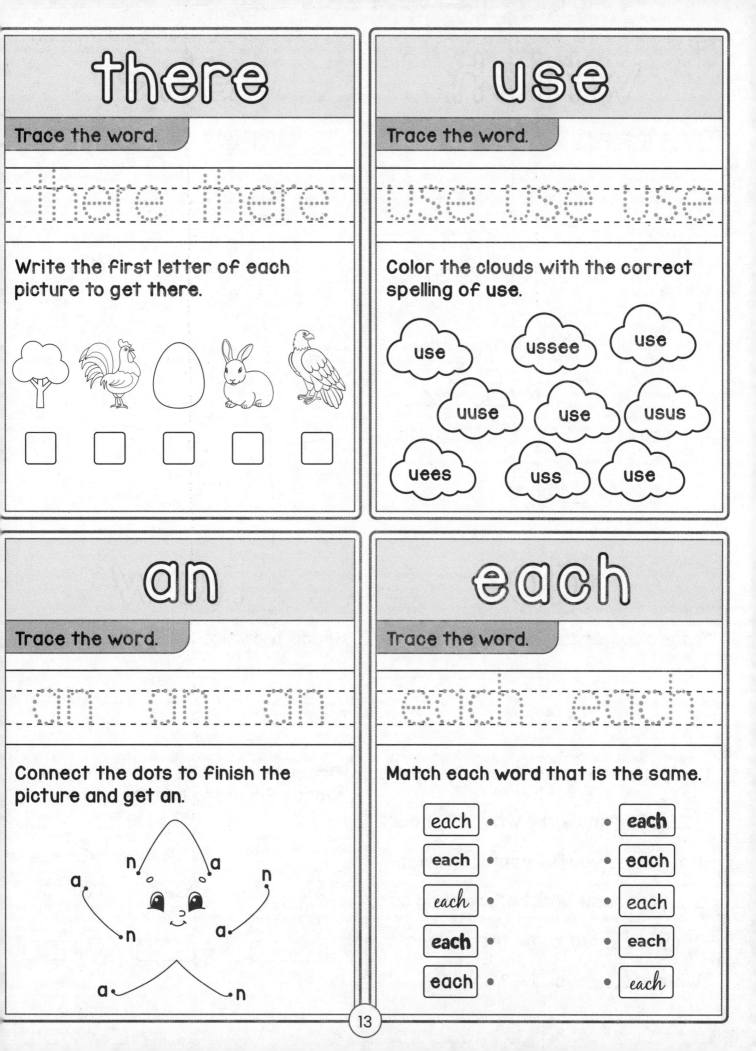

use

Trace the word.

use use use

Color the clouds with the correct spelling of use.

use   ussee   use

uuse   use   usus

uees   uss   use

an

Trace the word.

an an an

Connect the dots to finish the picture and get an.

n   a
a   n
a   n   a
a   n

each

Trace the word.

each each

Match each word that is the same.

each •   • each
each •   • each
each •   • each
each •   • each
each •   • each

13

which

which which

How many times can you spot which?

- your
- which
- the
- each
- there
- which
- can
- which

☐ times.

she

Trace the word.

she she she

Connect the dots to spell she. Find the word two times.

s   h
            e
e
   h   s

do

Trace the word.

do do do

Complete the sentences by using do.

- _____ you know the way to school
- How _____ you like your ice cream?
- ____your homework before going out.
- They _____ not know the answer.
- Where _____ you live?

how

Trace the word.

how how

Observe the icons and write new words from the letters of how.

h ☐   o ☐   w ☐

14

Let's Revise!

1. Fill in the blanks with the correct words. (when, and, your, from, was).

· John _____ Mira went to play.

· Cecelia got the book _____ the store.

· There _____ a dog rolling in the snow.

· _____ is the match?

· How is _____ mother?

2. Circle the articles in the given sentences.

· An apple a day keeps the doctor away.

· The ball is in your court.

· She is a bit under the weather.

· Humpty Dumpty sat on a wall.

· In rainy days, use an umbrella.

3. Underline the prepositions.

· The cat is in the hat.

· Mike went with his father to hike.

· The dog barks at her.

· Where did you come from?

· There are ghosts in the forest.

4. Use the given 2-letter words correctly. (of, to, on, be, by).

· The Queen _____ England died.

· This is like cherry _____ top.

· Take the road _____ the lake.

· Let's go _____ the playground.

· You _____ on your way.

their

Trace the word.

their their

Fill in the missing letters to complete their.

t		e		r
	h		i	r
t	h			
		e	i	r

if

Trace the word.

if if if

Color each space pink that has if. Color the rest with your choice.

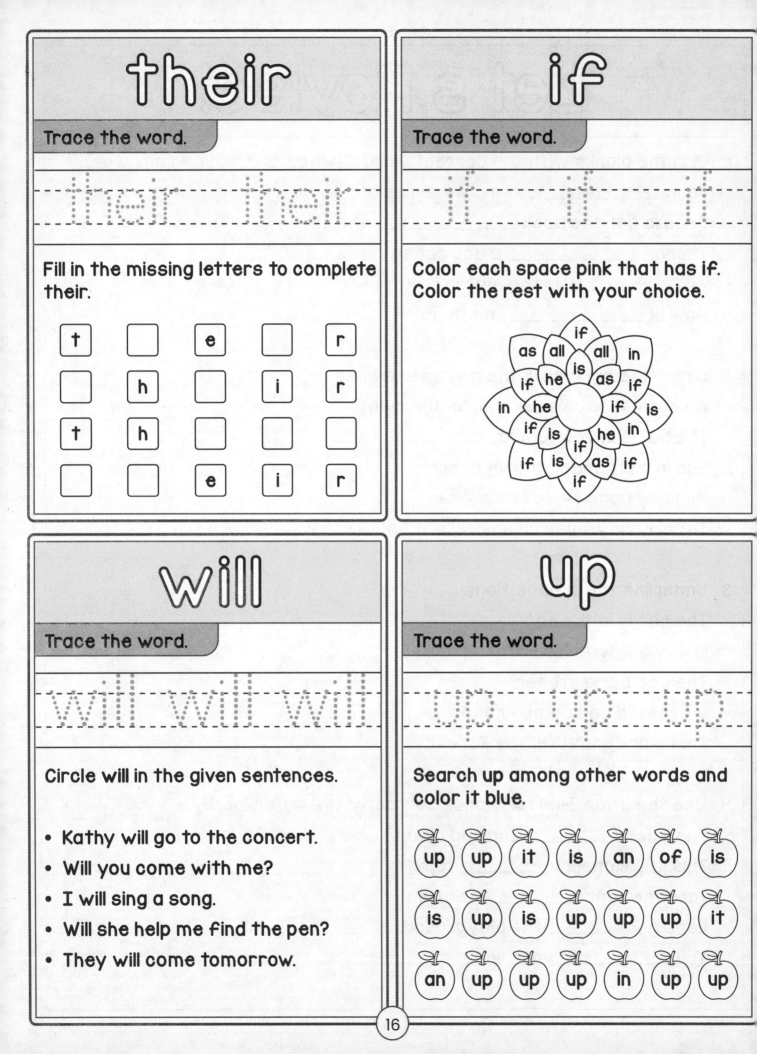

will

Trace the word.

will will will

Circle will in the given sentences.

- Kathy will go to the concert.
- Will you come with me?
- I will sing a song.
- Will she help me find the pen?
- They will come tomorrow.

up

Trace the word.

up up up

Search up among other words and color it blue.

up up it is an of is

is up is up up up it

an up up up in up up

other

Trace the word.

other other

Circle the initials of the words to get **other**.

owl

tree

hibiscus

elephant

rat

about

Trace the word.

about about

Color the correct code for each letter to get **about**.

	a	b	o	u	t
a	□	⬡	△	□	○
b	△	⬡	□	○	□
o	○	□	△	⬡	□
u	△	○	□	□	□
t	□	□	△	⬡	○

out

Trace the word.

out out out

Add and write new words with **out**.

cut + out =

out + source =

lay + out =

out + run =

with + out =

many

Trace the word.

many many

Rank the letters in the correct order to get **many**.

a m y n

_ _ _ _

y a n m

_ _ _ _

then

Trace the word.

then then

Match the same letters of then.

t •   • h

h •   • n

e •   • e

n •   • t

them

Trace the word.

them them

Replace the underlined words with them and then read aloud.

· She went with <u>Kathy and Alex</u>.

· Ask <u>Sean and Pearl</u> to come home.

----

these

Trace the word.

these these

Spot these in the box.

a	t	h	e	s	e	t
a	n	d	a	n	n	h
t	h	e	s	e	g	e
a	b	v	x	w	w	s
s	e	a	i	d	d	e

so

Trace the word.

so so so

Color the spaces with so in pink.

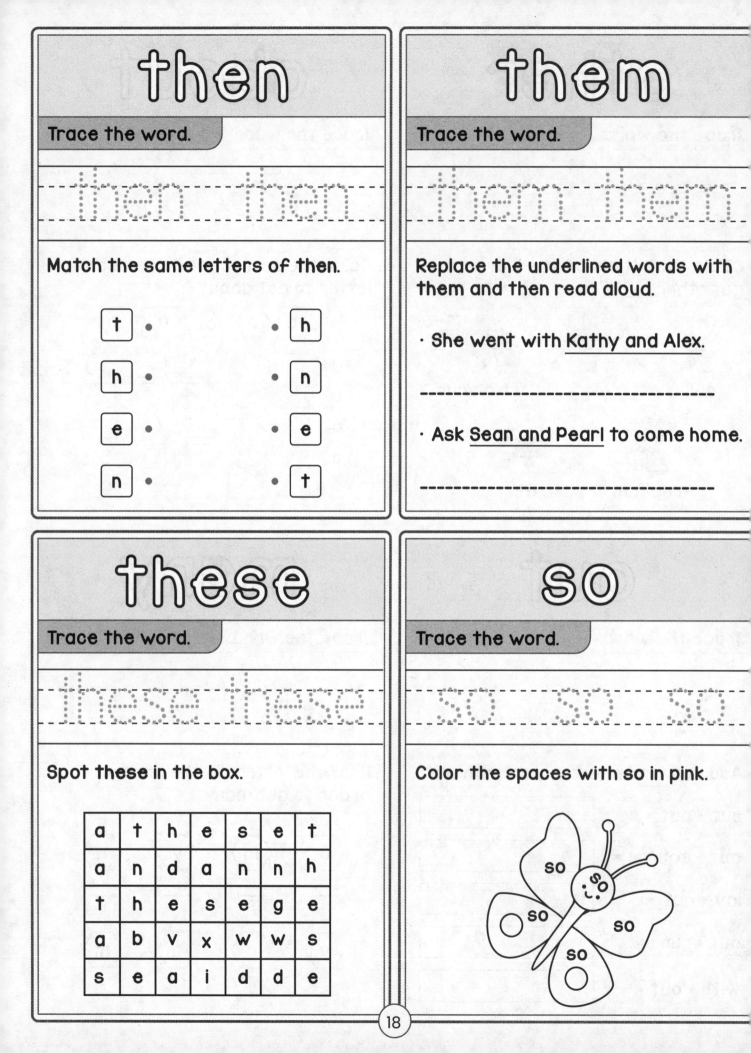

some

some some

Circle some in the given sentences.

· There are some oranges in the basket.
· Some fries would be nice.
· Would you like some water?
· Some people like to go skiing.
· Are some of your friends coming?

her

her her her

Spot her on the teapots. Count and write.

her · the · his · her
then · her · him · the

☐ times

would

would would

Match would written in same style.

would ·   · would
would ·   · WOUld
would ·   · would
WOUld ·   · would

make

make make

Write five sentences using make.

_____

_____

_____

_____

like

Trace the word.

like like like

Connect the dots with like to complete the picture.

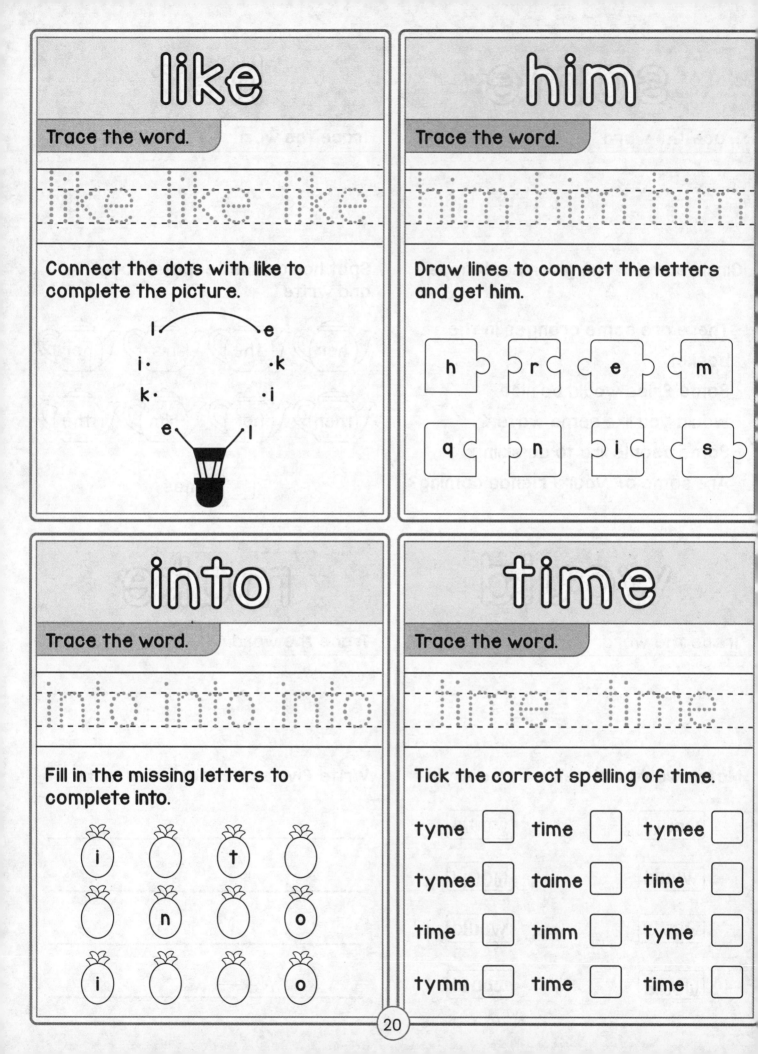

l — e
i· ·k
k· ·i
e l

him

Trace the word.

him him him

Draw lines to connect the letters and get him.

h   r   e   m

q   n   i   s

into

Trace the word.

into into into

Fill in the missing letters to complete into.

i   t

n   o

i   o

time

Trace the word.

time   time

Tick the correct spelling of time.

tyme ☐   time ☐   tymee ☐

tymee ☐   taime ☐   time ☐

time ☐   timm ☐   tyme ☐

tymm ☐   time ☐   time ☐

has

has has has

Match each has that is same.

has •   • has
has •   • has
has •   • has
has •   • has

look

Trace the word.

look   look

Write five words that end in -ook as look.

☐ ook   ☐ ook

☐ ook   ☐ ook

☐ ook

two

Trace the word.

two two two

Color the spaces with two written on them.

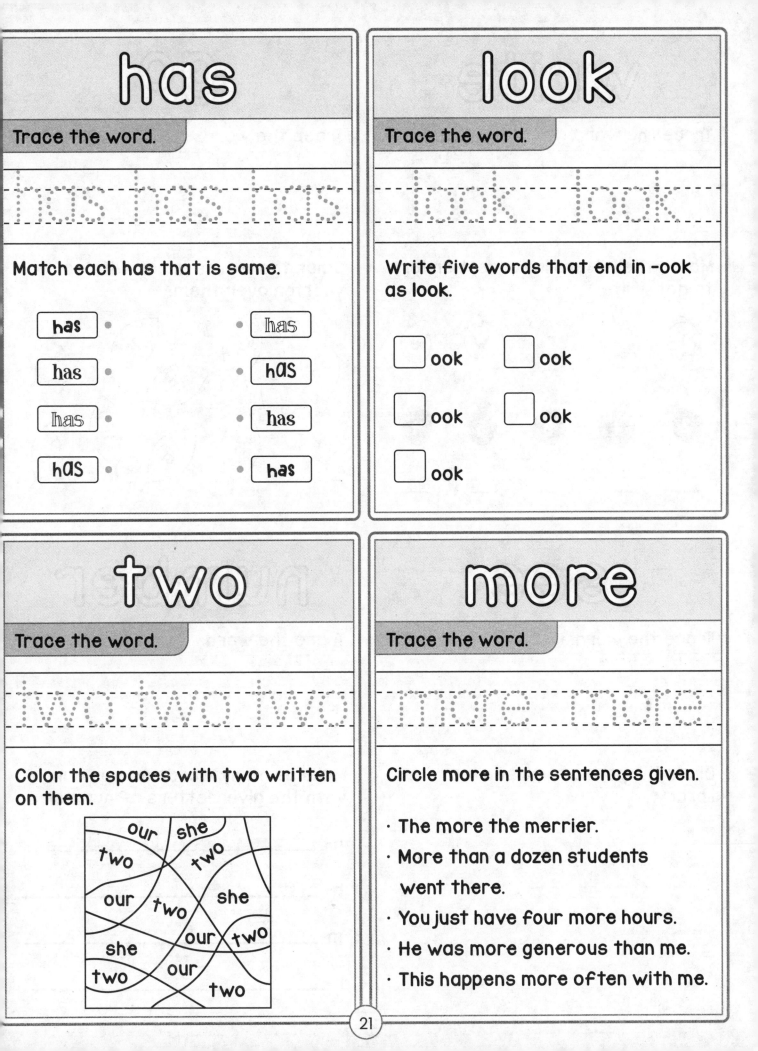

more

Trace the word.

more more

Circle more in the sentences given.

· The more the merrier.
· More than a dozen students
  went there.
· You just have four more hours.
· He was more generous than me.
· This happens more often with me.

21

write

Trace the word.

write write

Match the letters in correct order to get write.

i   t   r   w   e

2   1   3   5   4

___ ___ ___ ___ ___

go

Trace the word.

go go go

Color the leaves green with go written over them.

go   go   go   is
      is   if
      go   is   if   go

see

Trace the word.

see see see

Draw things that you see in a library.

number

Trace the word.

number

Make as many words as you can with the given letters of number.

n-_____

b-_____

m-_____

r-_____

no

Trace the word.

no   no   no

Answer the following questions in negative with a no.

· Is there any water in the fridge?

· Ans.

· Can you come with me to the park?

· Ans.

· Will you go to the barber shop?

· Ans.

way

Trace the word.

way   way

Help the cub find its **way** to its mother.

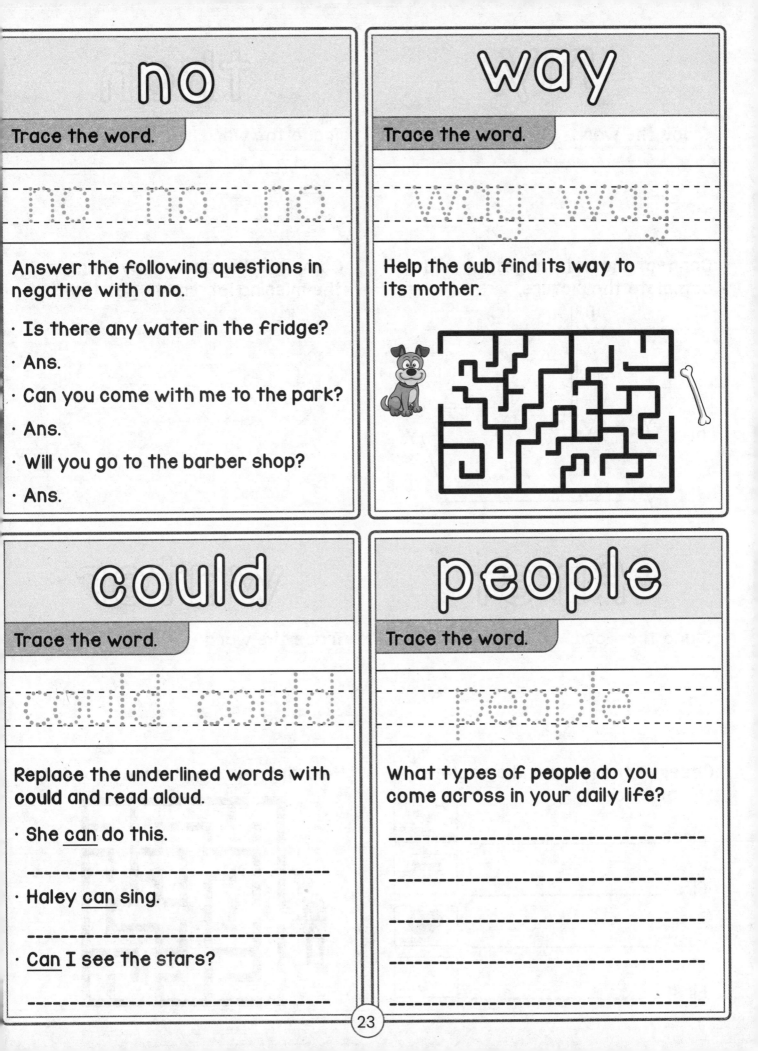

could

Trace the word.

could   could

Replace the underlined words with could and read aloud.

· She <u>can</u> do this.

· Haley <u>can</u> sing.

· <u>Can</u> I see the stars?

----

people

Trace the word.

people

What types of **people** do you come across in your daily life?

----

my

Trace the word.

my my my

Connect the dots to get my and complete the picture.

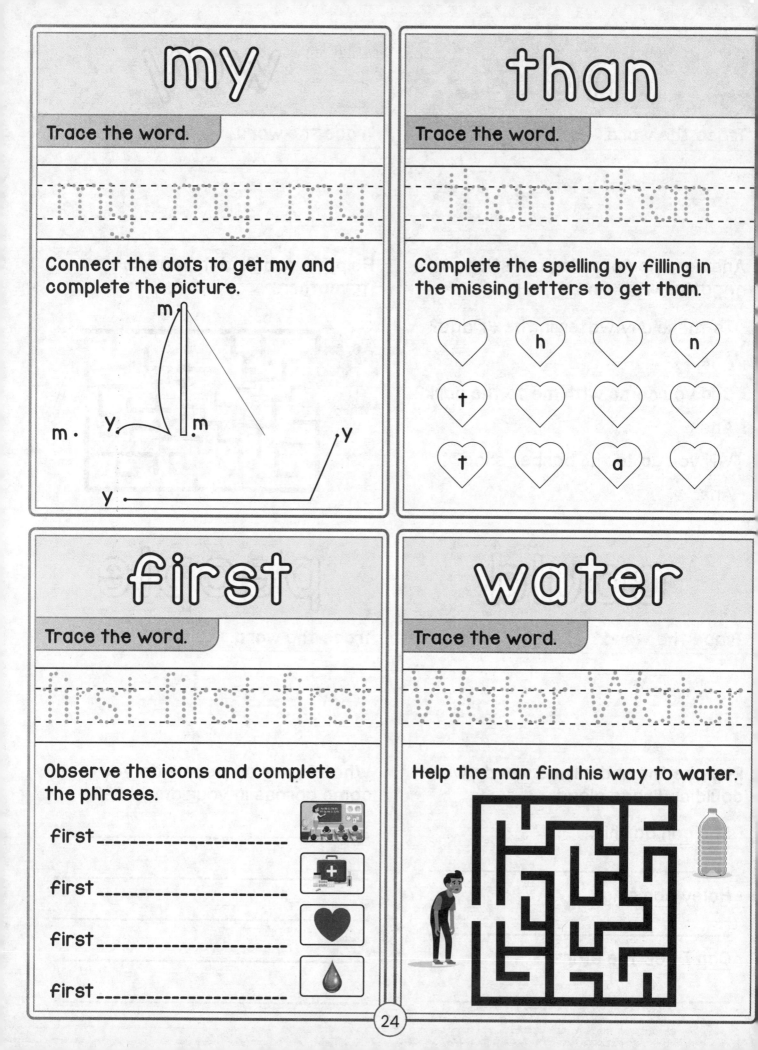

than

Trace the word.

than than

Complete the spelling by filling in the missing letters to get than.

first

Trace the word.

first first first

Observe the icons and complete the phrases.

first _____

first _____

first _____

first _____

water

Trace the word.

Water Water

Help the man find his way to water.

been

Trace the word.

been been

Identify the icons and circle the initials to get **been**.

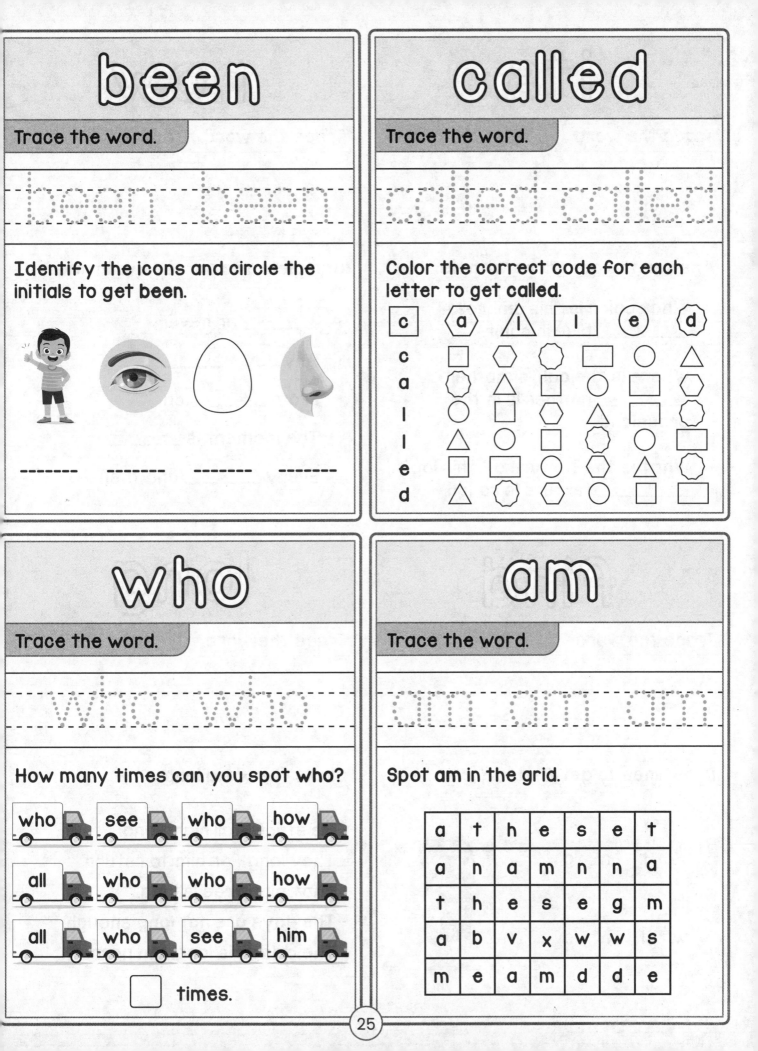

------- ------- ------- -------

called

Trace the word.

called called

Color the correct code for each letter to get **called**.

c	a	l	l	e	d

who

Trace the word.

who who

How many times can you spot who?

who	see	who	how
all	who	who	how
all	who	see	him

☐ times.

am

Trace the word.

am am am

Spot am in the grid.

a	t	h	e	s	e	t
a	n	a	m	n	n	a
t	h	e	s	e	g	m
a	b	v	x	w	w	s
m	e	a	m	d	d	e

its

Trace the word.

its its its

Answer the questions with its.

- What color is this umbrella?
  _____ blue in color.

- Where is the calf's mother?
  _____ mother is in the grassland.

- What is the texture of this log?
  _____ texture is rough.

now

Trace the word.

now now

Complete the phrases with now.

- _____ or never

- Any day _____

- From _____ on

- The moment is _____

- Every _____ and then

find

Trace the word.

find find find

Draw lines to get find.

f r n g

w i h d

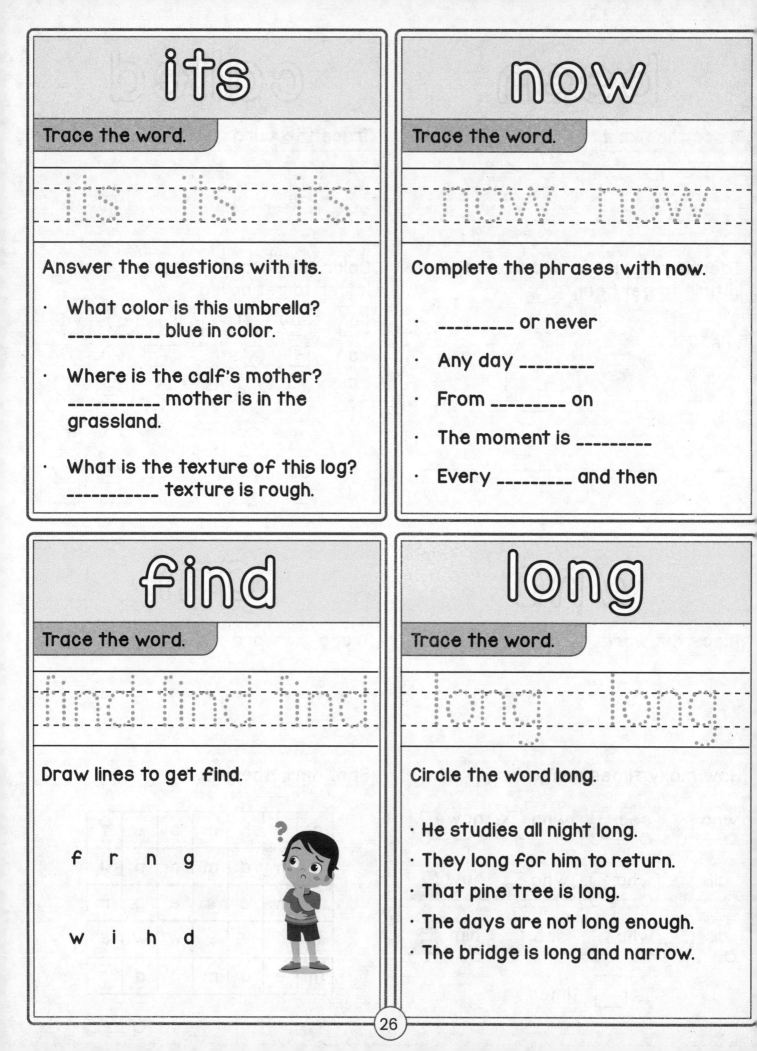

long

Trace the word.

long long

Circle the word long.

- He studies all night long.
- They long for him to return.
- That pine tree is long.
- The days are not long enough.
- The bridge is long and narrow.

down

Trace the word.

down down

Add **down** as given to get a new word.

down + fall = _____

tumble + down = _____

down + stream = _____

sun + down = _____

down + town = _____

day

Trace the word.

day day day

Add **day** at the beginning and write the new words.

_____ break

_____ time

_____ light

_____ care

did

Trace the word.

did did did

Color the spaces in orange with **did** written on it.

did | as | see | is | did

did | her | the | did | did

get

Trace the word.

get get get

Match the same fonts of **get**.

get •   • get

get •   • get

get •   • get

get •   • get

come

Trace the word.

come come

Color the clouds that have **come** written over it.

use come use
come use come
come the it

made

Trace the word.

made made

Complete the spelling of **made** by filling in the missing letters.

may

Trace the word.

may may

Circle **may** in the given words.

mayflower mayday maybe
mayonnaise maynard

part

Trace the word.

part part

Color the leaves with **part** written on them.

part as
part in part
part part
are in
are

let's revise!

1. Make five meaningful sentences using the words you have learned till now.

----

2. Use the correct question words to fill in the blanks. (which, who, what, how, when).

- _____ is your name?

- _____ do you leave for the airport?

- _____ one of these is better?

- _____ is your brother?

- _____ is your best friend?

3. Underline the words that show action.

- I think he will show his art.

- Did you follow them to the ground?

- They help Montana in her studies.

- Maya and Lily came to the theater.

4. Use the m-words correctly. (many, make, more, made, may).

- _____ I come in?

- They _____ a good company.

- There are _____ lakes around here.

over

Trace the word.

over over

Fill in the blanks with over.

- Turn _____ a new leaf
- Cast a shadow _____
- All _____ the lot
- Can't get _____ something
- A roof_____ one's head

new

Trace the word.

new new

Color the words that end with –ew. (new, flew, brew, crew, threw).

a	t	h	e	c	e	t	b
f	l	e	w	n	r	a	r
t	h	r	e	w	g	e	e
a	b	v	x	w	w	s	w
m	e	a	n	e	w	e	e

sound

Trace the word.

sound sound

Connect the letters to spell sound.

| h | e | o | a | n | e |

| l | s | t | u | j | d |

take

Trace the word.

take take

Circle take as many times you spot it.

our she
take take
our two take
she our two
take her
take

only

only only

Underline only in the given sentences.

- It's only a matter of time.
- Only you and I know this secret.
- This is the only road to the palace.
- Do this only if you want to.
- Only God can help her now.

little

Trace the word.

little little

Fill in the missing letters to spell little.

l · · t · l ·
· i · · t · e
· · · t t · ·

work

Trace the word.

work work

Add work as given to get new words.

_____ + shop = workshop

home + _____ =

_____ + load =

team + _____ =

_____ + flow =

know

Trace the word.

know know

Write how many times you spot know.

Know no now know her
that lag saw no now
know lag his knew know

[ ] times.

31

place

Trace the word.

place place

Fill in the boxes to form place.

p			p		p
l	l		l		
a		a		a	
	c		c		c
e	e		e		

years

Trace the word.

years years

Make as many words as you can from years.

----

live

Trace the word.

live live live

Draw the place where you live.

me

Trace the word.

me me me

Match each me that is same.

me	•	•	Me
me	•	•	me
Me	•	•	me
me	•	•	me

back

Trace the word.

back back

Read aloud the words and underline back.

backbone

backdrop

backyard

backpack

backward

give

Trace the word.

give give

Color the space red with give. Color the rest of the picture as per your choice.

most

Trace the word.

most most

Complete the following adjectives by adding most in the beginning.

_____ beautiful

_____ handsome

_____ intelligent

_____ powerful

_____ important

very

Trace the word.

very very

Spot very in the grid.

v	t	h	e	c	e	t	b
e	l	e	v	e	r	y	r
r	h	r	e	w	g	e	e
y	b	v	x	w	w	s	w
m	e	a	v	e	r	y	e

after

Trace the word.

after after

Circle each tree with the word **after**.

after things after very

our after just after

things

Trace the word.

things things

Color the letters with your favorite colors to get things.

a	b	c	d	e	f	g
h	i	j	k	l	m	n
o	p	q	r	s	t	u
v	w	x	y	z		

our

Trace the word.

our our our

Name the things that you can call **our** and write them.

our _____

our _____

our _____

our _____

our _____

just

Trace the word.

just just just

Spot **just** in the given words and underline it.

· justly   · justle

· justify   · justice

· adjust

· unjust

name

name name

Help Johny find the letters that spell name.

z n r o
c t e f
y d n
b a m

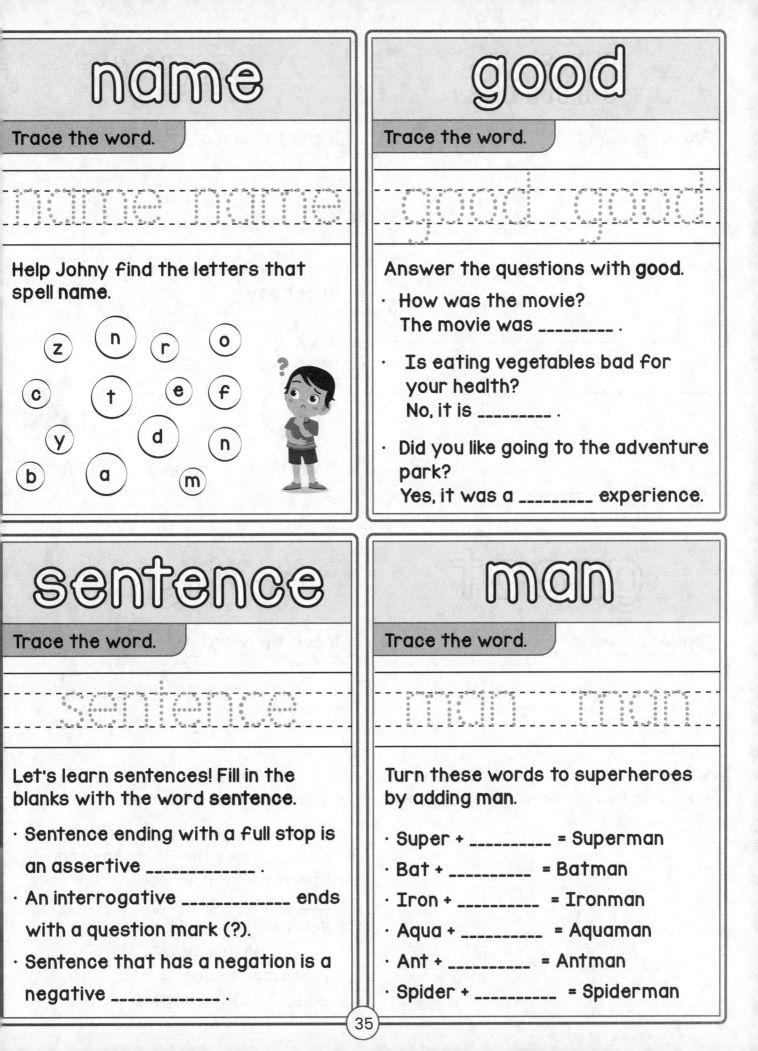

good

Trace the word.

good good

Answer the questions with **good**.

· How was the movie?
The movie was _____ .

· Is eating vegetables bad for your health?
No, it is _____ .

· Did you like going to the adventure park?
Yes, it was a _____ experience.

sentence

Trace the word.

sentence

Let's learn sentences! Fill in the blanks with the word **sentence**.

· Sentence ending with a full stop is an assertive _____ .

· An interrogative _____ ends with a question mark (?).

· Sentence that has a negation is a negative _____ .

man

Trace the word.

man man

Turn these words to superheroes by adding man.

· Super + _____ = Superman

· Bat + _____ = Batman

· Iron + _____ = Ironman

· Aqua + _____ = Aquaman

· Ant + _____ = Antman

· Spider + _____ = Spiderman

think

Trace the word.

think think

Write 3 sentences using think.

_____

_____

_____

say

Trace the word.

say say say

Circle the initials of the given words to get say.

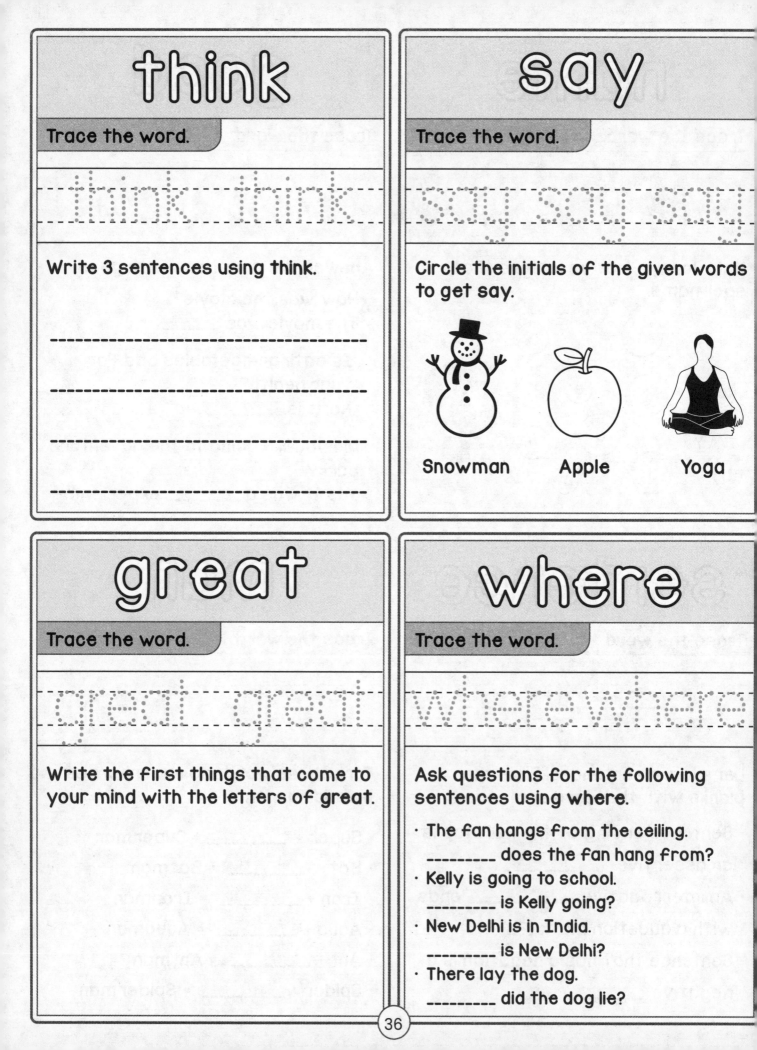

Snowman   Apple   Yoga

great

Trace the word.

great great

Write the first things that come to your mind with the letters of great.

where

Trace the word.

where where

Ask questions for the following sentences using **where**.

· The fan hangs from the ceiling.

_____ does the fan hang from?

· Kelly is going to school.

_____ is Kelly going?

· New Delhi is in India.

_____ is New Delhi?

· There lay the dog.

_____ did the dog lie?

help

Trace the word.

help   help

Add the given letters to make and learn new words.

help + s =

help + ed =

help + ing =

help + ful =

help + less =

through

Trace the word.

through

Hop on the letters of through and help the rabbit reach the carrot.

t	h	c	d	e
x	r	o	u	l
o	s	f	g	h
e	p	q	r	m

much

Trace the word.

much much

Make your own emojis for the given phrases.

Too <u>much</u> happy

Too <u>much</u> sad

Too <u>much</u> sleepy

Too <u>much</u> love

before

Trace the word.

before

Write the names of animals with the letters of the word **before**.

b ------------------------------

e ------------------------------

f ------------------------------

o ------------------------------

r ------------------------------

e ------------------------------

line

Trace the word.

line line line

Fill in the blanks with **line** to learn about different lines.

This is a straight _____   _____

This is a curved _____   ⌒

This is a horizontal _____   ‾

This is a vertical _____ |

right

Trace the word.

right   right

Complete the word pyramid for right.

r

r   i

r   i   g

r   i   g   h

r   i   g   h   t

too

Trace the word.

too too too

Match the words in same style.

too	•	•	too
too	•	•	too
too	•	•	**too**
too	•	•	too

means

Trace the word.

means

Draw the means of transport.

flies in air   runs on land

floats on water   runs on rails

old

old old old

Spot and circle the word **old** in the given passage.

An old woman lived in the countryside. She had an old husband. They lived in an old mansion. There was an old oak tree in the lawn of the old mansion. An old dog guarded their mansion. The old couple loved the dog very much.

any

Trace the word.

any any any

Connect the letters to spell **any**.

| p | a | t | r | w | y |

| s | e | l | n | d | q |

same

Trace the word.

same same

Write things from the letters of same.

s _____

a _____

m _____

e _____

tell

Trace the word.

tell tell tell

Circle **tell** in the given words.

satellite   foretell

intellect   immortelle

retelling   storyteller

intelligent   foretelling

boy

Trace the word.

boy boy boy

Replace the underlined letters with boy and write the new word.

cowgirl

girlhood

papergirl

girlish

tomgirl

follow

Trace the word.

follow follow

Color the shapes according to the codes of follow.

f	o	l	l	o	w
f					
o					
l					
l					
o					
w					

came

Trace the word.

came came

Spell came by filling in the missing letters correctly.

	a		e
c		m	e
	a	m	
c	a		

want

Trace the word.

want want

Color the correct spelling of want.

vant   Waunt   want

want   vaunt   vant

want   vaunt   vaunt

40

show

show show

Add show in the beginning to get new words.

_____ + case = _____

_____ + stopper = _____

_____ + biz = _____

_____ + piece = _____

_____ + room = _____

also

alsoalsoalso

Circle and color also.

also
after
hen
our
sky
also
aloof
take
our
also
two
her
also
two
also

around

around

Spot around in the grid.

a	r	o	u	n	d	t	b
e	l	e	v	e	r	y	r
r	h	a	r	o	u	n	d
y	b	v	x	w	w	s	w
m	a	r	o	u	n	d	e

form

form form

Fill in the blanks with form and learn various types of forms.

- You fill an application _____ to apply in school.
- To register, you fill a registration _____ .
- You place an order with an order _____ .
- To improve services, fill a feedback _____ .

let's revise!

1. Color the rhyming words with matching colors. (old, bold, live, give, man, tan)

b	o	l	d	d	r	e	s	s	g
c	r	m	a	n	w	e	a	r	i
o	y	a	r	d	t	a	n	t	v
o	l	d	e	s	i	d	e	n	e
l	a	r	e	l	i	v	e	s	s

2. Fill in the blanks with the correct adjectives. (little, great, good, new)

a. Blake was a _____ poet.

b. Alex bought a _____ book.

c. We have very _____ time left.

d. Tracy is a _____ singer.

3. Circle naming words in the given sentences.

a. That man walks too slow.

b. My mother gave me an orange.

c. Our cat sleeps and purrs all day.

d. Maverick is a good boy.

4. Use the appropriate words to complete the sentences. (where, sound, before, over)

a. How much time _____ we leave for the airport?

b. She went _____ her notes twice.

c. This is the _____ of a cricket chirping.

d. _____ did you place the candle?

three

Trace the word.

three three

Complete the given poem with the word three.

_____ blind mice, _____ blind mice, See how they run, see how they run, They all ran after the farmer's wife, who cut off their tails with a carving knife. Did you ever see such a thing in your life, as _____ blind mice?

small

Trace the word.

small small

Replace the underlined words with small and rewrite the sentences.

· She was a big girl.
·
· He needs only a tiny space.
·
· The wall has a little hole.
·

set

Trace the word.

set set set

Match the same font style for set.

set	·	·	set
set	·	·	set
Set	·	·	set
set	·	·	set

put

Trace the word.

put put put

Learn phrases and their meaning by filling in the blanks with put.

· _____ up with - to tolerate
· _____ on - to wear
· _____ down - to write
· _____ away - to clean up
· _____ out - to stop burning
· _____ off - to delay

43

end

Trace the word.

end end end

Circle **end** in the given words.

- blend
- spend
- friend
- trend
- lend

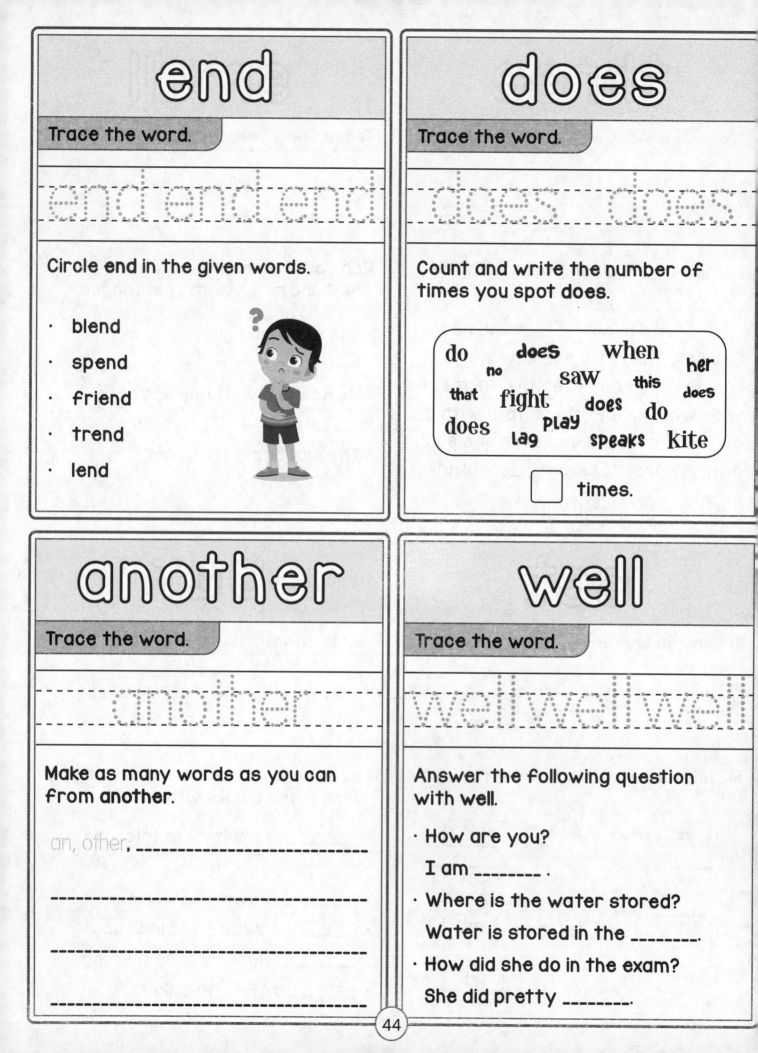

does

Trace the word.

does does

Count and write the number of times you spot **does**.

do   does   when   her
no   saw   this
that   fight   does   does
does   play   do
lag   speaks   kite

[ ] times.

another

Trace the word.

another

Make as many words as you can from **another**.

an, other, _____

_____

_____

well

Trace the word.

well well well

Answer the following question with **well**.

- How are you?

  I am _____ .

- Where is the water stored?

  Water is stored in the _____.

- How did she do in the exam?

  She did pretty _____.

large

Trace the word.

large large

Fill in the missing letters to spell large.

	a		g	e
l	l	r	g	
	a	r		e
l			g	

must

Trace the word.

must must

Join the dots to get must and complete the picture.

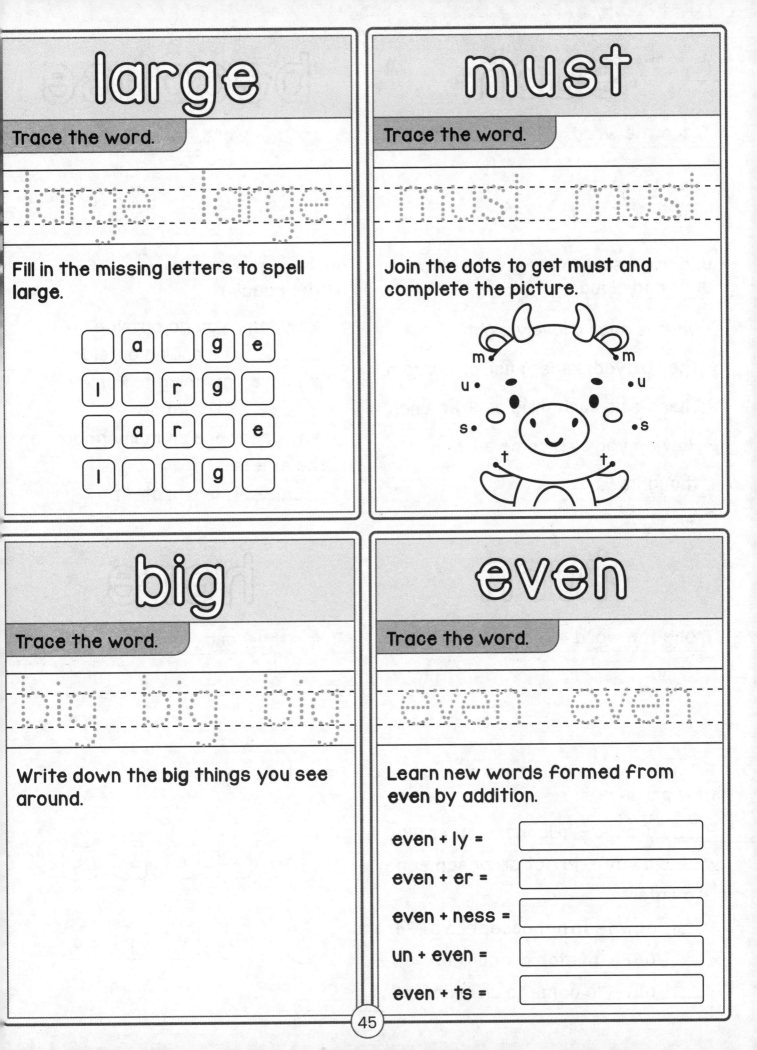

m •   • m
u •   • u
s •   • s
    t   t

big

Trace the word.

big big big

Write down the **big** things you see around.

even

Trace the word.

even even

Learn new words formed from **even** by addition.

even + ly = _____

even + er = _____

even + ness = _____

un + even = _____

even + ts = _____

such

such such

Underline such in the given sentences and read aloud.

· Oh, it is such a lovely sight!

· They played games such as carrom.

· There is no such thing as free lunch.

· How do you overcome such

thoughts?

because

Trace the word.

because

Answer the following questions with because.

· Why don't you go outside?

_____ it's chilling outside.

· Why are you going to Rome?

_____ I like Rome.

· Why are there so many people on the street?

_____ it is a protest.

turn

Trace the word.

turn turn turn

Fill in the blanks with turn and learn new phrases.

· _____ around - to look the other way

· _____ away - to not allow someone to enter

· _____ down - to not accept an offer

· _____ off - to stop a machine

· _____ out - to come to an event

here

Trace the word.

here here

Draw lines to get here.

t	r	e	w	e

l	h	g	r	a

why

Trace the word.

why why why

Circle why in the given sentences.

- Why are you crying?
- That is why climbing is difficult.
- Why do you think Susie loves Ross?
- Why is there no chalk on the board?
- Is this why you don't like going to school?

ask

Trace the word.

ask ask ask

Spot and color the bubbles with ask.

ask   is   he
as
as
it   ask   in   he
it   ask
ask
☐ times

went

Trace the word.

went went

Help Harry reach his parrot by following went.

v
s   o
e   t
n
w   p
c

men

Trace the word.

men men

Match the same pair of men.

men   •   •   MEN
MEN   •   •   men
men   •   •   men
men   •   •   men

47

read

Trace the word.

read read

Draw things you can **read**.

need

Trace the word.

need need

Color the alphabets to get **need**.

s	w	n	c	p	e	z
b	h	g	f	n	d	o
e	u	j	i	k	s	z
v	o	b	r	a		

land

Trace the word.

land land

Add **land** to get the names of places.

Fin + land =

Ice + land =

Ire + land =

Thai + land =

Queens + land =

different

Trace the word.

different

Write same or **different** in the given pictures.

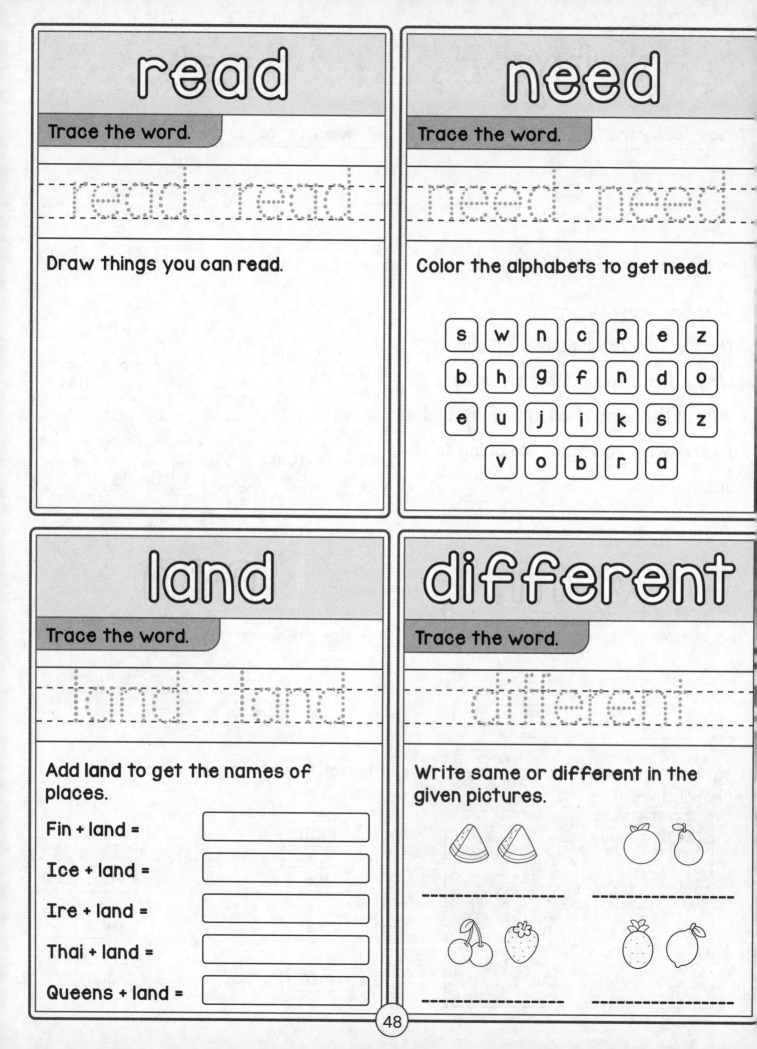

_____   _____

_____   _____

home

Trace the word.

home home

Draw a picture of your **home**.

us

Trace the word.

us   us   us

Trace and color the flowers with us written on them.

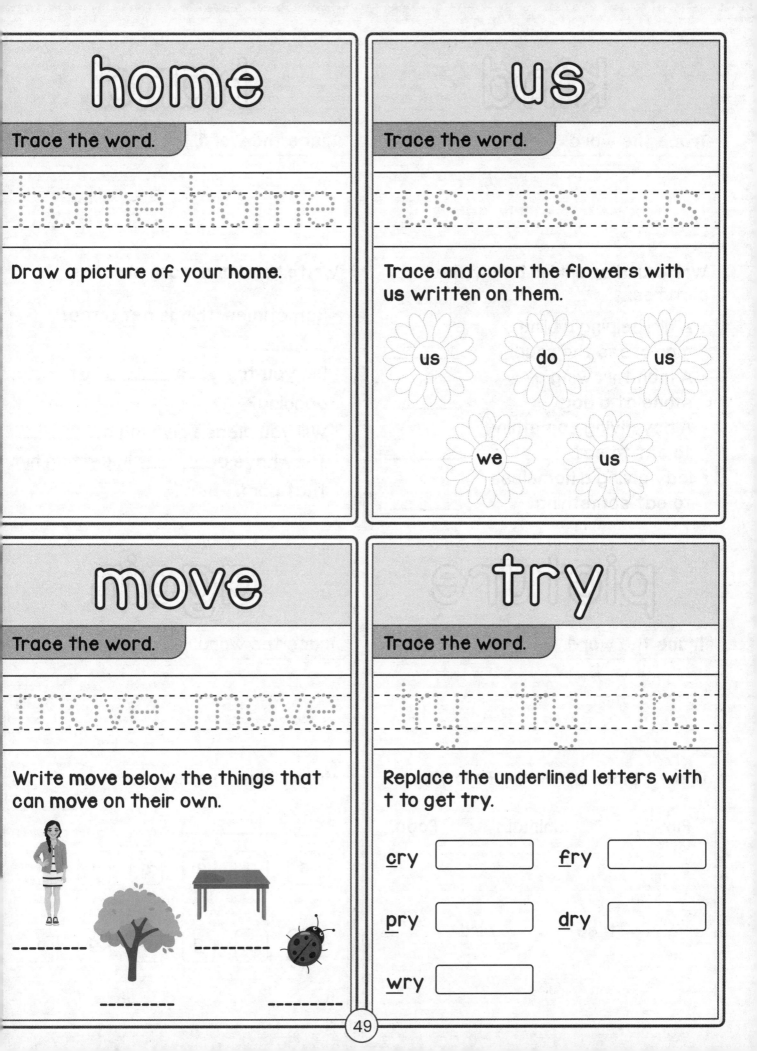

us   do   us

we   us

move

Trace the word.

move move

Write **move** below the things that can **move** on their own.

--------   --------

--------   --------

try

Trace the word.

try   try   try

Replace the underlined letters with t to get try.

<u>c</u>ry [   ]   <u>f</u>ry [   ]

<u>p</u>ry [   ]   <u>d</u>ry [   ]

<u>w</u>ry [   ]

49

kind

Trace the word.

kind   kind

Write **kind** or **unkind** below the pictures.

- A girl helping a blind man cross the road.   _____
- A man throwing a stone at a dog.   _____
- A boy giving something to cat to eat.   _____
- lady giving a homeless to eat something.   _____

hand

Trace the word.

hand   hand

Write **hand** and learn phrases.

· Sometimes, things get out of _____.
· Did you try your _____ at dancing?
· Will you please give me a _____.
· They have a _____ in getting him that part.

picture

Trace the word.

picture

Draw a picture for the following.

flower   animal.   food.

tree   bird

again

Trace the word.

again   again

Match lines to spell **again**.

| s | a | m | d | i | n |

| f | l | g | a | g | o |

change

Trace the word.

change

Color the word **change** in the given picture.

change more

change

change

were

here change type

off

Trace the word.

off off off

Fill **off** to complete the phrases.

1. be _____
2. bear _____
3. cut _____
4. doze _____
5. fall _____
6. put _____

7. _____ and on
8. _____ the bat
9. get _____ the can
10. take the gloves _____

play

Trace the word.

play play

Write **play** in the blanks that interest you.

· I want to _____ football.

· I like to _____ guitar.

· I want to _____ cricket.

· I like to _____ badminton.

· I want to learn how to _____ violin.

spell

Trace the word.

spell spell

Underline the initials of the given words to get spell.

s_____   p_____   e_____

s_____   l_____

air

air air air

Underline air in the given words.

fair

chair

stairs

hairpin

airplane

away

away away

Add away to the words to get new words.

· give + _____ = giveaway

· take + _____ = takeaway

· straight + _____ = straightaway

· _____ + ness = awayness

· break + _____ = breakaway

animal

animal

Which is an animal? Write in the space provided.

_____   _____   _____

_____   _____   _____

house

house house

Let's learn the different types of houses! Underline house.

Beach house: A house near a beach
Igloo: A snow house
Farmhouse: A house on the farm
Ranch: A house to breed animals
Townhouse: A house in town

52

learn

learn learn

Spot learn in the grid.

b	o	l	e	a	r	n	s	s	g
c	r	m	a	n	w	e	a	r	i
o	y	a	r	l	e	a	r	n	v
l	e	a	r	n	i	d	e	n	e
l	a	r	e	l	e	a	r	n	s

page

Trace the word.

page page

Match the same font style for page.

page •   • page

page •   • page

page •   • page

page •   • page

letter

Trace the word.

letter letter

Spell letter by filling the blanks.

	e		t		r
l		t		e	
	e	t			r
l	e		t		

mother

Trace the word.

mother

Write five sentences for your mother.

----

answer

answer

Make as many words as you can from answer.

wear, _____

_____

_____

found

found found

Complete the calculations to get found.

round - r + f =

ground - gr + f =

sound - s + f =

around - ar + f =

bound - b + f =

study

study study

Connect the letters to spell study.

a   s   u   n   y

w   o

p   d

t   e   l

still

still still still

Fill in the blanks with still and read the sentences aloud.

· Jericho is _____ recovering.

· That bird lay _____ on the ground.

· Drake shots _____ pictures.

· They became _____ upon hearing footsteps.

· Maxine _____ lives with her parents.

54

learn

learn learn

Spot learn in the grid.

l	e	a	r	n	e	t
a	n	a	m	n	n	a
t	l	e	a	r	n	m
a	b	v	x	w	w	s
m	e	l	e	a	r	n

should

Trace the word.

should

Color the letters to get should.

a	b	c	d	e	f	g
h	i	j	k	l	m	n
o	p	q	r	s	t	u
v	w	x	y	z		

America

Trace the word.

America

Let's learn! Underline America in the sentences given.

· America has fifty states.
· Washington, D.C. is the capital of America.
· America has fifty stars in its flag.
· The largest freshwater lake in the world is in America.
· America has all five climate zones.

world

Trace the word.

world world

Trace the outlines to get the map of the world.

let's revise!

1. Write three words ending with the same letters as the given words.

three _____, _____, _____

well _____, _____, _____

need _____, _____, _____

kind _____, _____, _____

still _____, _____, _____

2. Complete the crossword for the given words with the help of clues.
(small, large, turn, went, home, read, picture, change)

Across
5. It is the only constant
6. You live here permanently
7. Books are meant to be _____
8. Whale is a _____ mammal

Down
1. To change or transform
2. In Pictionary, you draw this
3. The past tense of go
4. It is little, only with 5 letters

3. Spot and color the given 3-letter words in the picture.
(set, put, end, big, why, ask, men, try, off, air)

set	spot	some	lion	men	practice
past	the	put	little	draw	off
this	ask	table	air	you	why
give	day	chair	end	glass	plane
big	word	image	stair	try	night

high

high high

Write the first thing you can think of with the letters of high.

h [ ]   h [ ]

i [ ]   i [ ]

g [ ]   g [ ]

h [ ]   h [ ]

every

Trace the word.

every every

Add every to get a new word.

every + one = [ ]

every + day = [ ]

every + man = [ ]

every + thing = [ ]

every + where = [ ]

near

Trace the word.

near near

Write near in the given blanks and read aloud.

The tree is far, but the lamp is

The man is far, but the woman is

The stable is far, but the horse is

The sea is far, but the land is

----

add

Trace the word.

add add add

Make two words from the letters of add.

----

food

Trace the word.

food   food

Circle the items that are considered food for humans.

between

Trace the word.

between

Circle the initials to get **between**.

- B a t
- E g g
- T r o o p
- W o o l
- E l e p h a n t
- E y e
- N e s t

own

Trace the word.

own   own

Make as many words as you can from **own**.

----

below

Trace the word.

below below

Trace the letters to get **below**.

country

country

Draw and color the national flag of your **country**.

plant

plant plant

Which is your favorite **plant**. Why?

----

last

last last last

Fill in the blanks with **last**.

· They caught the _____ train.

· He finished in the _____ position.

· _____ year was merry.

· She gave her assignment

· on the _____ day.

school

school

How do you reach your **school**? Write it in the space provided.

----

father

Trace the word.

father

Help the father reach his child.

keep

Trace the word.

keep keep

Color the letters of keep in your favorite colors and read aloud.

tree

Trace the word.

tree tree tree

Solve the calculations to spell tree.

· free – f + t = _____

· spree – sp + t = _____

· three – th + t = _____

· agree – ag + t = _____

· degree – deg + t = _____

never

Trace the word.

never never

Write five things you never want to do.

· I never want to _____.

· I never want to _____.

· I never want to _____.

· I never want to _____.

· I never want to _____.

start

Trace the word.

start   start

What are the things you want to start doing? Fill in the blanks.

I want to start _____.

I want to start _____.

I want to start _____.

I want to start _____.

I want to start _____.

city

Trace the word.

city city city

Color the words that rhyme with city.

dog	kitty	pity
speaks	pop	bitty
witty	saw	mine

Earth

Trace the word.

Earth   Earth

Trace the outline to get a picture of the Earth.

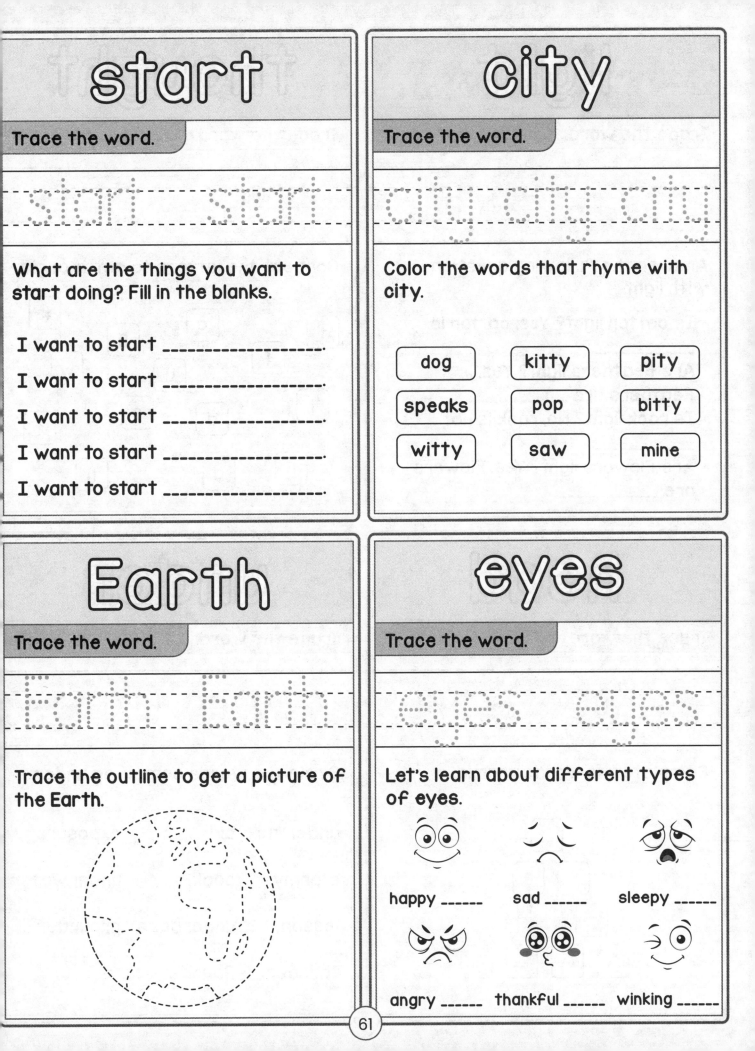

eyes

Trace the word.

eyes   eyes

Let's learn about different types of eyes.

happy _____   sad _____   sleepy _____

angry _____   thankful _____   winking _____

light

Trace the word.

light   light

Answer the following questions with light.

· Is cotton light? Yes, cotton is

_____.

· Are feathers light? Yes, feathers are _____.

· Is rock light? No, rock is not

_____.

· Are flowers light? Yes, Flowers are _____.

thought

Trace the word.

thought

Connect the letters to get thought.

k

t   o   g

l   w

u

i   s

d   t

h   a   h

head

Trace the word.

head   head

Complete the word pyramid.

h

h e

h e a

h e a d

under

Trace the word.

under under

Circle the words containing under.

underline	bid	exposure
stormy	cook	underwater
lesson	underpass	grounder
thunder	founder	

story

story story

Write a short story.

_____

_____

_____

saw

Trace the word.

saw saw

Make three words from the letters of saw.

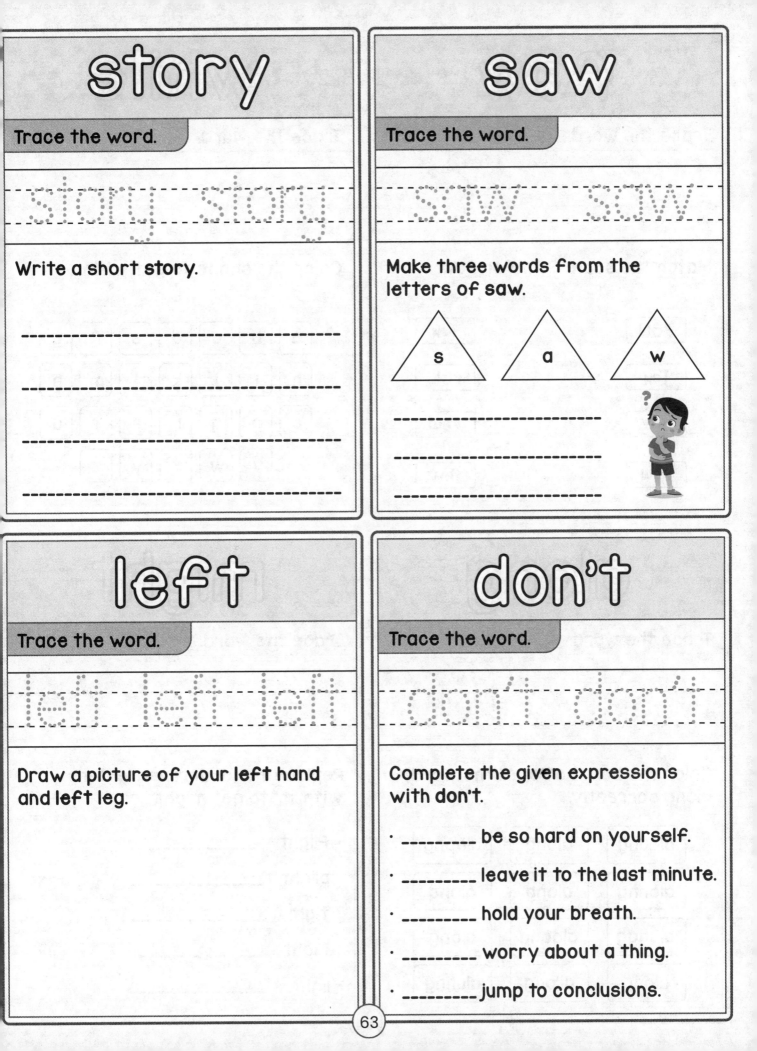

s   a   w

_____

_____

_____

left

Trace the word.

left left left

Draw a picture of your **left** hand and **left** leg.

don't

Trace the word.

don't don't

Complete the given expressions with **don't**.

· _____ be so hard on yourself.

· _____ leave it to the last minute.

· _____ hold your breath.

· _____ worry about a thing.

· _____ jump to conclusions.

few

Trace the word.

few few few

Match the same font for few.

fEW •	• Few
Few •	• fEW
few •	• Few
Few •	• few

while

Trace the word.

while   while

Color the shape to get while.

a	b	c	d	e	f	g
h	i	j	k	l	m	n
o	p	q	r	s	t	u
	v	w	x	y	z	

along

Trace the word.

along along

Color the box that spell the word along correctly.

alaung	along	aloong
alonng	along	along
alongg	aloong	along
along	allong	alunng

might

Trace the word.

might might

Replace the underlined letters with 'm' to get might.

· flight _____
· plight _____
· tight _____
· fight _____
· light _____

close

close close

Add these to get new words with **close**.

close + d =

en + close =

close + ly =

dis + close =

close + r =

something

Trace the word.

something

Make as many words as you can with **something**.

some, thing, _____

_____

_____

_____

seem

Trace the word.

seem seem

Fill in the boxes to spell **seem**.

	e		m
s		e	
		e	m
s	e		

next

Trace the word.

next next

Help the frog reach the pond by following **next**.

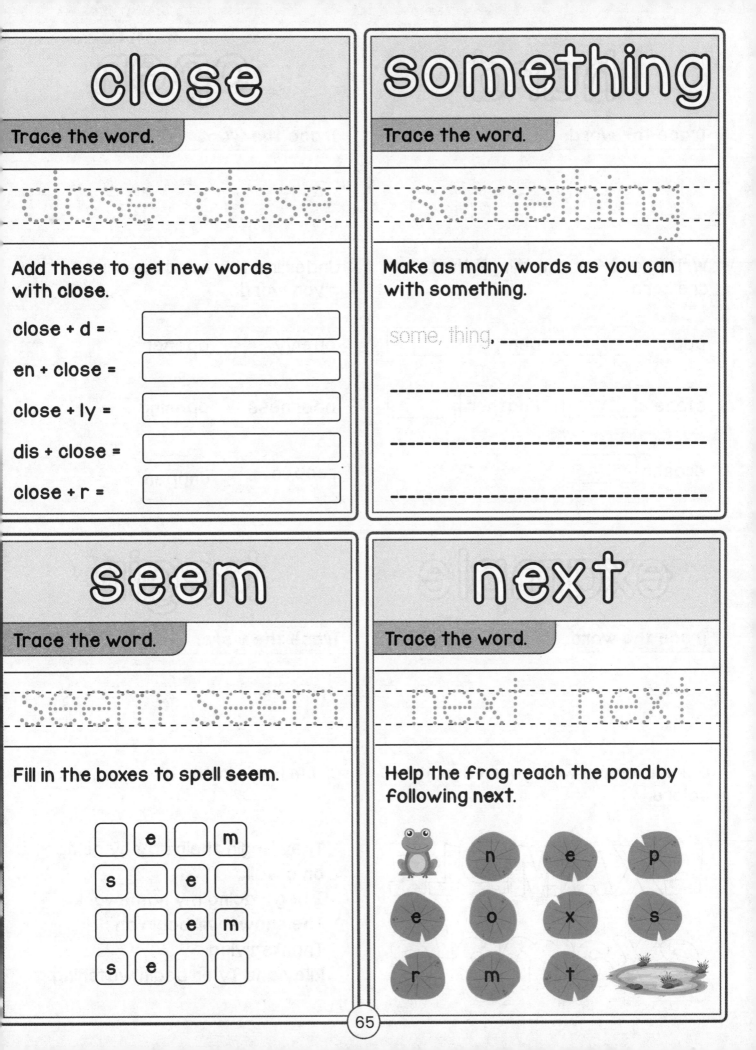

hard

Trace the word.

hard hard

Write hard for the things that are hard.

paper _____ pen _____

stone _____ feather _____

eraser _____

open

Trace the word.

open open

Underline the word open in the given words.

openly   opener

openness   opening

reopen

unopen

example

Trace the word.

example

Color **example** with your favorite colors.

EXAMPLE

example

begin

Trace the word.

begin begin

Circle **begin** in the given sentences.

- They begin their day by going on a walk.
- I begin doing my homework.
- The shows will begin on Thanksgiving.
- Riley and Tyler begin watching

life

life life life

Match the pairs of life with same font style.

life • • life

life • • life

life • • **life**

life • • life

always

always

Tick the correct color code for always.

a	l	w	a	y	s
a	□	⬡	⬡	▭	○	△
l	⬡	△	□	○	□	⬡
w	○	□	⬡	△	○	□
a	△	○	□	⬡	○	▭
y	□	□	○	⬡	△	⬡
s	△	⬡	⬡	○	□	□

those

those those

Connect the lines to get those.

t	t	o	w	s	e	l

d	h	h	a	s	e	p

both

both both

Color the oranges with both on them.

both   her   both   his   both

end   both   night   both   day

paper

Trace the word.

paper paper

Let's learn about papers! Underline paper as many times as you see it.

There are many types of papers. Our books and copies are made of paper. Most houses get newspaper in the morning. There is craft paper for art and craft. Paintings are mostly done on canvas paper.

together

Trace the word.

together

Color the letters to get together.

r	a	t	b	d	f	e
h	k	j	i	o	c	g
l	m	g	s	q	p	h
	e	u	n	z	t	

got

Trace the word.

got got got

Observe and write the names of icons from the letters of got.

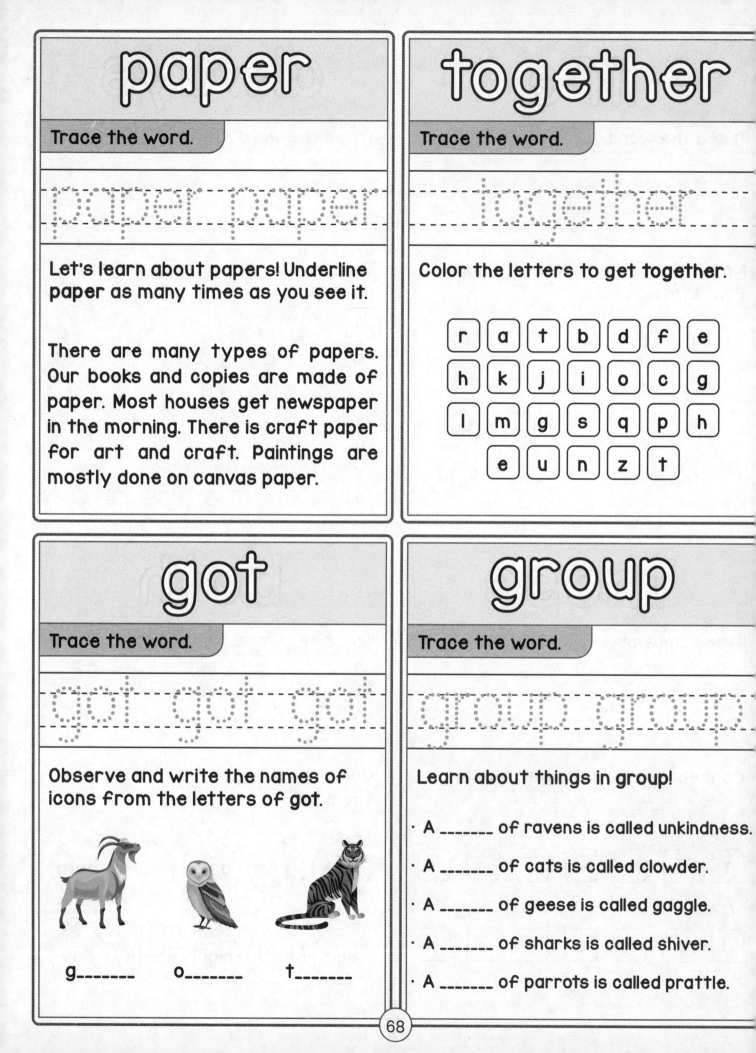

g_____   o_____   t_____

group

Trace the word.

group group

Learn about things in group!

· A _____ of ravens is called unkindness.

· A _____ of cats is called clowder.

· A _____ of geese is called gaggle.

· A _____ of sharks is called shiver.

· A _____ of parrots is called prattle.

let's revise!

1. Fill in the blanks with the correct words. (between, last, under, high, food)

- _____ is the fuel for energy in living beings.

- My cat sits _____ the table.

- Hannah speaks in a _____ pitch.

- Sarah could not choose _____ the two.

- I met my family _____ Christmas.

2. Color the rhyming words with matching colors.

   (last, fast, food, mood, add, mad, fight)

b	o	l	a	s	t	e	f	m	f
f	o	o	d	n	w	e	i	o	a
o	y	a	a	d	t	a	g	o	s
o	l	d	d	s	i	d	h	d	t
l	m	a	d	l	i	v	t	s	s

3. Rewrite the sentences with the opposites of the words highlighted.

- Can you jump high? Can you jump _____?

- Is your school near? Is your school _____?

- Do you give driving lessons? Do you _____ driving lessons?

- Do you never wear glasses? Do you _____ go to the cinema?

- When does the play start? When does the play _____?

4. Fill in the correct letters to get the words and complete the lyrics.

   (something, life, country, don't, life, story)

- C ___ u ___ t ___ y roads, take me home.

- Is this the real ___ i f ___? Is this just fantasy?

- It's a love ___ ___ or ___ ___, baby, just say, "Yes".

- I d ___ t wanna talk about the way that it was.

- Goin' out tonight, changes into s ___ ___ e t ___ i n ___ red.

often

often often

Complete the spelling by filling in the missing letters to get **often**.

	f		e	
o		t		n
			e	n
o	f	t		

run

Trace the word.

run run run

Circle **run** as many times as you spot it.

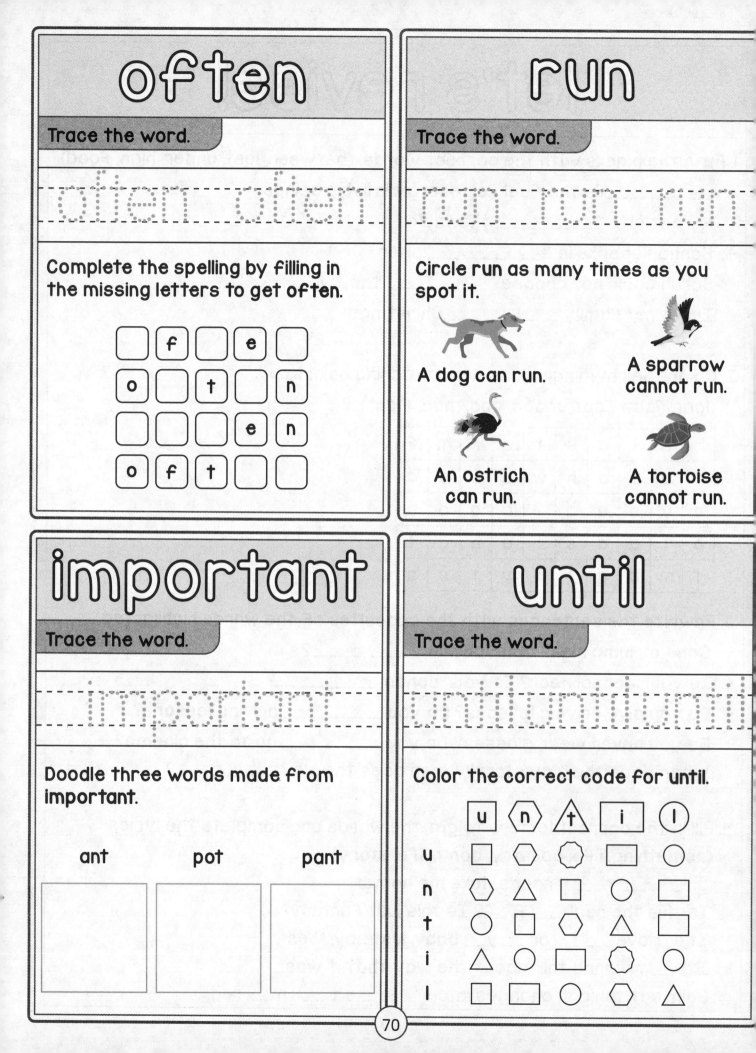

A dog can run.

A sparrow cannot run.

An ostrich can run.

A tortoise cannot run.

important

Trace the word.

important

Doodle three words made from **important**.

ant	pot	pant

until

Trace the word.

until until until

Color the correct code for **until**.

70

children

Trace the word.

children

How many times can you spot children? Count and write.

c	h	i	l	d	r	e	n	b
e	l	e	v	e	r	y	r	r
r	c	h	i	l	d	r	e	n
y	b	v	x	w	w	s	w	w
m	c	h	i	l	d	r	e	n

side

Trace the word.

side   side

Match the same font for side.

Side •   • side

side •   • Side

side •   • side

side •   • side

feet

Trace the word.

feet feet feet

Fill **feet** in the blanks and complete the sentences.

· _____ are parts of legs.

· Human _____ have ten toes in total.

· Heel is also a part of _____ .

· _____ also have ankles.

car

Trace the word.

car car car

Join the dots to get a car. Color it.

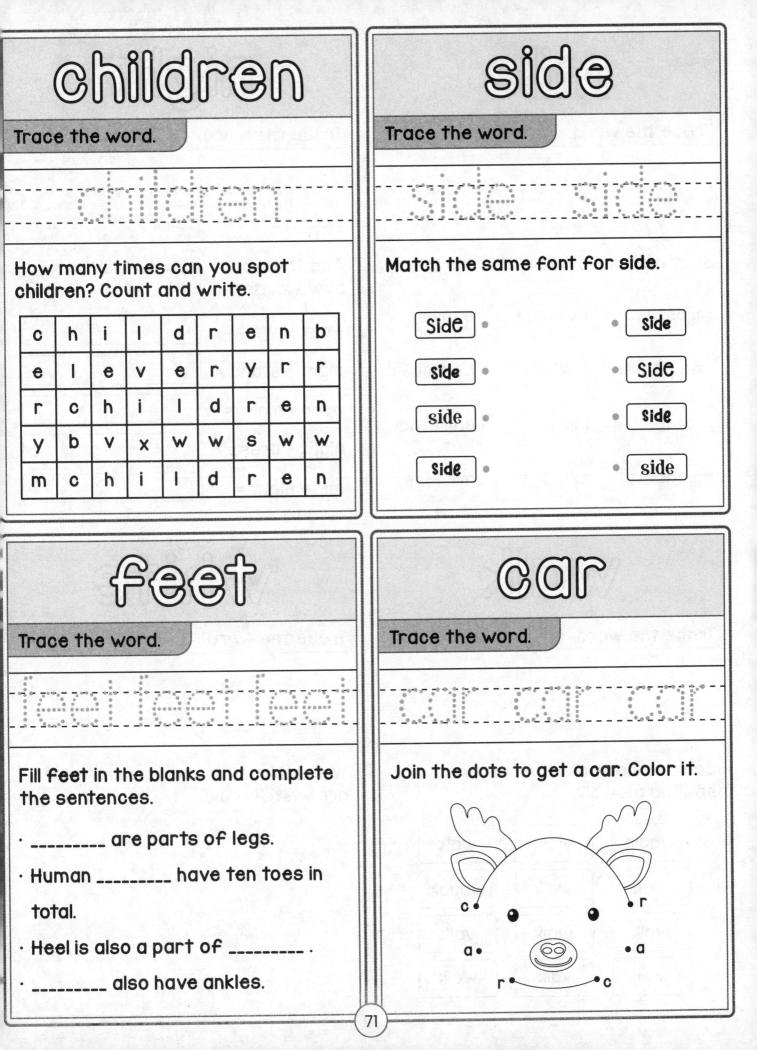

mile

Trace the word.

mile mile

Spot and circle mile in the words.

milestone	outsmile	besmile
chamomile	smiley	facsimiles
smiles	miler	semilethal
mileposts	mileage	smileless

night

Trace the word.

night night

Add the words. Now, write the new words.

fort + night = [ ]

night + stand = [ ]

over + night = [ ]

night + dress = [ ]

mid + night = [ ]

walk

Trace the word.

walk walk

Color the object with correct spelling of walk.

waulk	walk	walk
wok	walk	wauck
walk	walk	volk
walk	valk	walk

white

Trace the word.

white white

Write things around yourself that are white in color.

sea

Trace the word.

sea sea sea

Circle **sea** as many times as you see it.

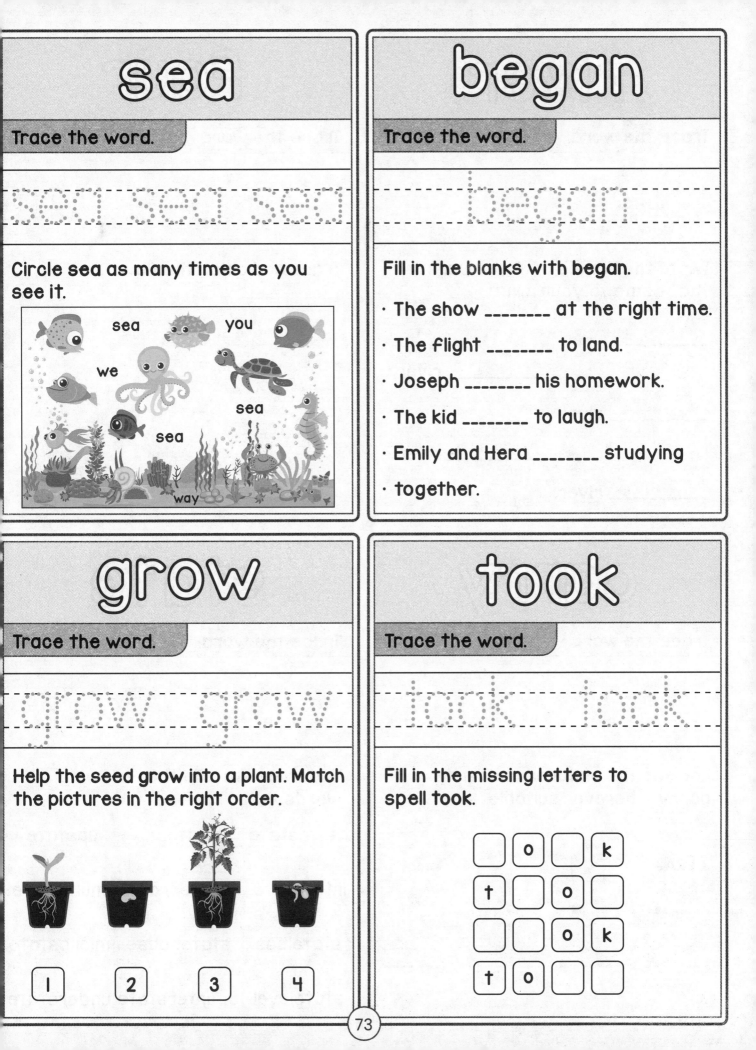

began

Trace the word.

began

Fill in the blanks with **began**.

· The show _____ at the right time.

· The flight _____ to land.

· Joseph _____ his homework.

· The kid _____ to laugh.

· Emily and Hera _____ studying

· together.

grow

Trace the word.

grow grow

Help the seed grow into a plant. Match the pictures in the right order.

1   2   3   4

took

Trace the word.

took took

Fill in the missing letters to spell took.

	o		k
t		o	
	t	o	k
t	o		

river

Trace the word.

river   river

Write the names of five rivers that come to your mind.

_____river

_____ river

_____ river

_____ river

_____ river

four

Trace the word.

four   four

Trace and color the **four**.

four

four

carry

Trace the word.

carry   carry

Look at the pictures and write **carry** wherever suitable.

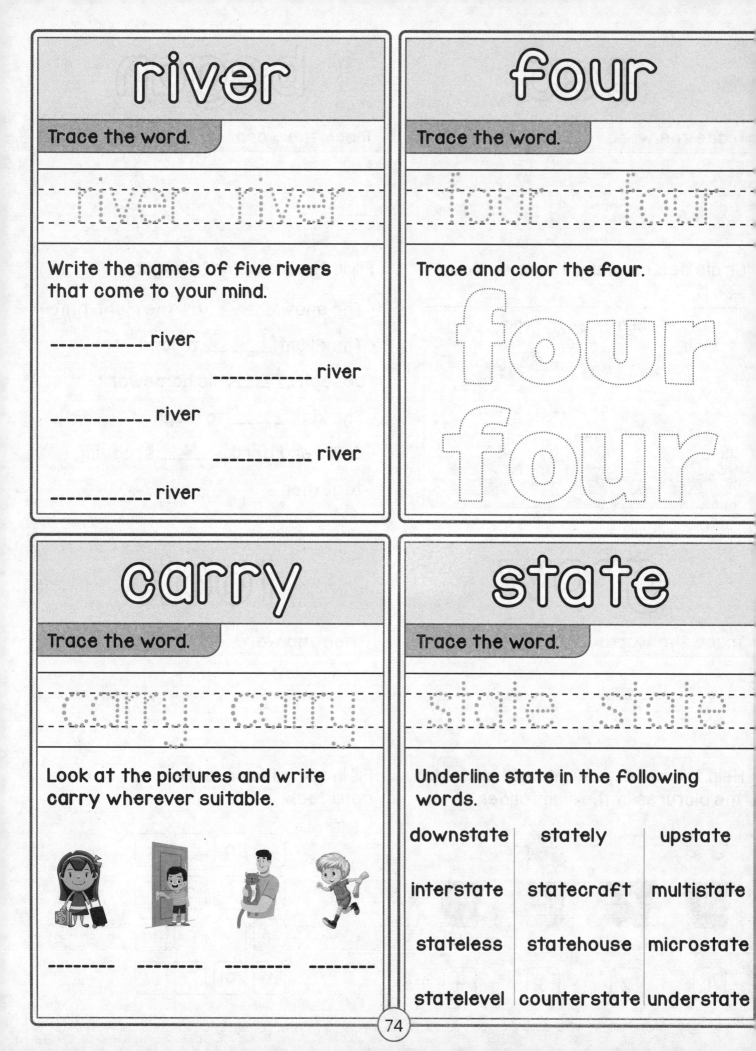

_____   _____   _____   _____

state

Trace the word.

state   state

Underline **state** in the following words.

downstate	stately	upstate
interstate	statecraft	multistate
stateless	statehouse	microstate
statelevel	counterstate	understate

once

Trace the word.

once   once

Write 3 sentences using the word once.

----

book

Trace the word.

book   book

Add these letters to get new words.

pre + book =

book + ish =

re + book =

book + ly =

un + book =

hear

Trace the word.

hear   hear

Which organ is used to **hear**?

Ears are used to_____ .

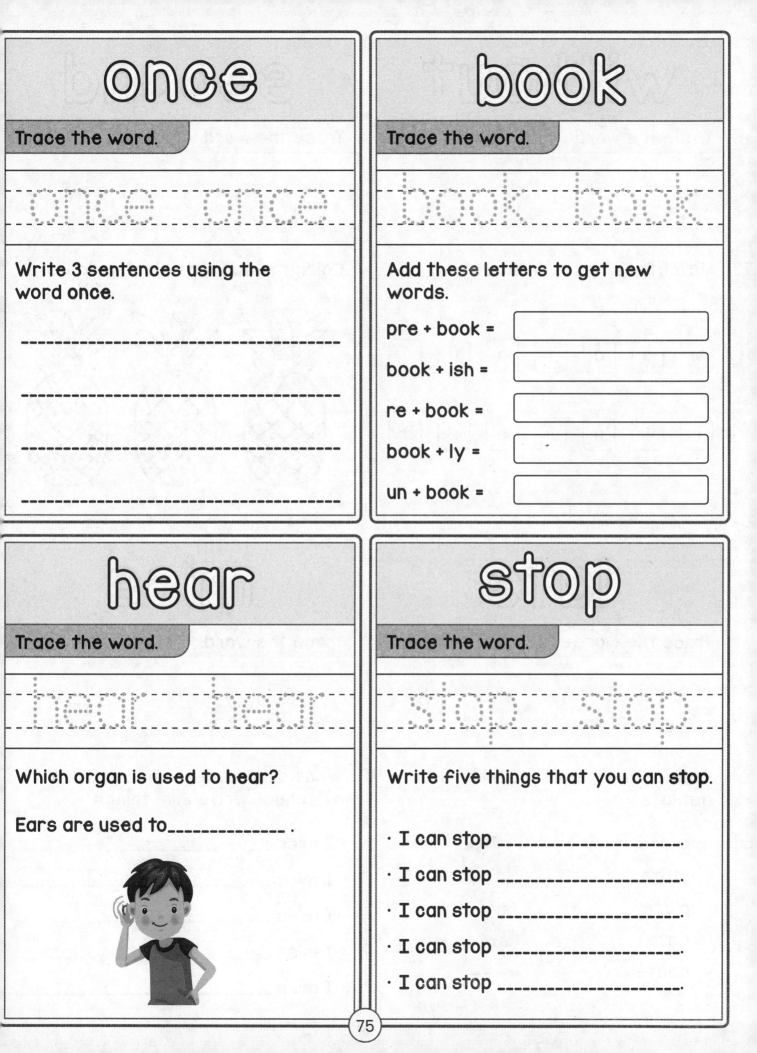

stop

Trace the word.

stop   stop

Write five things that you can **stop**.

· I can stop _____.

· I can stop _____.

· I can stop _____.

· I can stop _____.

· I can stop _____.

without

Trace the word.

without

Match lines to get **without**.

| w | a | q | t | o | u | l |

| r | i | p | h | e | z | t |

second

Trace the word.

second

Color the **second** object yellow.

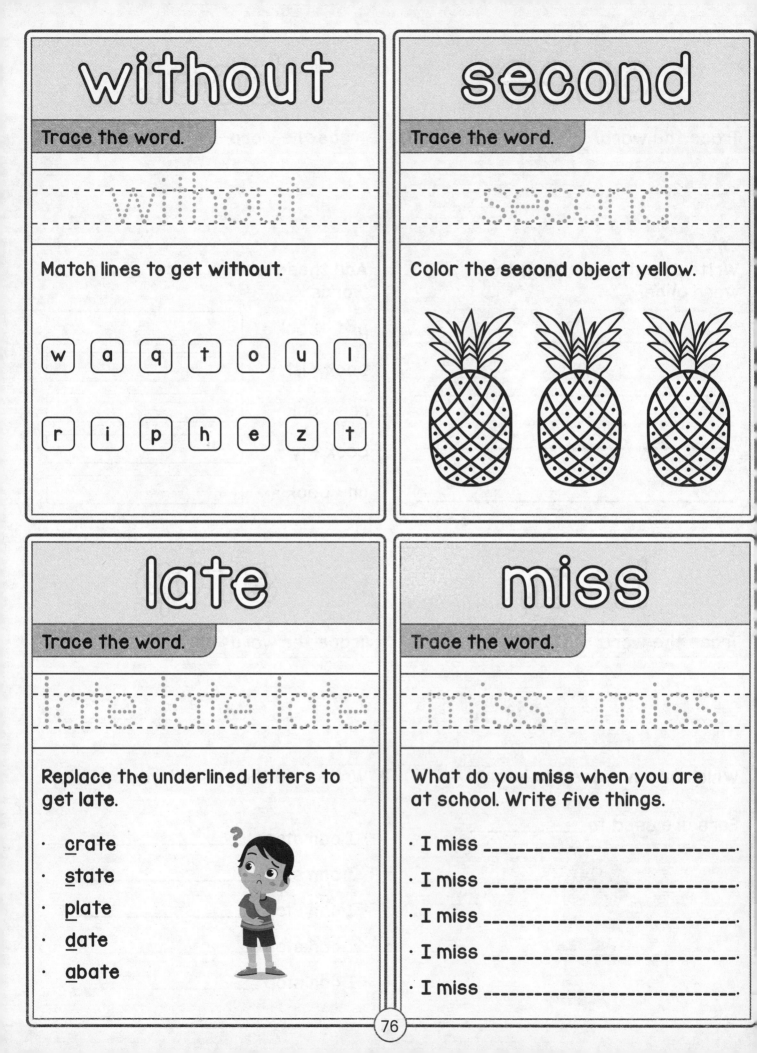

late

Trace the word.

late late late

Replace the underlined letters to get **late**.

- <u>c</u>rate
- <u>s</u>tate
- <u>p</u>late
- <u>d</u>ate
- <u>a</u>bate

miss

Trace the word.

miss   miss

What do you **miss** when you are at school. Write five things.

- I miss _____.
- I miss _____.
- I miss _____.
- I miss _____.
- I miss _____.

idea

Trace the word.

idea idea

Circle the initials of the words to spell **idea**.

- Ice _____
- Dog _____
- Eye _____
- Apple _____

enough

Trace the word.

enough

Fill in the blanks with **enough**.

- We don't have _____ space.
- _____ of this nonsense!
- There is not _____ room for toys.
- Jess has said _____.

eat

Trace the word.

eat eat eat

Write **eat** below the things you can eat?

_____ _____ _____ _____

_____ _____ _____ _____

face

Trace the word.

face face

Draw emojis for given **faces**.

smiley face   angry face

crying face   happy face

watch

Trace the word.

watch watch

Complete the sentence with watch.

· I have a digital _____.

· Sheila owns an analog _____.

· They like to _____ sunrise together.

· You are not going anywhere under my _____.

far

Trace the word.

far far far

Color far as many times as you see it.

sea far her his far

far try far here day

Indian

Trace the word.

Indian Indian

Write the names of a famous Indian.

_____

_____

_____

real

Trace the word.

real real real

How many times can you spot real? Count and write.

Know no real now real
this real
real lag real no now
know real his real real

☐ times.

78

almost

Trace the word.

almost

Join the dots to get almost.

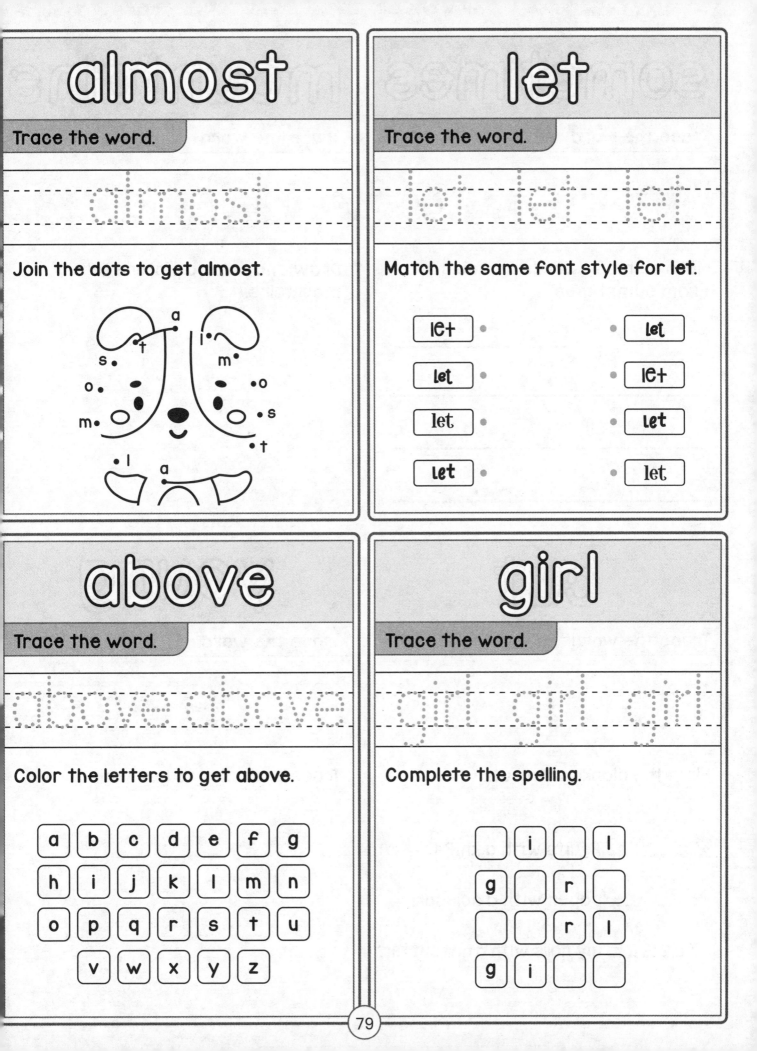

let

Trace the word.

let let let

Match the same font style for let.

let+	•	•	let
let	•	•	le+
let	•	•	let
let	•	•	let

above

Trace the word.

above above above

Color the letters to get above.

a	b	c	d	e	f	g
h	i	j	k	l	m	n
o	p	q	r	s	t	u
	v	w	x	y	z	

girl

Trace the word.

girl girl girl

Complete the spelling.

	i		l
g		r	
		r	l
g	i		

sometimes

Trace the word.

sometimes

Make as many words as you can from **sometimes**.

some, time, _____

_____

_____

_____

mountains

Trace the word.

mountains

Draw and color a picture of mountains.

cut

Trace the word.

cut cut cut

Fill in the blanks with **cut**.

· I _____ fruits with a knife.

· I _____ paper with a scissor.

· I _____ my nails with a nail cutter.

young

Trace the word.

young young

Trace and color to get **young**.

young

YOUNG

talk

Trace the word.

talk talk talk

Color the space with correct spelling of talk.

talk	taulk	talk
talk	tok	talk
tauck	talk	taulk
talk	taulk	taulk

soon

Trace the word.

soon soon

Write **soon** in the blanks to complete the sentences.

· _____ everything is going to be over.

· We need to go out _____.

· The play starts _____.

· He is _____ going to become a

list

Trace the word.

list list list

Make a list of things you want to do.

_____

_____

_____

_____

song

Trace the word.

song song

Fill in the blanks with **song**.

· I sing a _____.

· He sings a _____.

· She sings a _____.

· They sing a song _____.

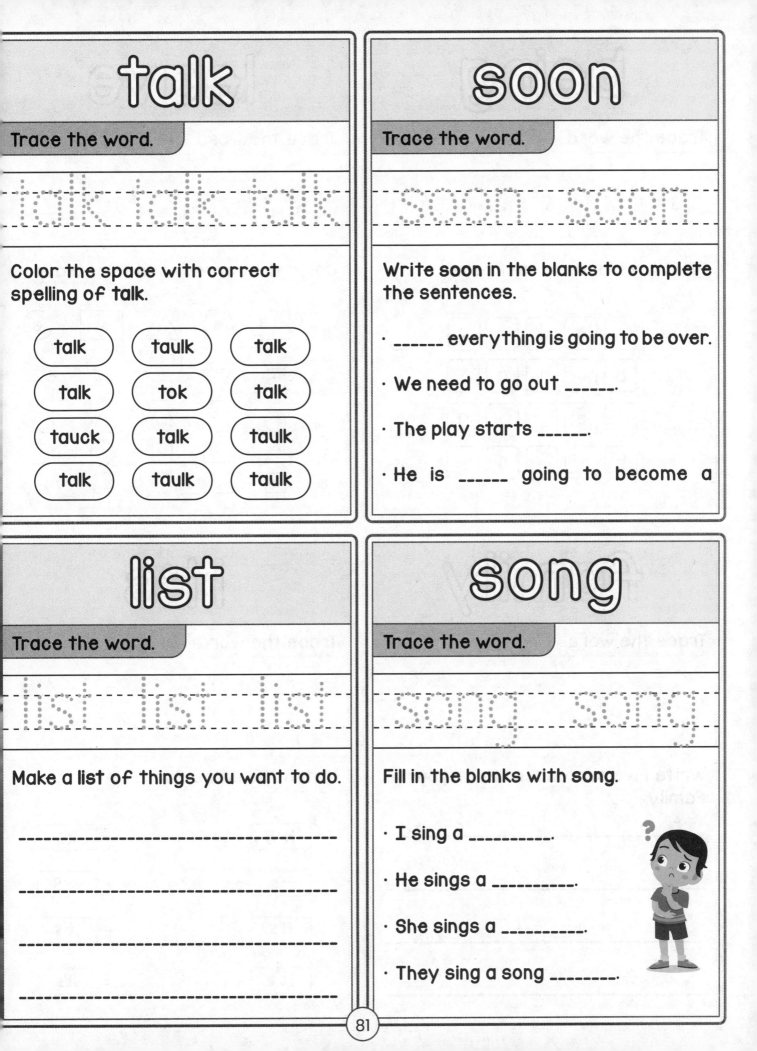

being

Trace the word.

being being

Fill in the blanks to spell being.

	e	i		g
b		i	n	
		e		g
b			n	

leave

Trace the word.

leave leave

Color the correct code for leave.

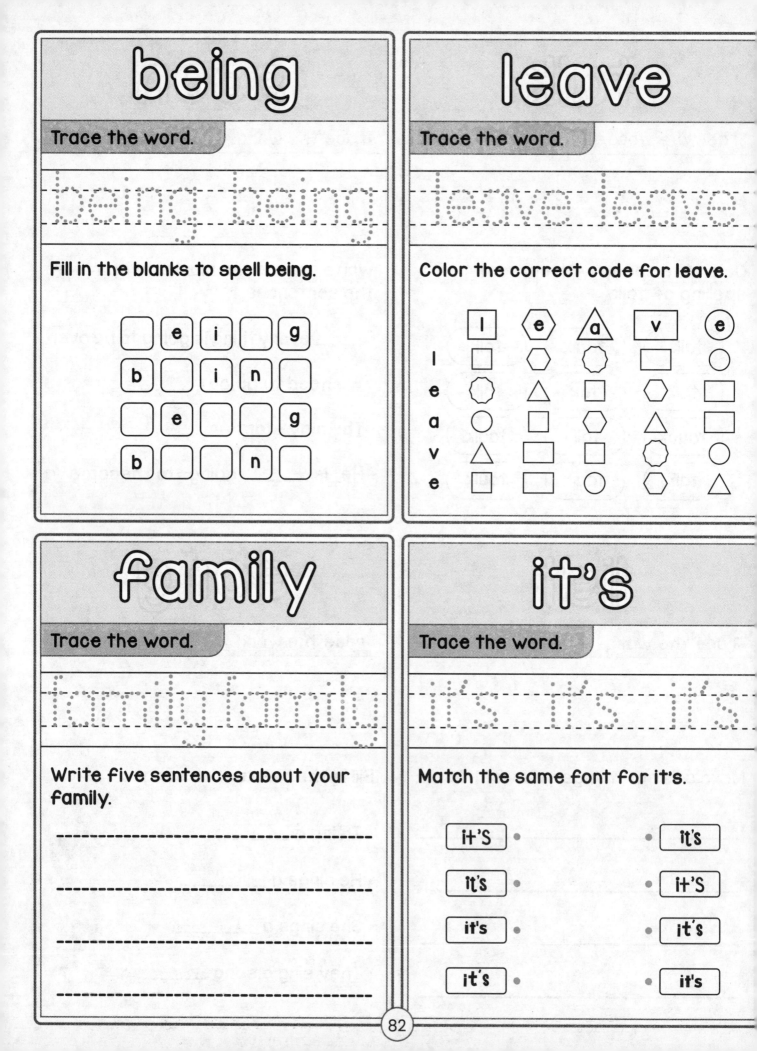

family

Trace the word.

family family

Write five sentences about your family.

----

it's

Trace the word.

it's it's it's

Match the same font for it's.

it's •   • it's

it's •   • it's

it's •   • it's

it's •   • it's

let's revise!

1. Color the given words in the picture. (sea, hear, book, girl, talk, walk, high, jump)

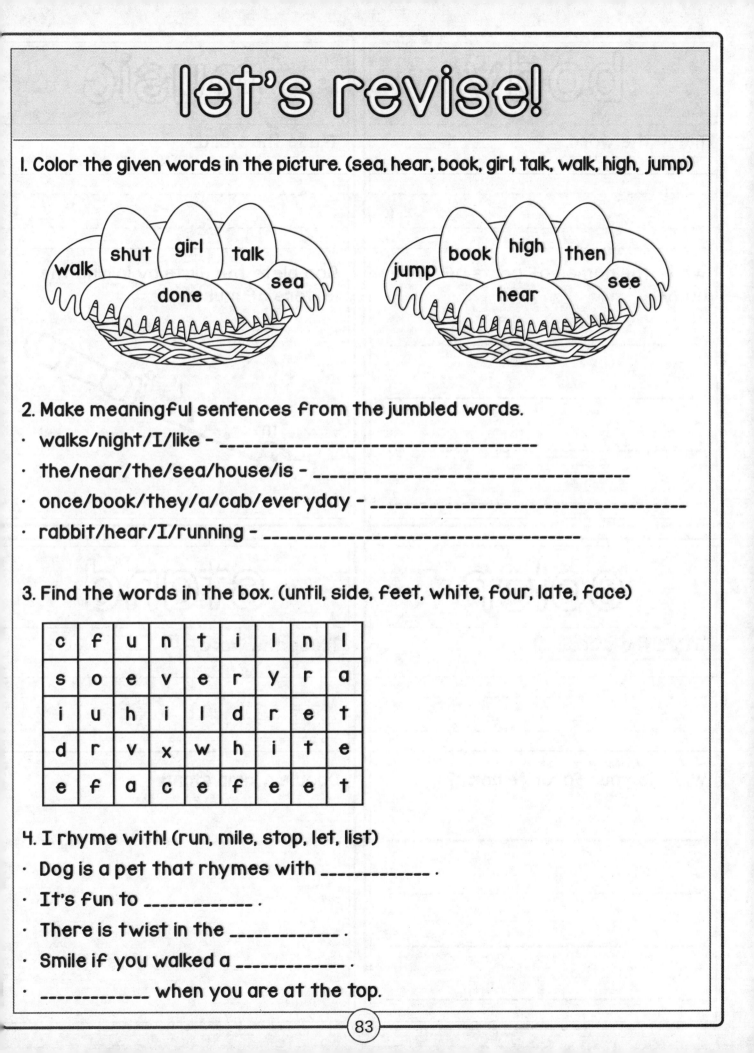

walk shut girl talk done sea

jump book high then hear see

2. Make meaningful sentences from the jumbled words.

· walks/night/I/like – _____

· the/near/the/sea/house/is – _____

· once/book/they/a/cab/everyday – _____

· rabbit/hear/I/running – _____

3. Find the words in the box. (until, side, feet, white, four, late, face)

c	f	u	n	t	i	l	n	l
s	o	e	v	e	r	y	r	a
i	u	h	i	l	d	r	e	t
d	r	v	x	w	h	i	t	e
e	f	a	c	e	f	e	e	t

4. I rhyme with! (run, mile, stop, let, list)

· Dog is a pet that rhymes with _____ .

· It's fun to _____ .

· There is twist in the _____ .

· Smile if you walked a _____ .

· _____ when you are at the top.

body

Trace the word.

body body

Write the names of parts of your body.

----

music

Trace the word.

music music

Complete the flute by joining the letters of music.

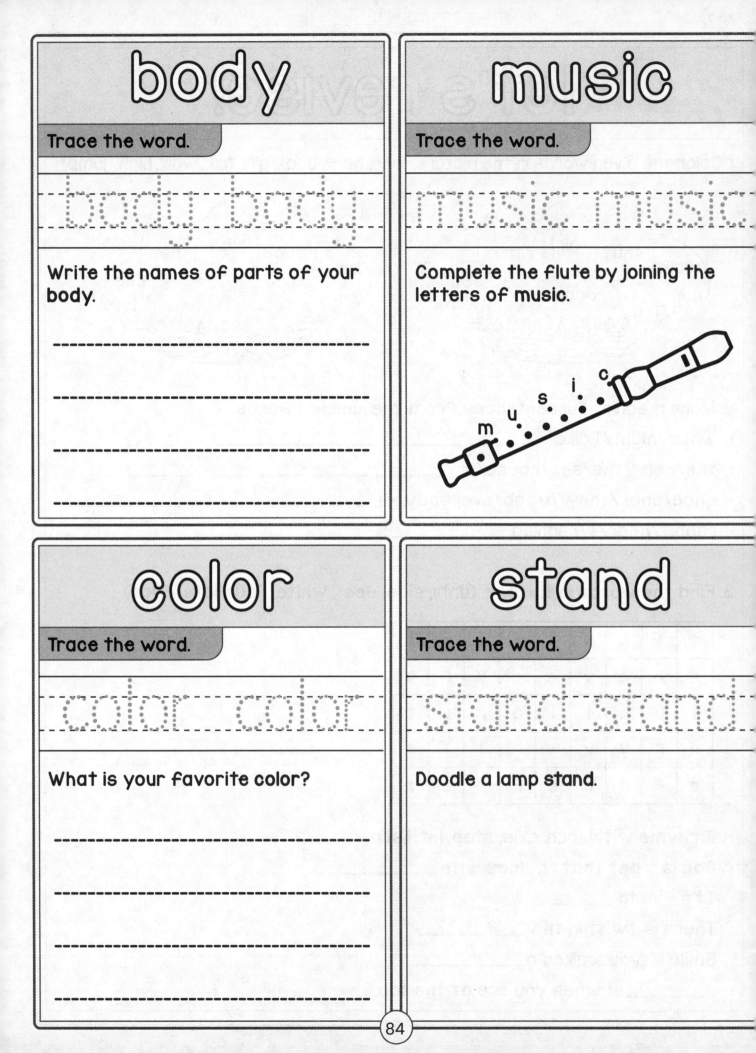

m u s i c

color

Trace the word.

color color

What is your favorite color?

----

stand

Trace the word.

stand stand

Doodle a lamp stand.

sun

Trace the word.

sun sun sun

Doodle a cute Sun.

questions

Trace the word.

questions

Write **questions** you want to ask your teacher?

----

fish

Trace the word.

fish fish fish

Draw a **fish** in water and color it.

area

Trace the word.

area   area

Complete the names of the given icons with the letters of **area**.

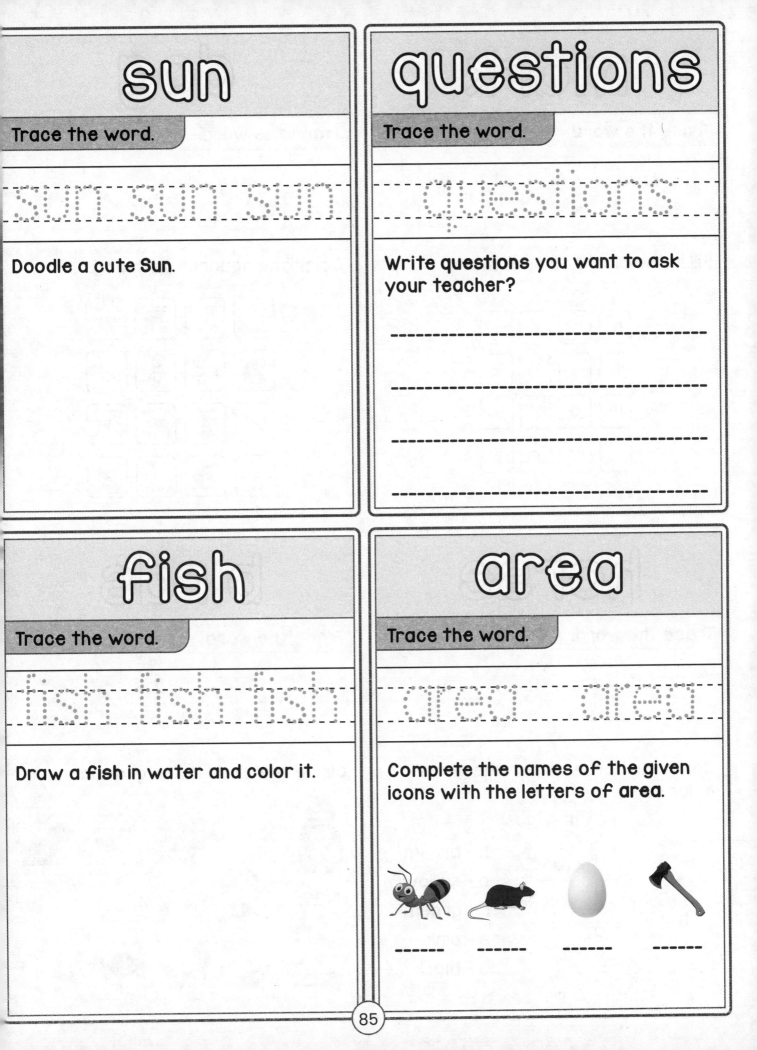

------   ------   ------   ------

mark

Trace the word.

mark mark

Fill in the blanks to spell mark.

m		r	
b		r	k
m	a		
		r	k

dog

Trace the word.

dog dog do

Color the squares with dog.

horse

Trace the word.

horse horse

Color the horse as per the given color key.

h – brown
o – yellow
r – green
s – pink
e – black

birds

Trace the word.

birds birds

Circle the birds in the given icons.

problem

Trace the word.

problem

Tick the words formed from problem.

- prom
- limb
- emblem
- bore
- mob

complete

Trace the word.

complete

How many times you spot complete?

complete	complete
women	always
between	complete
complete	something

room

Trace the word.

room room

Add room to words to get new words.

bed + room =

class + room =

board + room =

store + room =

cloak + room =

knew

Trace the word.

knew knew

Circle the things that rhyme with knew.

- scroll
- screw
- grow
- threw
- drew
- dam

since

since since

Complete the sentences with **since**.

The prince is not well

_____ yesterday.

_____ how long have you been watching us?

ever

Trace the word.

ever ever

Underline **ever** in the following words.

everlasting   forever   never

revere   believer   whosoever

fever   evergreen   whatsoever

piece

Trace the word.

piece piece

Check out the fruit and complete the sentences with **piece**.

· This is a _____ of an avocado.

· This is a _____ of an apple.

· This is a _____ of a pineapple.

· This is a _____ of a turnip.

told

Trace the word.

told told

Replace the underlined letters to get **told**.

· **b**old _____

· **f**old _____

· **h**old _____

· **c**old _____

· **m**old _____

usually

Trace the word.

usually

Circle the letters that spell **usually** from the jumbled words. Circle the right set.

d, u, k, o, s, u, f, a, w, q, l, l, p, d, y

s, t, u, f, f, s, k, j, u, a, w, o, l, y, l, r, y

u, g, r, s, a, e, u, a, c, c, b, l, l, f, y

x, m, v, u, b, s, k, o, u, a, p, z, l, r, h, y

didn't

Trace the word.

didn't didn't

Match the same font for **didn't**.

didn't •   • didn't

didn't •   • didn't

didn't •   • didn't

didn't •   • didn't

friends

Trace the word.

friends

Write the names of your **friends**.

----

easy

Trace the word.

easy easy

Color **easy** in your favorite colors.

EASY

heard

heard heard

Color the letters to get heard.

a	b	c	d	e	f	g
h	i	j	k	l	m	n
o	p	q	r	s	t	u
	v	w	x	y	z	

order

Trace the word.

order order

Add these letters to get words related to order.

dis + order =

order + ly =

pre + order =

order + less =

post + order =

red

Trace the word.

red red red

Draw and color a thing that is red.

door

Trace the word.

door door

Doodle a picture of the door of your house.

90

sure

Trace the word.

sure sure

Complete the word pyramid.

s
s u
s u r
s u r e

become

Trace the word.

become

Make as many words as you can from **become**.

come, be,_____

_____

_____

_____

top

Trace the word.

top top top

Draw a picture of a toy **top**.

ship

Trace the word.

ship ship ship

Color the word ship and help the **ship** reach the shore.

his	card	clean	ship
his	clean	visit	ship
	ship	ship	his
	ship	card	him

across

Trace the word.

across across

Circle the initials to get **across**.

apricot   camera   rope

octopus   sun   ship

today

Trace the word.

today today

Fill in the boxes to get **today**.

t			a	
	o	d		y
			d	a
t	o			y

during

Trace the word.

during during

Color the space with correct spelling of **during**.

during   duree   dureeng

during   dewring   during

during   duree   during

duree   dureeng   taulk

short

Trace the word.

short short

Fill in the blanks with **short**.

A giraffe is tall while a goat

is _____

A lamp is _____while a lamp

post is tall.

A tree is tall while its leaf

is _____

better

Trace the word.

better better

Color the correct code for better.

b	e	t	t	e	r
b					
e					
t					
t					
e					
r					

best

Trace the word.

best best

Complete the given calculation to get best.

test - t + b =

vest - v + b =

jest - v + b =

nest - v + b =

pest - v + b =

however

Trace the word.

however

Make as many words as you can from however.

how, ever,_____

_____

_____

_____

low

Trace the word.

low low low

Write the things you can think of with the letters of low.

l -

o -

w -

93

hours

Trace the word.

hours hours

Let's learn time. Fill in the blanks with **hours**.

· It's 2 _____ 45 minutes.

· It's 5 _____ 30 minutes.

· It's 8 _____ 15 minutes.

· It's 3 _____ 25 minutes.

black

Trace the word.

black black

Write the things that are **black**.

----

products

Trace the word.

products

Connect the letters to get study.

| w | r | o | c | t | h | j | n |

| l | p | d | u | s | a | m | b |

happened

Trace the word.

happened

Color the letters to get **happened**.

b	c	h	f	v	q	p
e	t	j	e	g	i	h
a	o	s	d	w	r	p
u	n	m	l	k

whole

Trace the word.

whole whole

Circle whole in the following words.

wholesome   wholeness

wholesale   wholefood

blowholes   wholemeal

measure

Trace the word.

measure

Color the words formed from measure.

ease   me   sure

war   see   star

sea   joker   play

remember

Trace the word.

remember

Fill in the blanks with **remember** and complete the lyrics.

_____ me though I have to say goodbye.

_____ me, don't let it make you cry.

_____ me though I have to travel far.

_____ me each time you hear a sad guitar.

early

Trace the word.

early early

Trace words formed from the letters of early.

ear   year

yale

waves

waves waves

Draw waves of a sea.

reached

reached

Unscramble the letters of the word **reached** from the jumbled words. Circle the right letters.

· r, s, e, d, f, a, c, k, h, g, e, l, d, w, e

· c, m, r, e, w, h, l, a, c, k, y, t, h, e, d, s, p

· z, c, g, r, j, m, e, a, b, c, n, h, e, l, x, w, d

· b, r, q, l, e, s, a, f, h, c, j, h, w, r, e, k, d

listen

listen listen

Complete the following sentences with **listen**.

· I _____ to music.

· Students _____ to their

   teachers.

· You _____ to me.

· Children _____ to their parents.

wind

wind wind

Add the following words to get new words.

wind + er = [   ]

re + wind = [   ]

wind + ow = [   ]

un + wind = [   ]

up + wind = [   ]

let's revise!

I. Fill in the blanks with appropriate words. (fish, dog, horse, birds)

· _____ is the most common pet animal.

· We can find _____ under water.

· _____ fly high in the sky.

· My _____ lives in its stable.

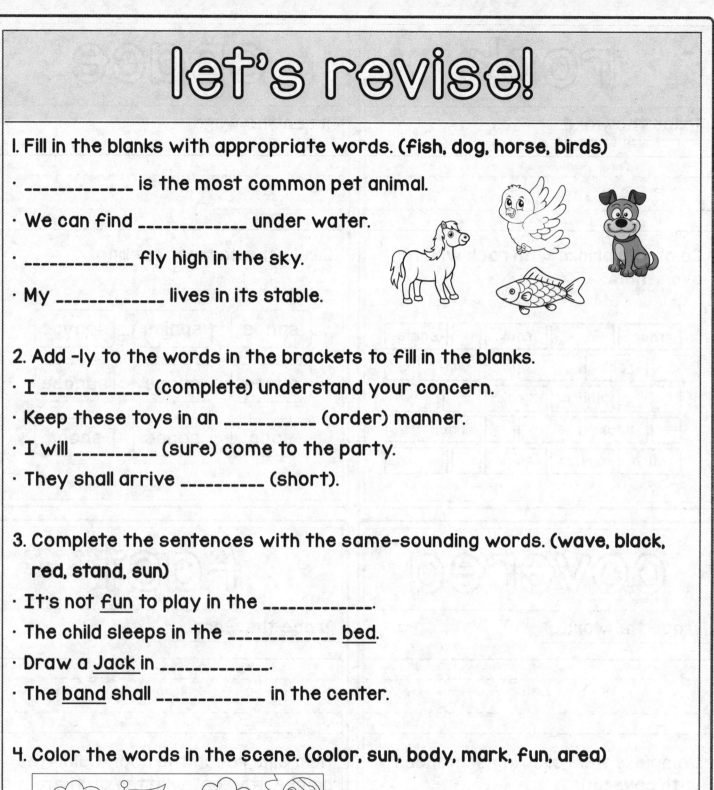

2. Add -ly to the words in the brackets to fill in the blanks.

· I _____ (complete) understand your concern.

· Keep these toys in an _____ (order) manner.

· I will _____ (sure) come to the party.

· They shall arrive _____ (short).

3. Complete the sentences with the same-sounding words. (wave, black, red, stand, sun)

· It's not <u>fun</u> to play in the _____.

· The child sleeps in the _____ <u>bed</u>.

· Draw a <u>Jack</u> in _____.

· The <u>band</u> shall _____ in the center.

4. Color the words in the scene. (color, sun, body, mark, fun, area)

rock

Trace the word.

rock rock rock

Color the bricks with **rock** written over them.

then		rock		same
	rock			write	
	shift	rock		
	rock		rock	
sure	dream	rock	

space

Trace the word.

space space

Circle the correct spelling.

space	spaice	spayce
space	space	spacee
spac	space	space

covered

Trace the word.

covered

Complete the following sentences with **covered**.

· The stone is _____ in moss.

· The sky was _____ in bubbles.

· The killer _____ his tracks.

· Mary _____ her notebook with ribbons.

fast

Trace the word.

fast fast fast

Help Gina reach the door. Color the block with **fast** written on them.

and

fast

fast fast

dog fast cat

fast small

fast day

with

several

Trace the word.

several

Connect the dots to get **several** and finish the picture.

hold

Trace the word.

hold hold

Fill in the blanks with **hold**.

· Will you _____ this for me, please?

· _____ on a second, I'll be back.

· Don't put me on _____.

· My dog likes to _____ the ball.

himself

Trace the word.

himself

Color the correct code for each letter.

h   i   m   s   e   l   f

h
i
m
s
e
l
f

toward

Trace the word.

toward

Circle the initials of the words to get **toward**.

tree   owl   water

apple   rat   dog

five

Trace the word.

five five five

Learn about shapes with five.

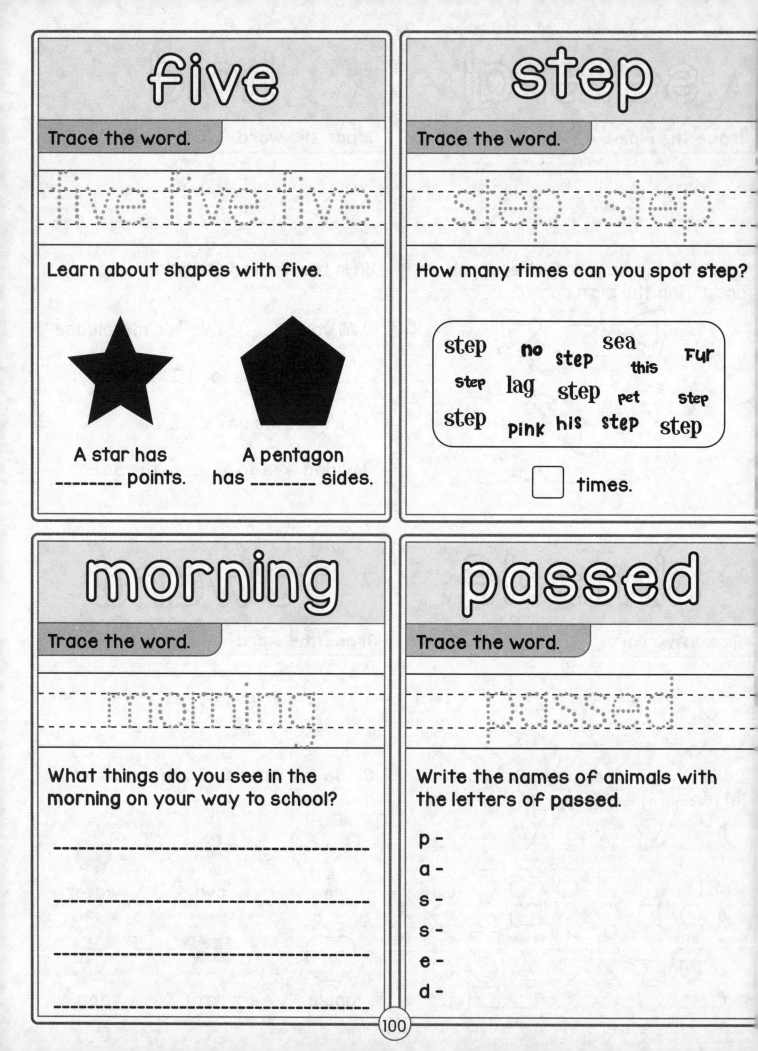

A star has _____ points.

A pentagon has _____ sides.

step

Trace the word.

step step

How many times can you spot **step**?

step   no   step   sea   fur
step   lag   step   this
step   pink   his   pet   step
step   pink   his   step   step

☐ times.

morning

Trace the word.

morning

What things do you see in the morning on your way to school?

----

passed

Trace the word.

passed

Write the names of animals with the letters of passed.

p -

a -

s -

s -

e -

d -

vowel

Trace the word.

vowel vowel

Underline vowels as you spot it.

In English, there are five vowels. These five vowels are a, e, i, o, and u. Sounds starting with vowels and called vowel sounds.

true

Trace the word.

true   true

Match the same font for true.

+rue •	• true
true •	• +rue
true •	• **true**
true •	• true

hundred

Trace the word.

hundred

Trace color to and get **hundred**.

hundred

hundred

against

Trace the word.

against

Let's learn phrases! Read them aloud.

· Your words <u>against</u> mine

· <u>Against</u> all odds

· <u>Against</u> your will

· A race <u>against</u> time

· A black mark <u>against</u>

pattern

Trace the word.

pattern

Trace the pattern.

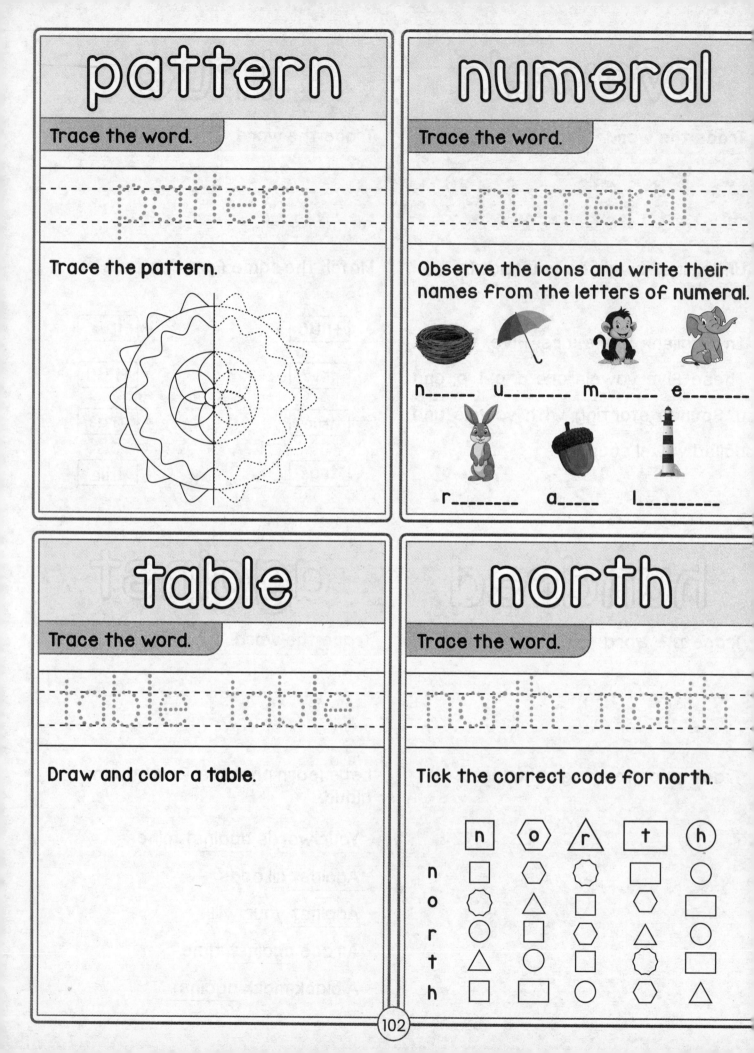

numeral

Trace the word.

numeral

Observe the icons and write their names from the letters of numeral.

n_____   u_____   m_____   e_____

r_____   a_____   l_____

table

Trace the word.

table table

Draw and color a table.

north

Trace the word.

north north

Tick the correct code for north.

	n	o	r	t	h
n	□	⬡	⬡	□	○
o	⬡	△	□	⬡	□
r	○	□	⬡	△	○
t	△	○	⬡	⬡	□
h	□	□	○	⬡	△

slowly

Trace the word.

slowly

Fill in the blanks with **slowly**.

· I walk _____.

· A tortoise walks _____.

· They jumped _____.

· Jason runs _____.

· I can stop _____.

money

Trace the word.

money

Draw the leaf of a money plant.

map

Trace the word.

map map

Trace the outline of the physical map of the world.

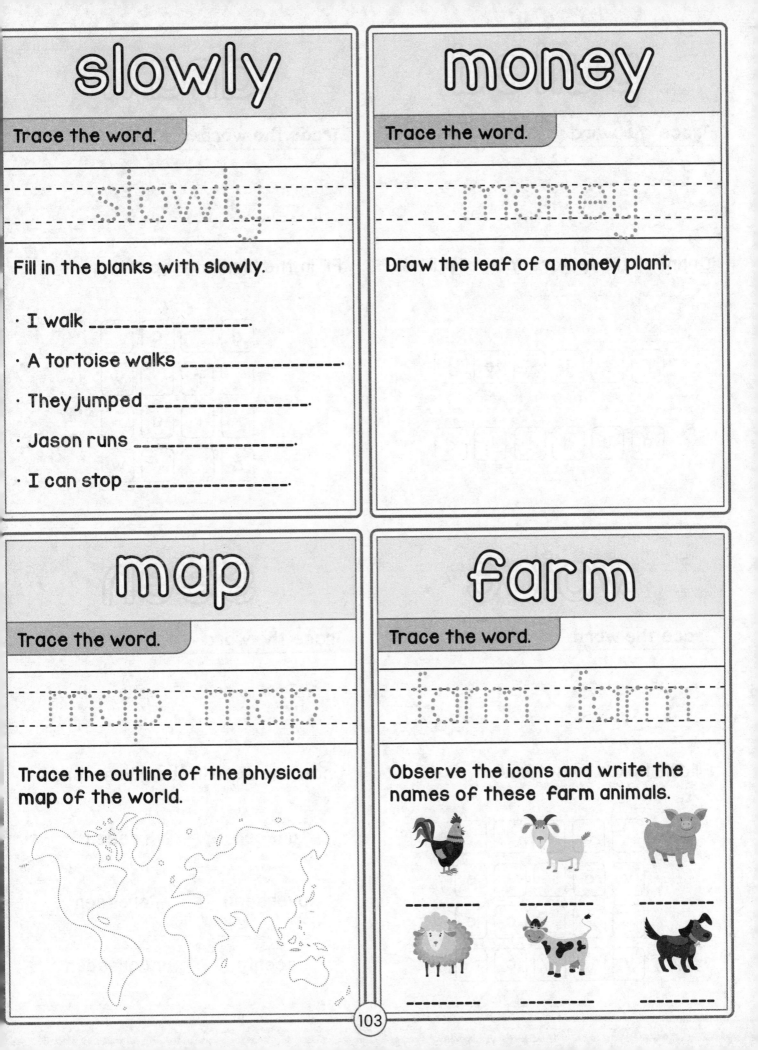

farm

Trace the word.

farm farm

Observe the icons and write the names of these farm animals.

_____ _____ _____

_____ _____ _____

pulled

pulled

Connect the letters to spell pulled.

| p | s | l | f | e | j |

| a | u | d | l | k | d |

draw

Trace the word.

draw draw

Fill in the blanks to spell draw.

d		a	
	r		w
	r	a	
d			w

voice

Trace the word.

voice voice

Fill the boxes to get voice.

	o	i		
v	o			e
			c	e
v			c	

seen

Trace the word.

seen seen

Underline seen in the given words.

unseen   reseen

overseen   foreseen

seenly   unforeseen

104

cold

Trace the word.

cold   cold

Draw a thing that is cold.

cried

Trace the word.

cried   cried

Draw an emoji face for cried.

plan

Trace the word.

plan   plan

Add the following to get new words from plan.

plan + ned =

un + plan =

plan + ing =

plan + er =

notice

Trace the word.

notice   notice

Make as many words as you can from notice.

no, ice,_____

_____

_____

_____

south

Trace the word.

south south

Tick the correct color code for south.

	s (□)	o (⬡)	u (△)	t (□)	h (○)
s	□	⬡	⬡	□	○
o	⬡	△	□	⬡	□
u	○	□	⬡	△	○
t	△	○	□	⬡	□
h	□	□	○	⬡	△

sing

Trace the word.

sing sing

You sing with this on stage. What is it?

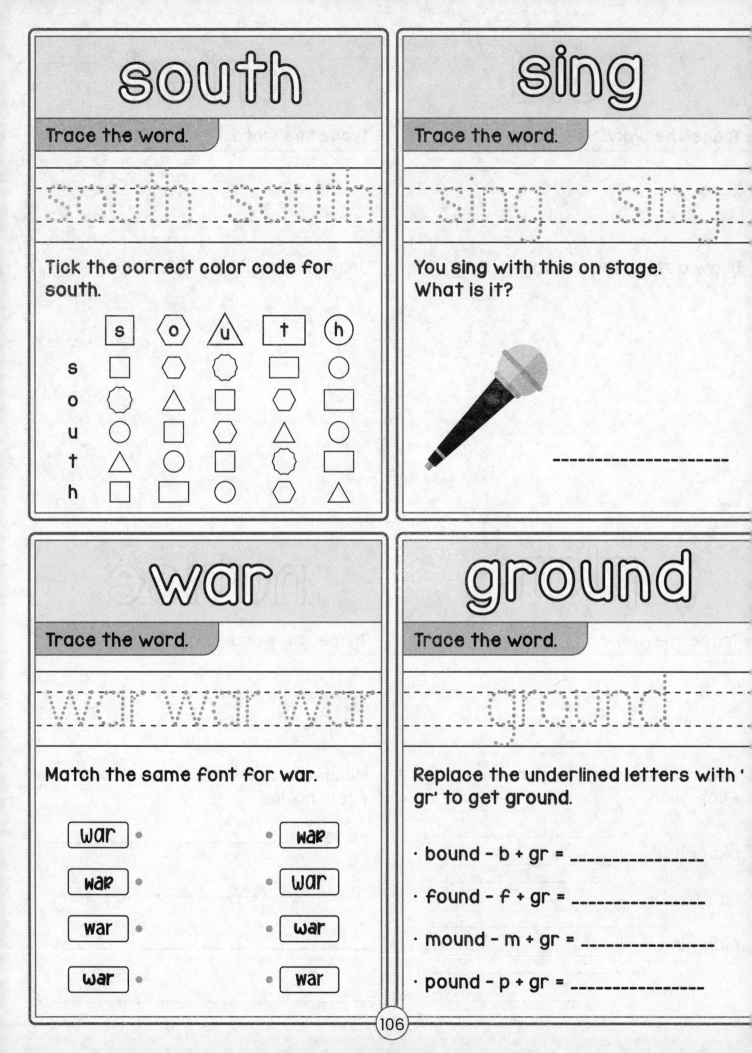

_____

war

Trace the word.

war war war

Match the same font for war.

war	•	•	war
war	•	•	war
war	•	•	war
war	•	•	war

ground

Trace the word.

ground

Replace the underlined letters with ' gr' to get ground.

· bound – b + gr = _____

· found – f + gr = _____

· mound – m + gr = _____

· pound – p + gr = _____

fall

Trace the word.

fall fall fall

Tick the pictures that show **fall**.

king

Trace the word.

king king

A king wears this on his head.
What is it?

----

town

Trace the word.

town town

Noddy lives in this **town**. What is it?

i'll

Trace the word.

i'll i'll i'll

Color the stars that have **i'll**
written on them.

i'll   is   no   i'll

so   i'll   i'll   he

unit

Trace the word.

unit unit

Fill in the blanks with **unit** to learn the standard units.

· The SI _____ of time is second.

· The SI _____ of length is meter.

· The SI _____ of mass is kilogram.

· The SI _____ of volume is liter.

figure

Trace the word.

figure figure

Circle the initials to get **figure**.

fish   ice   grapes

unhappy   radio   eye

certain

Trace the word.

certain

Color the letters to get **certain**.

a	b	c	d	e	f	g
h	i	j	k	l	m	n
o	p	q	r	s	t	u
	v	w	x	y	z	

field

Trace the word.

field field

Draw and color a **field** of grass.

travel

travel travel

Join the dots to get travel.

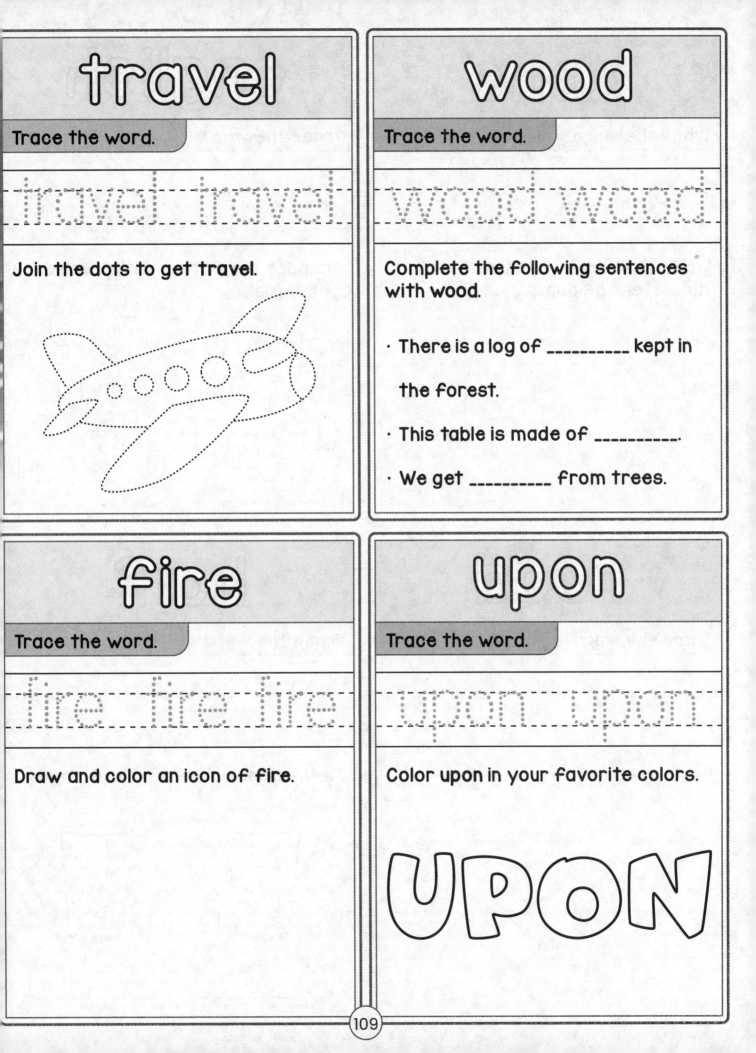

wood

Trace the word.

wood wood

Complete the following sentences with wood.

· There is a log of _____ kept in

the forest.

· This table is made of _____.

· We get _____ from trees.

fire

Trace the word.

fire fire fire

Draw and color an icon of fire.

upon

Trace the word.

upon upon

Color upon in your favorite colors.

UPON

109

done

Trace the word.

done done

Write the names of animals with the letters of **done**.

d -

o -

n -

e -

english

Trace the word.

english

Connect the letters with lines to get english.

a n q i p

e u k a s

l g l x h

n

road

Trace the word.

road road

Draw a road to the mountains.

half

Trace the word.

half half half

Is the glass **half-full** or **half-empty**?

let's revise!

1. Circle the given words in the shape. (covered, hold, step, himself, morning, vowel, true, map, slowly, draw, seen, notice, plan, sing, war, ground, certain, figure)

covered sing figure hold
type
tiger
world
certain
long draw map he honey crown color
war morning above
down slowly true vowel should
day ground is himself step stand
notice
mountains plan at seen
view
girl

2. Add -ed to the given words to get their past forms.

present	past
remember	
rock	
farm	
travel	

3. Rearrange the words to form meaningful sentences.

· today/the/across/sailed/ship

· decision/hours/ best/the/in/was/it

· wind/the/space/filled/whole/the

111

finally

Trace the word.

finally

Write the first thing that comes to your mind with the letters that spell finally.

f -   l -

i -   l -

n -   y -

a -

wait

Trace the word.

wait   wait

Add letters to wait to get new words.

a + wait =

wait + er =

wait + ress =

wait + list =

out + wait =

correct

Trace the word.

correct

Circle the correct spelling.

correct   coorect   correct

correct   coreect   correctt

correcct   correct   coorect

oh

Trace the word.

oh   oh   oh

Match the same font for oh.

Oh •   • oH

oH •   • Oh

oh •   • **oh**

oh •   • oh

112

quickly

Trace the word.

quickly

Fill in the blanks with **quickly** to complete the sentences.

· _____ run to the ground.

· She _____ went to the market.

· The mother _____ found the cookies.

· My father rushed to the

· airport _____.

person

Trace the word.

person

Circle the images that denote a **person**.

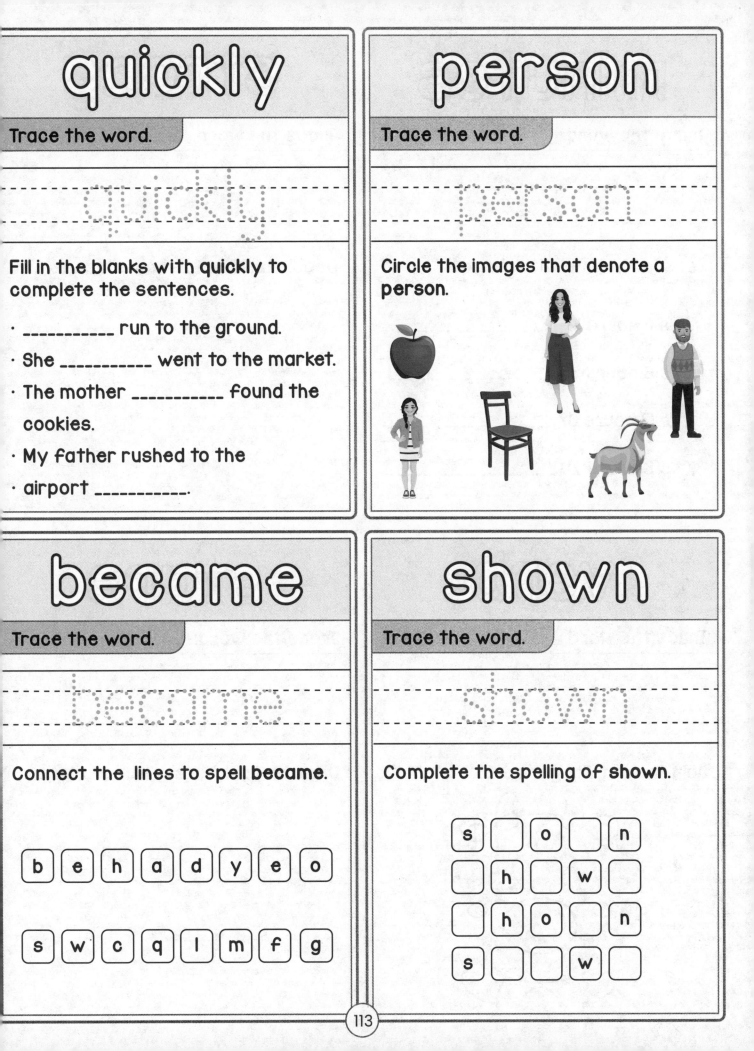

became

Trace the word.

became

Connect the lines to spell **became**.

b	e	h	a	d	y	e	o

s	w	c	q	l	m	f	g

shown

Trace the word.

shown

Complete the spelling of **shown**.

s		o		n
	h		w	
	h	o		n
s			w	

minutes

Trace the word.

minutes

Let's learn time with **minutes**.

It's 3 hours 10 _____.

It's 6 hours 45 _____.

It's 12 hours 37 _____.

It's 8 hours 20 _____.

strong

Trace the word.

strongstrong

Doodle an icon to show **strong**.

verb

Trace the word.

verb verb

Join the dots to get **verb**.

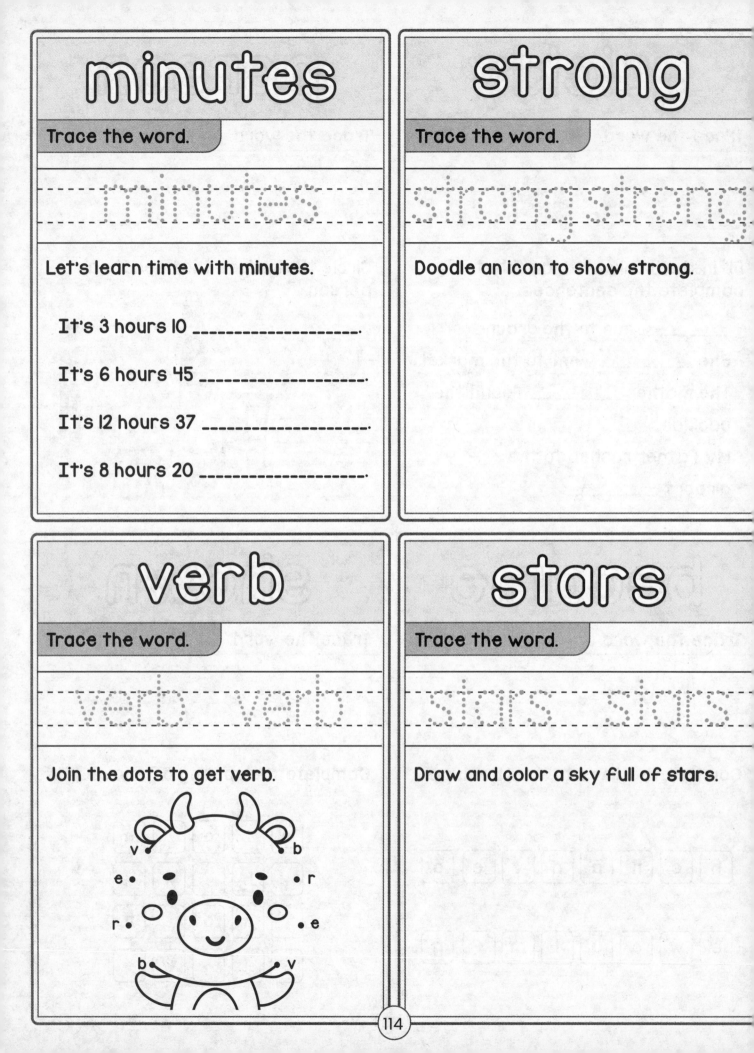

stars

Trace the word.

stars stars

Draw and color a sky full of **stars**.

front

Trace the word.

front front

Draw the **front** of the house you live in.

feel

Trace the word.

feel feel feel

Write down the things you can **feel**.

----

fact

Trace the word.

fact fact fact

Color each kiwi brown that has **fact** written over it.

as   fact   is

fact   of   fact

inches

Trace the word.

inches inches

Spot **inches** 3 times and color it.

c	f	i	n	c	h	e	s	l
s	o	e	v	e	r	y	r	a
i	i	n	c	h	e	s	e	t
d	r	v	x	w	h	i	t	e
i	n	c	h	e	s	e	e	t

street

Trace the word.

street street

Follow the **street** to reach the house.

decided

Trace the word.

decided

Fill in the blanks with **decided**.

Our parents _____ to go for a vacation.

The principal _____ to take school for a picnic.

The prince _____ to propose the princess.

contain

Trace the word.

contain

Make as many words as you can from **contain**.

on, coat_____

_____

_____

course

Trace the word.

course

Trace the letters to spell **course**.

course

surface

Trace the word.

surface

Follow the letters and help Pinocchio reach the water surface.

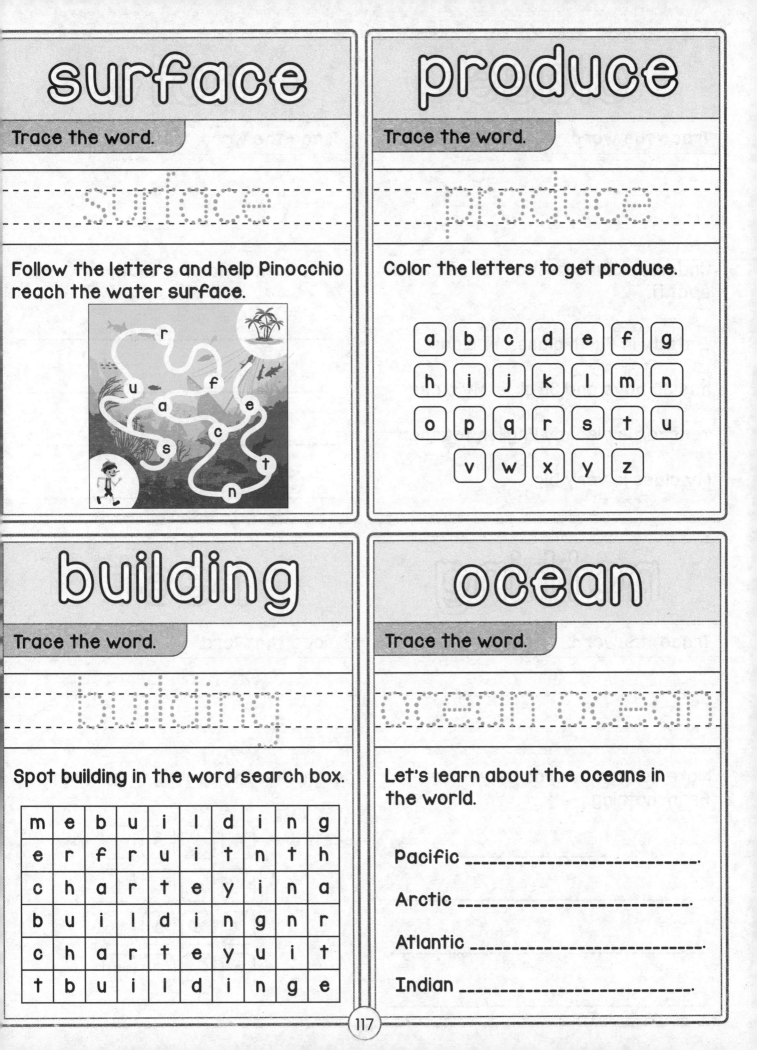

produce

Trace the word.

produce

Color the letters to get produce.

a	b	c	d	e	f	g
h	i	j	k	l	m	n
o	p	q	r	s	t	u
v	w	x	y	z

building

Trace the word.

building

Spot **building** in the word search box.

m	e	b	u	i	l	d	i	n	g
e	r	f	r	u	i	t	n	t	h
c	h	a	r	t	e	y	i	n	a
b	u	i	l	d	i	n	g	n	r
c	h	a	r	t	e	y	u	i	t
t	b	u	i	l	d	i	n	g	e

ocean

Trace the word.

ocean ocean

Let's learn about the **oceans** in the world.

Pacific _____.

Arctic _____.

Atlantic _____.

Indian _____.

117

class

Trace the word.

class class

Underline class as many time as you spot it.

I study in fifth class. My class

has 30 boys and 35 girls. My class

teacher is also my English teacher.

My class is very big.

note

Trace the word.

note note

Write a note to your mother.

----

nothing

Trace the word.

nothing

Make as many words as you can from nothing.

on, thing, _____

----

rest

Trace the word.

rest rest rest

Complete the spelling to get rest.

r		s	
	e		t
	e	s	
r			t

118

carefully

Trace the word.

carefully

Tick the pictures where the things are done **carefully**.

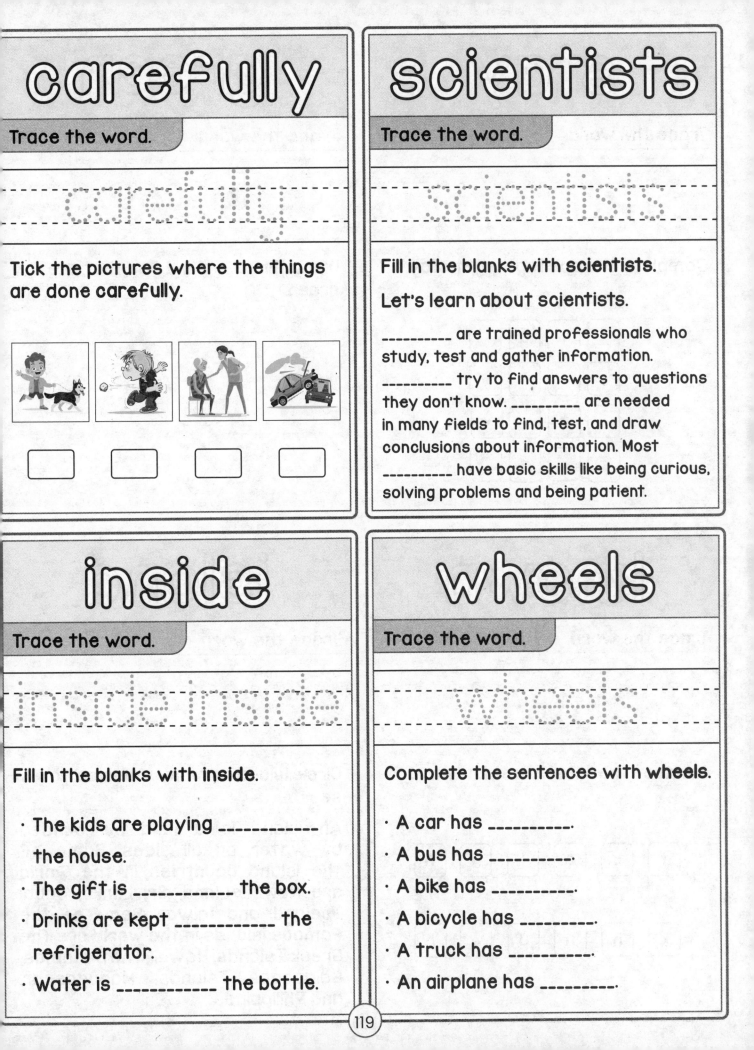

☐ ☐ ☐ ☐

scientists

Trace the word.

scientists

Fill in the blanks with **scientists**.

Let's learn about scientists.

_____ are trained professionals who study, test and gather information. _____ try to find answers to questions they don't know. _____ are needed in many fields to find, test, and draw conclusions about information. Most _____ have basic skills like being curious, solving problems and being patient.

inside

Trace the word.

inside inside

Fill in the blanks with **inside**.

· The kids are playing _____ the house.
· The gift is _____ the box.
· Drinks are kept _____ the refrigerator.
· Water is _____ the bottle.

wheels

Trace the word.

wheels

Complete the sentences with **wheels**.

· A car has _____.
· A bus has _____.
· A bike has _____.
· A bicycle has _____.
· A truck has _____.
· An airplane has _____.

stay

Trace the word.

stay   stay

Complete the spelling to get stay.

	t	a	
s			y
	t		y
s		a	

green

Trace the word.

green green

Draw things around you that are green.

known

Trace the word.

known

Connect the lines to get known.

| t | k | o | l | g | n |

| k | h | n | u | w | h |

island

Trace the word.

island island

Circle island as many times as you see it.

An island is a land surrounded by water on all sides. Some of the island countries in the world are New Zealand, Sri Lanka, Cuba, Iceland, and Taiwan. Some of the famous islands in the world are The Greek Islands, Hawaii, The Bahamas, Galapagos Islands, Madagascar, and Philippines.

week

Trace the word.

week week week

Let us learn the days of the **week**.

less

Trace the word.

less less less

Complete the qualities by adding less.

- _____ careful
- _____ populated
- _____ scary
- _____ thoughtful
- _____ fearful

machine

Trace the word.

machine

Doodle an easy **machine** at your home.

base

Trace the word.

base base

Help the soldier reach its **base**. Color the path with letters that spell **base**.

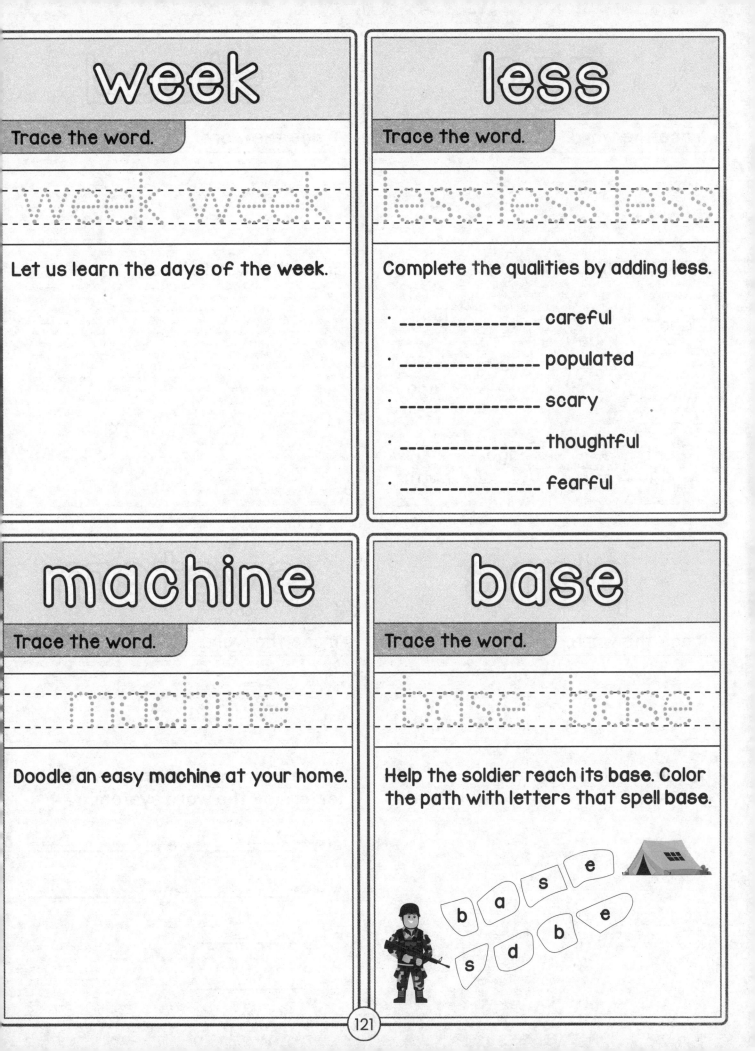

121

ago

Trace the word.

ago ago

Color the objects with **ago**.

ago
day
ago
her
him
ago
here
ago
ago
ago
with

stood

Trace the word.

stood stood

Trace the word stood.

stood

plane

Trace the word.

plane plane

Doodle an air plane.

system

Trace the word.

system

Write the names of animals with the letters of the word system.

s - _____   e - _____

y - _____   m - _____

s - _____

t - _____

let's revise!

1. Use the given -ly ending words appropriately. (finally, quickly, carefully)

· The nurse _____ dressed the wound.

· India _____ won the match.

· James moved aside _____.

2. Complete the sentences with the right words. (strong, building, verbs, stars, plane, minutes)

· Do all the _____ twinkle?

· Are you as _____ as her?

· The time is two _____ to two.

· All action words are called _____.

· A fire can be seen in the _____.

· An air _____ flies in the sky.

3. Write three words that end with the same letters as the given ones.

· Wh**eel**: _____, _____, _____

· Sh**own**: _____, _____, _____

· R**est**: _____, _____, _____

· Gr**een**: _____, _____, _____

behind

behind

Circle the word **behind**.

· I sit behind Anna in class.
· There is a garden behind my house.
· The seats were placed one behind the other.
· 'Behind every successful man is a woman.'

ran

ran ran ran

Complete the sentences with **ran**.

· He <u>ran</u> beside her.
· The dog <u>ran</u> behind the girl.
· The police <u>ran</u> to catch the thief.
· The students <u>ran</u> to the ground.

round

round round

Draw and color a **round** figure.

boat

boat boat

Doodle a **boat** in a lake.

game

Trace the word.

game game

Write about the **game** you like to play.

_____

_____

_____

_____

force

Trace the word.

force force

Complete the spelling to get **force**.

	o	r		e
f			c	
	o		o	
f		r		e

brought

Trace the word.

brought

Replace the underlined letters with **br** to get **brought**.

- <u>s</u>ought
- <u>f</u>ought
- <u>b</u>ought
- <u>w</u>rought
- <u>th</u>ought

understand

Trace the word.

understand

Unscramble the word **understand** from the jumbled letters. Circle the right letters.

- u, z, n, d, w, e, q, r, s, h, t, l, a, n, o, d
- p, u, m, n, v, d, e, x, r, s, y, t, s, a, b, n, l, d
- c, a, r, u, n, d, e, r, s, t, a, n, d, p, i, e, q
- u, n, l, d, e, r, a, q, x, e, s, t, l, q, r, s, a, n, d

125

warm

Trace the word.

warm warm

Tick against the season that is **warm**.

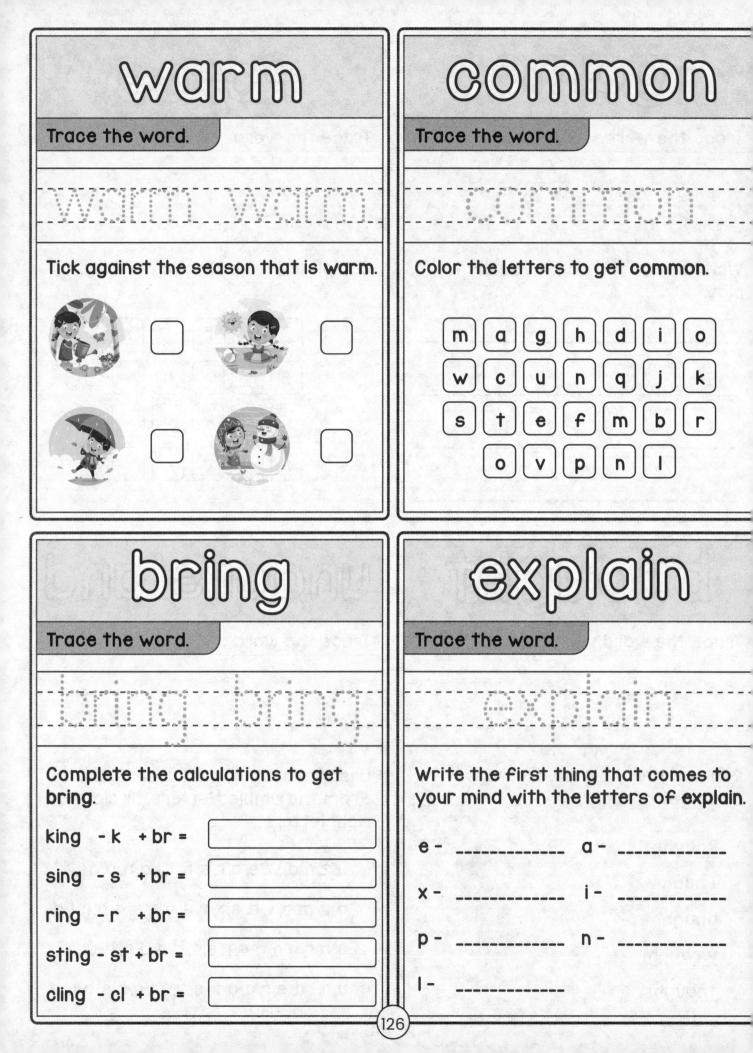

common

Trace the word.

common

Color the letters to get **common**.

m	a	g	h	d	i	o
w	c	u	n	q	j	k
s	t	e	f	m	b	r
o	v	p	n	l		

bring

Trace the word.

bring bring

Complete the calculations to get **bring**.

king   – k   + br = _____

sing   – s   + br = _____

ring   – r   + br = _____

sting – st + br = _____

cling – cl + br = _____

explain

Trace the word.

explain

Write the first thing that comes to your mind with the letters of **explain**.

e - _____   a - _____

x - _____   i - _____

p - _____   n - _____

l - _____

dry

Trace the word.

dry dry dry

Tick against the season that is dry.

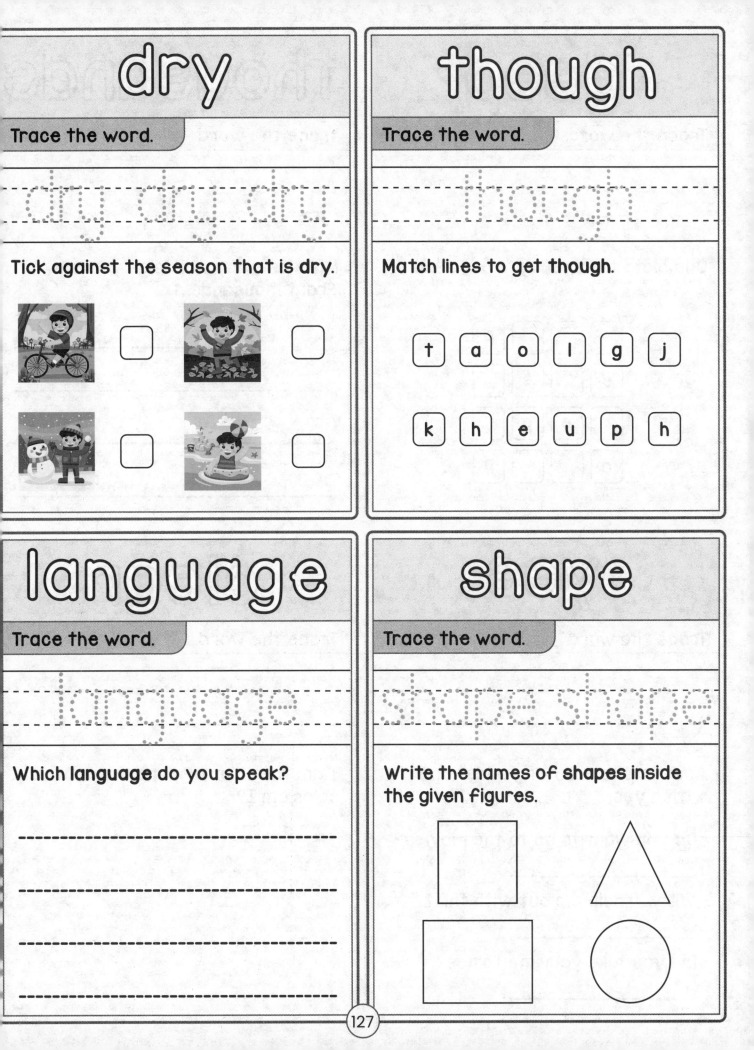

though

Trace the word.

though

Match lines to get though.

| t | a | o | l | g | j |

| k | h | e | u | p | h |

language

Trace the word.

language

Which language do you speak?

\-

\-

\-

shape

Trace the word.

shape shape

Write the names of shapes inside the given figures.

deep

Trace the word.

deep deep

Complete the spelling to get **deep**.

	e		p
d		e	
	e	e	
d			p

thousands

Trace the word.

thousands

Make as many words as you can from **thousands**.

us, sand, _____

_____

_____

_____

yes

Trace the word.

yes yes yes

Answer the following questions with a **yes**.

· Do you want to go to the movies?

_____.

· Will you help me out with this?

_____.

· Did you take your medicines?

_____.

clear

Trace the word.

clear clear

I am the color of pure water. Which color am I?

equation

Trace the word.

equation

Use + and = to complete the equations.

1 ▢ 1 ▢ 2

2 ▢ 2 ▢ 4

2 ▢ 1 ▢ 3

1 ▢ 2 ▢ 3

yet

Trace the word.

yet yet yet

Match the same font for yet.

Yet	•	•	yet
yet	•	•	Yet
yet	•	•	yet
yet	•	•	yet

government

Trace the word.

government

Learn the types of government.

· democratic _____.

· autocratic _____.

· monarchy _____.

· theocratic _____.

filled

Trace the word.

filled filled

Fill in the blanks with **filled**.

· The smell of flowers _____ the air.

· Her laughter _____ the house like happiness.

· The glass is half- _____.

· The garbage can is _____ to the brim.

heat

Trace the word.

heat heat heat

Complete the spelling to get **heat**.

	e		t
h		a	
	e	a	
h			t

full

Trace the word.

full full full

Circle the bottle that is **full**.

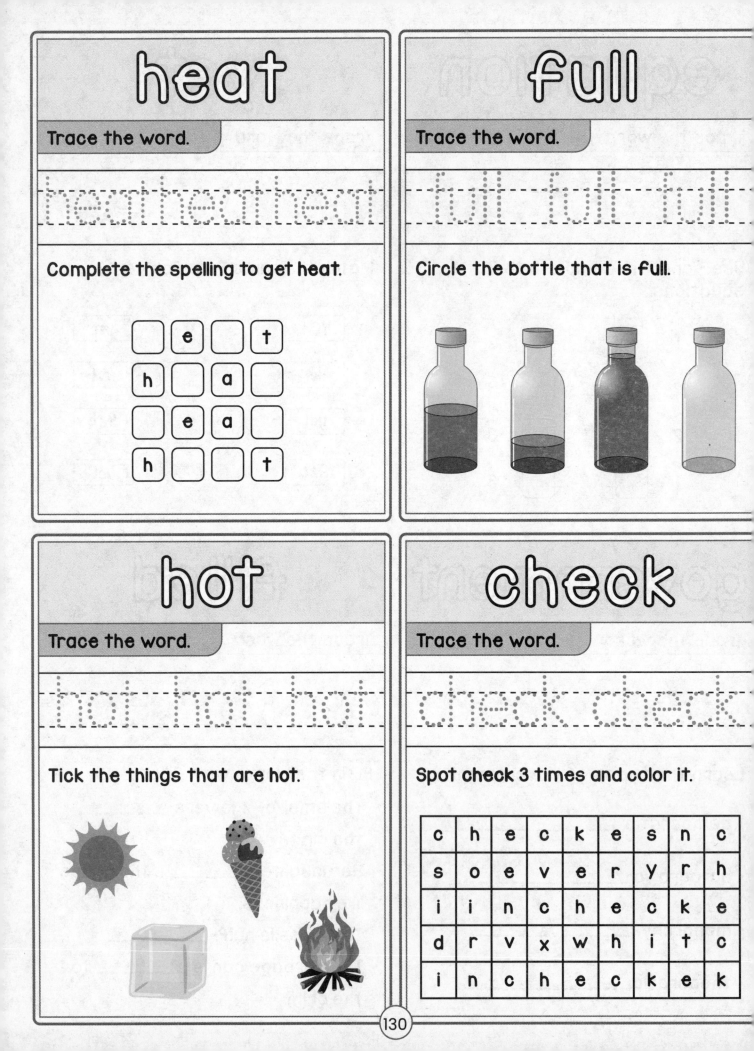

hot

Trace the word.

hot hot hot

Tick the things that are hot.

check

Trace the word.

check check

Spot **check** 3 times and color it.

c	h	e	c	k	e	s	n	c
s	o	e	v	e	r	y	r	h
i	i	n	c	h	e	c	k	e
d	r	v	x	w	h	i	t	c
i	n	c	h	e	c	k	e	k

object

object object

Draw and color an object of your choice.

am

am am am

Match the same font for am.

am	•	•	am
am	•	•	am
am	•	•	am
am	•	•	am

rule

rule rule rule

Write one rule you like to follow.

----

among

among

Trace and color the word among.

among

noun

Trace the word.

noun noun

Any name, place, animal, thing, or feeling is called noun.

Identify the nouns and underline them.

- Flowers are pretty.
- John has beautiful hair.
- The lion gave birth to cubs.
- America is a democratic country.

power

Trace the word.

power power

Color the letters to get power.

a	b	c	d	e	f	g
h	i	j	k	l	m	n
o	p	q	r	s	t	u

v	w	x	y	z

cannot

Trace the word.

cannot cannot

Make two three-letter words from cannot.

----

able

Trace the word.

able able

Fill in the boxes with missing letters to spell able.

a			e

| | b | l | |

| a | b | | |

| | | l | e |

six

Trace the word.

six six six

Complete the sentences with six.

· An over in a cricket match has _____ balls.
· Half a dozen is _____.
· Add _____ to two and get eight.

size

Trace the word.

size size

Match lines to get size.

| t | s | o | z | g | j |

| k | h | i | u | e | h |

dark

Trace the word.

dark dark

I am the opposite of light and you cannot see in me. Who am I?

_____

ball

Trace the word.

ball ball ball

Add these words to ball and learn new games.

foot + ball = _____

basket + ball = _____

hand + ball = _____

foos + ball = _____

volley + ball = _____

material

Trace the word.

material

Answer the following questions.

· Which material is used to make sweaters?

· Which material can goats eat?

----

special

Trace the word.

special

Write 3 sentences about your special day.

----

heavy

Trace the word.

heavy heavy

Circle the things that are heavy.

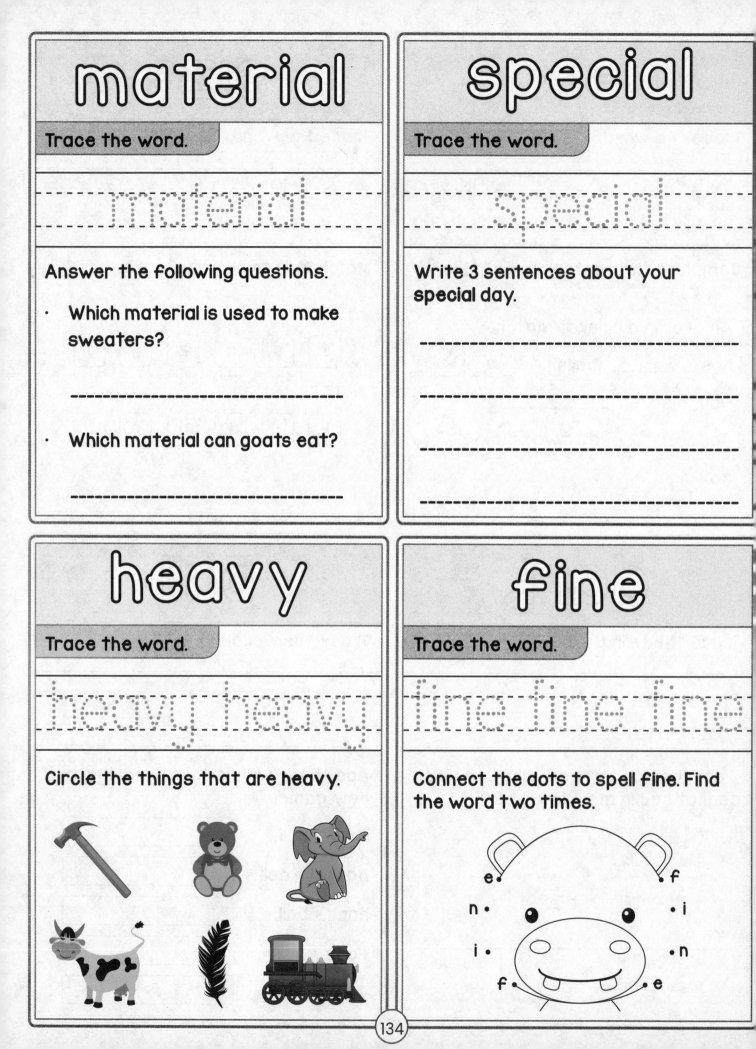

fine

Trace the word.

fine fine fine

Connect the dots to spell fine. Find the word two times.

pair

Trace the word.

pair pair pair

Color the things in pair.

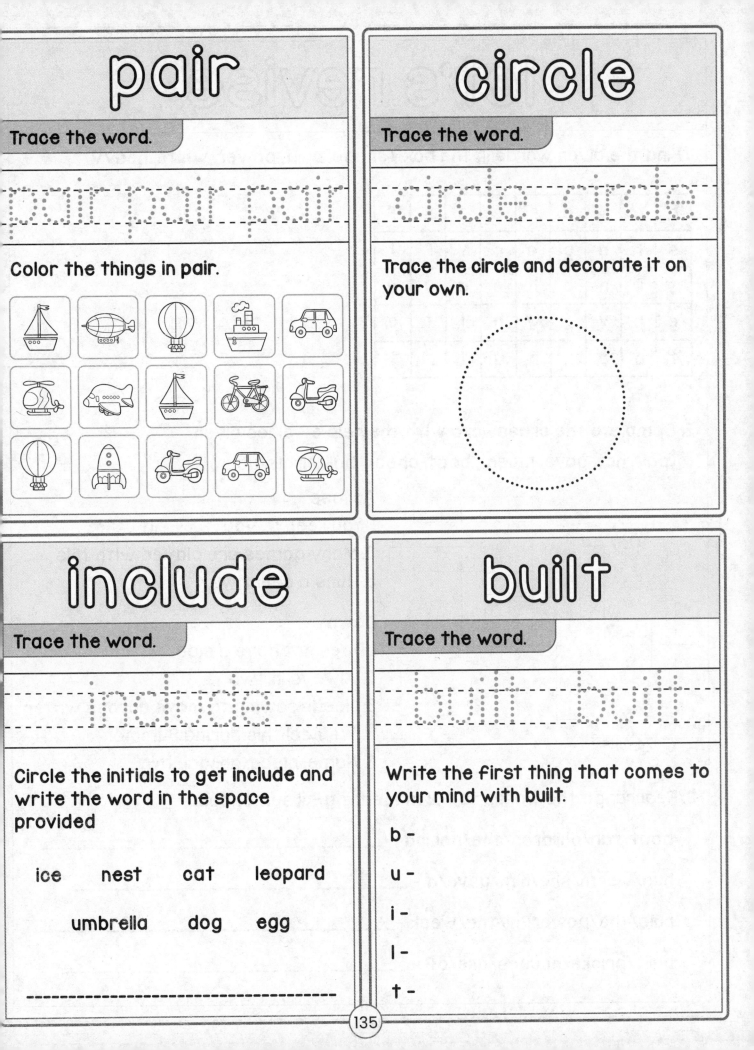

circle

Trace the word.

circle circle

Trace the circle and decorate it on your own.

include

Trace the word.

include

Circle the initials to get include and write the word in the space provided

ice   nest   cat   leopard

umbrella   dog   egg

_____

built

Trace the word.

built built

Write the first thing that comes to your mind with built.

b –

u –

i –

l –

t –

let's revise!

1. Find the given words in the box. (shape, built, power, white, heavy)

p	o	w	e	r	e	s	n	f
s	h	a	p	e	r	y	r	i
y	i	n	c	h	e	a	v	y
e	r	v	x	w	h	i	t	e
t	n	c	h	b	u	l	i	t

2. Complete the crossword with the help of clues given.

(pair, hot, government, boat, check, ball, circle, noun)

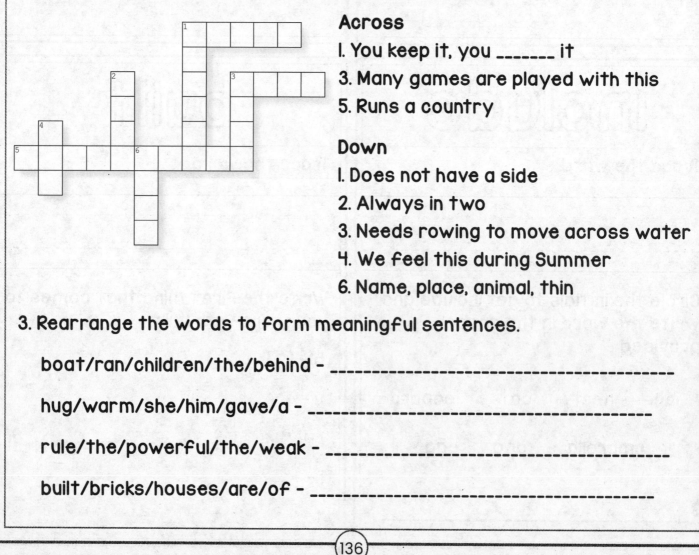

Across

1. You keep it, you _____ it
3. Many games are played with this
5. Runs a country

Down

1. Does not have a side
2. Always in two
3. Needs rowing to move across water
4. We feel this during Summer
6. Name, place, animal, thin

3. Rearrange the words to form meaningful sentences.

boat/ran/children/the/behind – _____

hug/warm/she/him/gave/a – _____

rule/the/powerful/the/weak – _____

built/bricks/houses/are/of – _____

can't

can't can't

Fill in the blanks with can't.

· Can a cheetah play video games?
No, it _____.
· A news anchor _____ come
out of the TV.
· Stop! You _____ cross the red
light.
· An elephant _____ climb a tree.

matter

matter

Complete the word matter in pyramid.

m
m a
m a t
m a t t
m a t t e
m a t t e r

square

square

**Circle the objects that are square
in shape.**

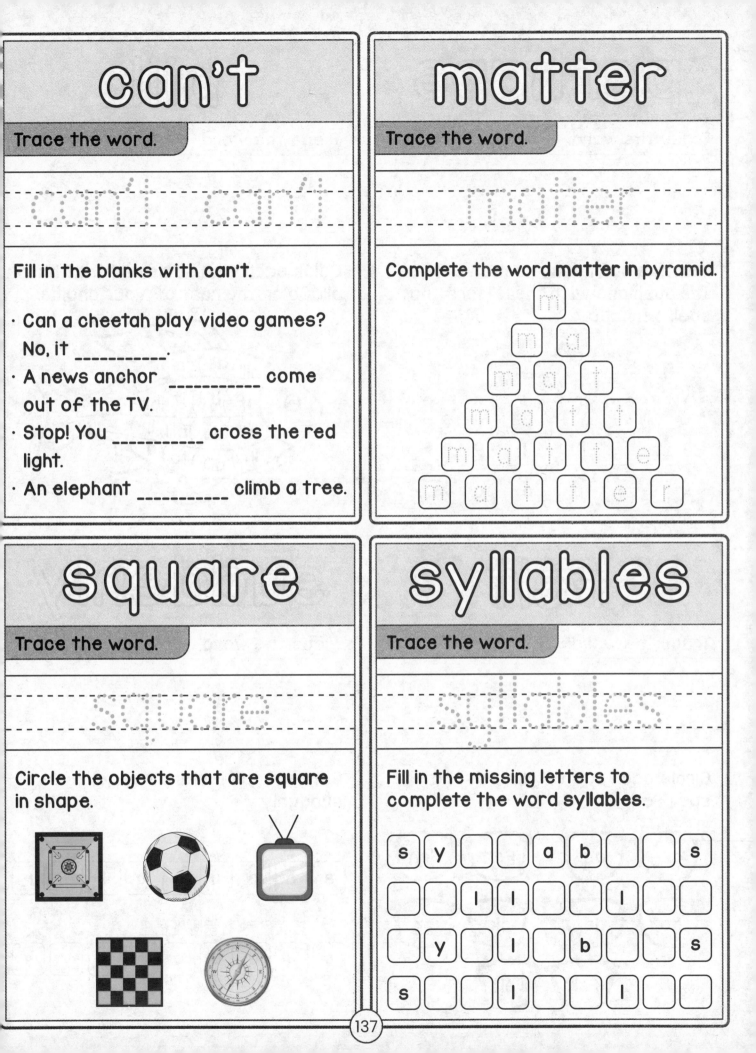

syllables

syllables

**Fill in the missing letters to
complete the word syllables.**

s	y		a	b		s
		l			l	
	y		l		b		s
s				l		

137

perhaps

Trace the word.

perhaps

Help the cat reach its mat. Color the cushions with the letters that spell perhaps.

p	a	b	e	r
e	r	h	a	p
n	b	m	q	o	s
x	z	p	p	p

bill

Trace the word.

bill bill bill

Color each fish scale red that has bill. Color the rest of your choice.

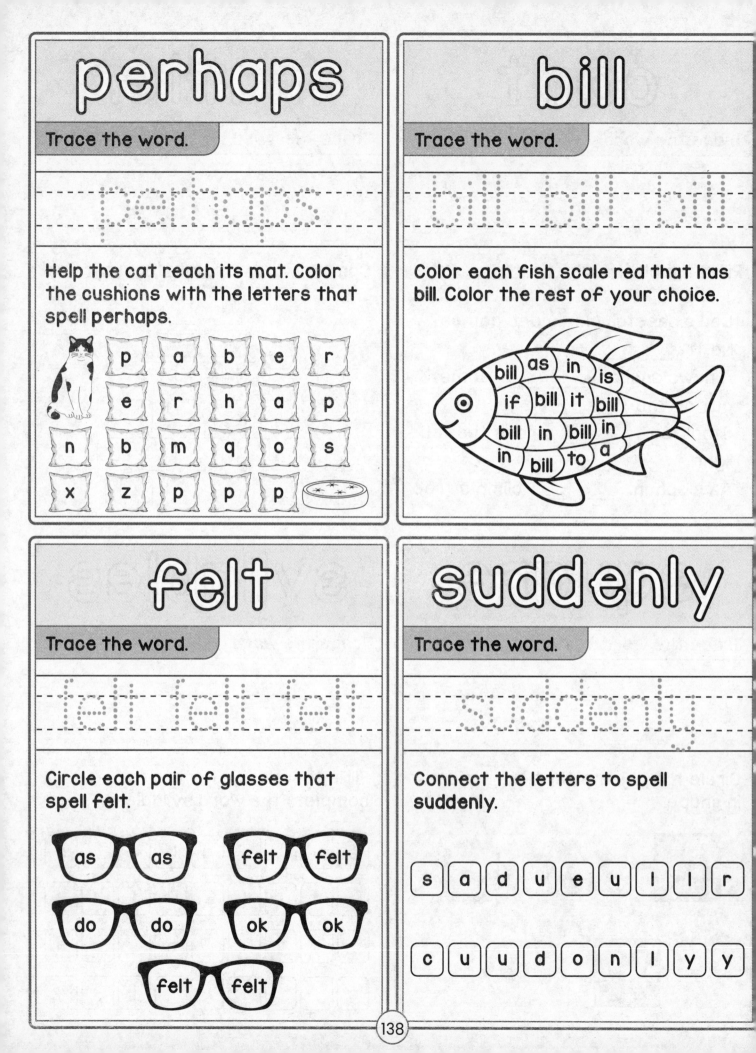

felt

Trace the word.

felt felt felt

Circle each pair of glasses that spell felt.

as as   felt felt

do do   ok ok

felt felt

suddenly

Trace the word.

suddenly

Connect the letters to spell suddenly.

s	a	d	u	e	u	l	r

c	u	u	d	o	n	l	y	y

test

Trace the word.

test test test

Fill in the missing letters to complete the word test.

t	e		t
	e		t
t		s	
t			t

direction

Trace the word.

direction

What does each arrow say?

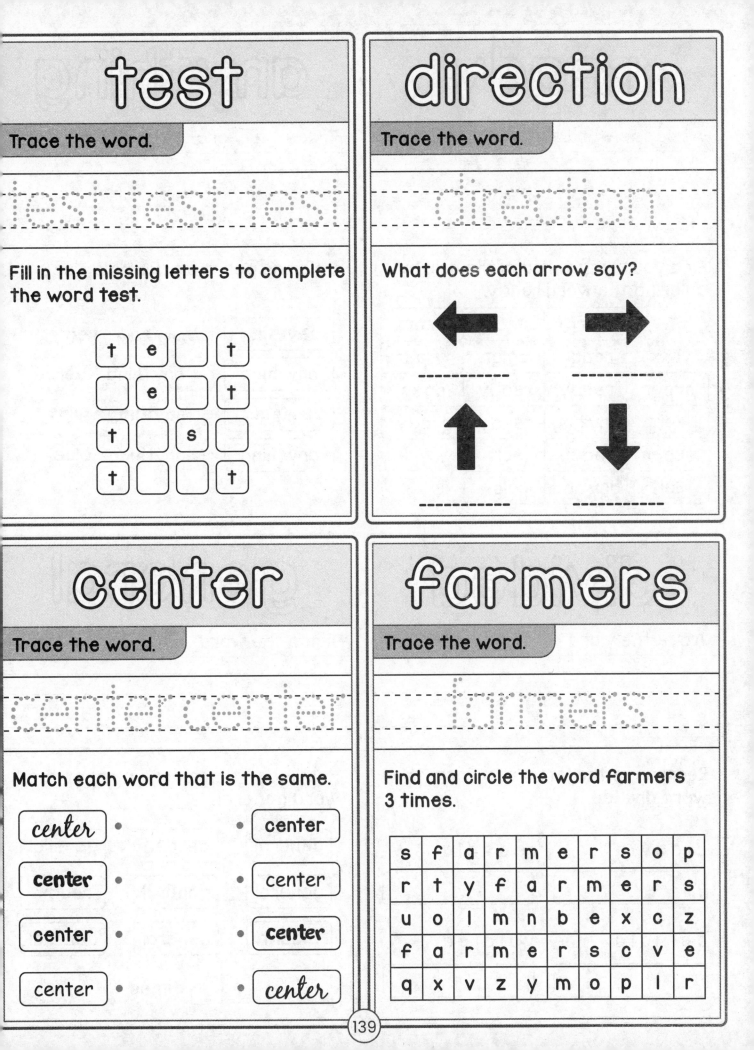

‑‑‑‑‑‑‑‑‑‑   ‑‑‑‑‑‑‑‑‑‑

‑‑‑‑‑‑‑‑‑‑   ‑‑‑‑‑‑‑‑‑‑

center

Trace the word.

center center

Match each word that is the same.

center	•	•	center
center	•	•	center
center	•	•	center
center	•	•	center

farmers

Trace the word.

farmers

Find and circle the word farmers 3 times.

s	f	a	r	m	e	r	s	o	p
r	t	y	f	a	r	m	e	r	s
u	o	l	m	n	b	e	x	c	z
f	a	r	m	e	r	s	c	v	e
q	x	v	z	y	m	o	p	l	r

ready

Trace the word.

ready ready

Find your way through the grid by coloring the word **ready**.

	energy	smart	smart
	ready	color	find
super	ready	ready	does
felt	anyting	ready	ready
super	ready	felt	
felt	anyting	color	

anything

Trace the word.

anything

Color as per the given color key.

anything	*anything* – red
anything	anything – yellow
anything	**anything** – green
anything	anything – blue

divided

Trace the word.

divided

Rearrange the letters to form the word **divided**.

d i e d v i d

i e d v d i d

d e i v d i d

v d i d i e d

general

Trace the word.

general

How many times can you spot the word **general**?

general	divided	general
general	general	ready
smart	general	general

☐ times

energy

energy energy

Color the letters to find energy.

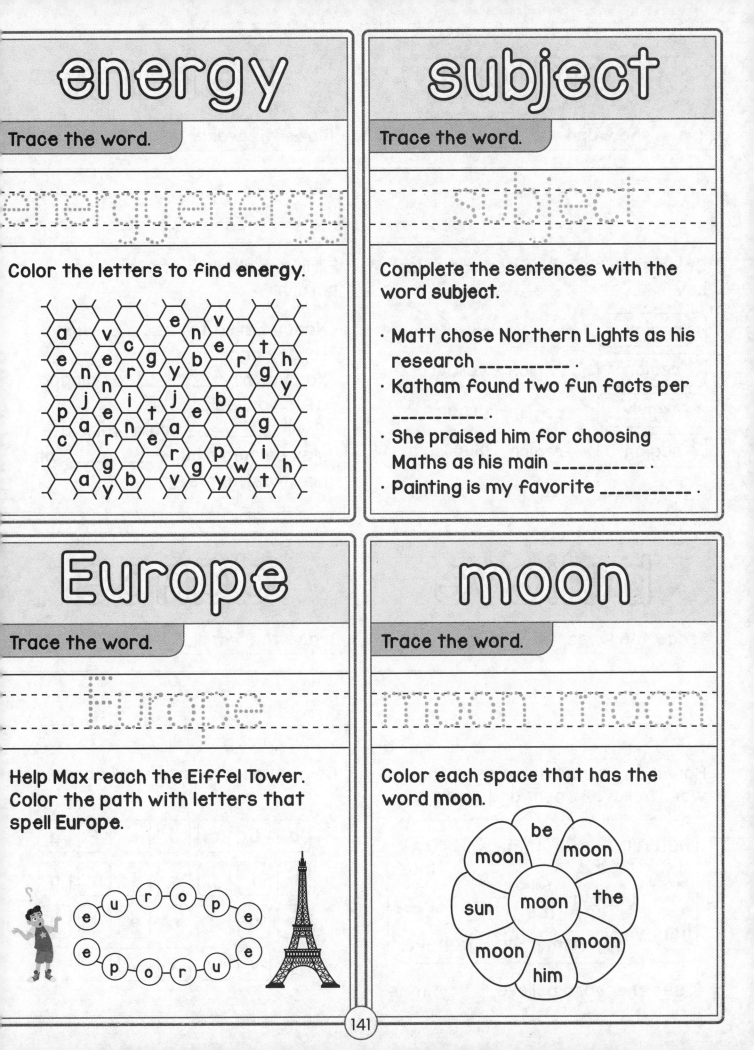

subject

Trace the word.

subject

Complete the sentences with the word **subject**.

· Matt chose Northern Lights as his research _____ .
· Katham found two fun facts per _____ .
· She praised him for choosing Maths as his main _____ .
· Painting is my favorite _____ .

Europe

Trace the word.

Europe

Help Max reach the Eiffel Tower. Color the path with letters that spell **Europe**.

moon

Trace the word.

moon moon

Color each space that has the word **moon**.

141

region

Trace the word.

region region

Color each space as per the color key.

region	region – red
region	region – yellow
region	**region** – green
region	region – blue

return

Trace the word.

return return

Fill in the blanks with the word return.

· Nancy failed to _____ her library books.
· Kamya will _____ to Chicago after a week.
· I will _____ from work late.
· Max earned a huge _____ on his investments.

believe

Trace the word.

believe

How many times do you see the word believe? Count and write.

believe   the   believe   her
the   this   time
believe   believe
believe   his   her   believe
believe   her   time   this   believe

I see the word believe ☐ times.

dance

Trace the word.

dance dance

Color the letters to spell dance.

a	b	c	d	e	f	g
h	i	j	k	l	m	n
o	p	q	r	s	t	u
v	w	x	y	z		

members

Trace the word.

members

Fill in the missing letters to spell members.

	e	m		e		s
		m			r	s
m			b	e		
m	e				r	s

picked

Trace the word.

pickedpicked

Match each word that is the same.

picked •   • picked

picked •   • picked

picked •   • **picked**

picked •   • *picked*

simple

Trace the word.

simple

Noddy lives in this town. What is its name? Spot the word 2 times.

s	i	m	p	l	e	t
w	e	l	p	m	i	s
n	n	w	o	t	w	n
s	i	m	p	l	e	e

cells

Trace the word.

cells cells

Color the oranges that make up the word cells.

c	e	l	l	s	o
l	c	e	l	l	s
c	l	l	l	e	c

paint

Trace the word.

paint paint

Spot the word paint.

s	f	p	a	i	n	t	p	o	p
p	a	i	n	t	r	m	a	r	a
u	o	t	n	i	a	p	i	c	i
f	a	r	m	e	r	s	n	v	n
q	t	n	i	a	p	o	t	l	t

mind

Trace the word.

mind mind

Circle the first letter of each word to spell mind. Write it in the blank.

meerkat

iguana

narhwal

dolphin

love

Trace the word.

love love love

Color each heart with the word love.

love   the   love   off

love   him   ask   love

see   love   love   did

cause

Trace the word.

cause cause

Find and underline the word cause in the set of letters.

gnogcausekgkkgt

negcauseththotth

frcausengrnjghhtoh

nvibnibngntcause

causempthpthpth

rain

Trace the word.

rain rain rain

Spot and highlight the word rain 4 times.

s	r	a	i	n	e	r
w	e	r	a	i	n	a
r	a	i	n	t	w	i
s	r	a	i	n	e	n

exercise

Trace the word.

exercise

Find the word **exercise**. Draw a line to connect the letters.

s	e	s	e	d	c	e	s	r

c	s	x	d	r	d	i	t	e

eggs

Trace the word.

eggs eggs

Fill in the missing letters to write the word eggs.

e		g	
	g		s
		g	s
e	g		

train

Trace the word.

train train

Match each word that is the same.

train •   • train

train •   • train

train •   • **train**

train •   • train

blue

Trace the word.

blue blue blue

Connect the dots to spell **blue**. Find the word 2 times.

l   u
b   e
b
e
i
u

wish

Trace the word.

wish   wish

Complete the word pyramid.

w
w i
w i s
w i s h

drop

Trace the word.

drop   drop

Circle the word **drop**.

· The cops asked the thief to drop his weapons.

· Carla and Martha always drop their feeders in the playground.

· Let us drop the subject.

· Kindly drop my son to school.

developed

Trace the word.

developed

Find your way through the maze. Color the word **developed** red.

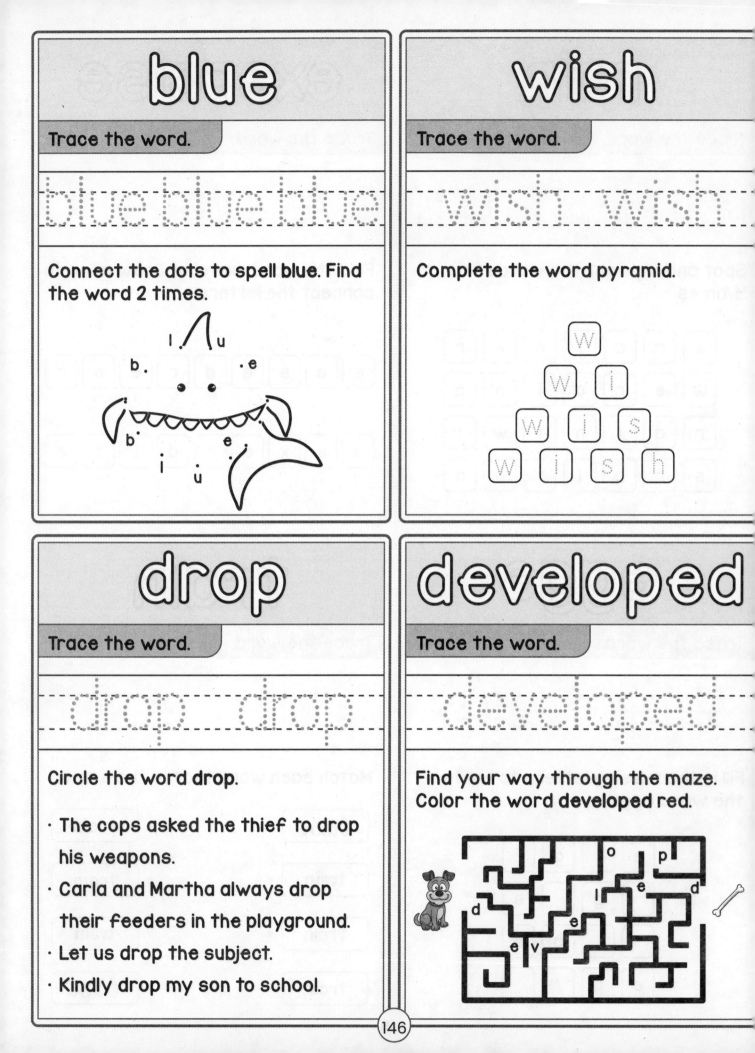

window

Trace the word.

window

Write the first letter of each picture and find the hidden word.

___hale   ___ce   ___est

___oor   ___wl   ___heel

difference

Trace the word.

difference

Find the word **difference** 3 times.

s	f	p	a	i	n	t	p	o	p
d	i	f	f	e	r	e	n	c	e
u	o	t	n	i	a	p	i	c	i
d	i	f	f	e	r	e	n	c	e
q	t	n	i	a	p	o	t	l	t
e	c	n	e	r	e	f	f	i	d

distance

Trace the word.

distance

Read the sentences and underline the word **distance**.

- They are watching them from a distance.
- I cycled the short distance home.
- A coyote howled in the distance.
- The distance is thirty miles.

heart

Trace the word.

heart heart

Match each word that is the same.

heart •

heart •

heart •

heart •

• heart

• heart

• **heart**

• *heart*

site

Trace the word.

site site site

How many times can you spot site?

believe   the   Site   her
Site   the   believe   this   site
believe   Site   site   believe
believe   her   site   this   Site

I see the word site ⬚ times.

sum

Trace the word.

sumsumsum

Fill in the word sum to get some new words.

· _____ mer
· as_____ e
· _____ mit
· re_____ e
· _____ mon
· gyp_____

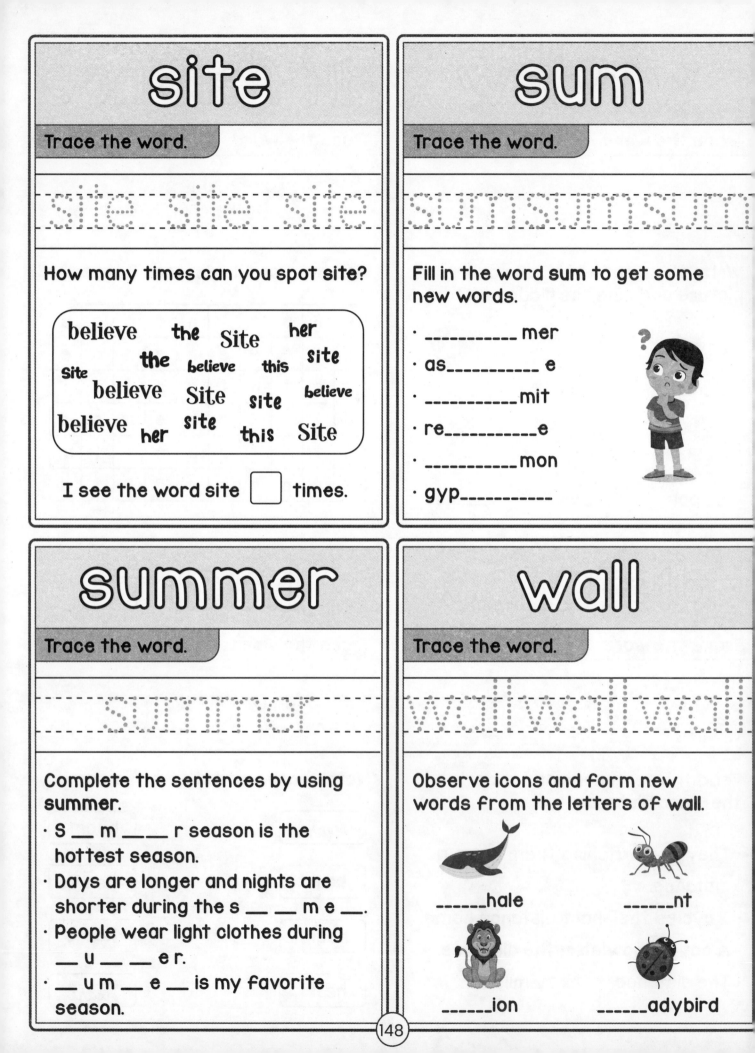

summer

Trace the word.

summer

Complete the sentences by using summer.

· S __ m ___ r season is the hottest season.
· Days are longer and nights are shorter during the s __ __ m e __.
· People wear light clothes during __ u __ __ e r.
· __ u m __ e __ is my favorite season.

wall

Trace the word.

wall wall wall

Observe icons and form new words from the letters of wall.

_____hale   _____nt

_____ion   _____adybird

let's revise!

1. State whether the statements show sum or difference of the numbers.

- _____ of 200 and 210 is 410.
- _____ of 400 and 200 is 200.
- _____ of 750 and 50 is 700.
- _____ of 50 and 750 is 800.
- _____ of 100 and 25 is 75.

2. Add –ed to the given words to get their past forms.

develop	
pick	
subject	

3. Fill in the blanks with the right word in the sentences.

   (return, dance, paint, love, wish, exercise)

- I just _____ dancing.
- His friends did not _____ back.
- Can you _____ the tango?
- Could you _____ this wall?
- We _____ you every success.
- Eat healthily and _____ regularly.

4. I rhyme with! (blue, test, hill, moon)

- Hey Bill, don't climb up the _____ .
- Give your best when writing a _____ .
- Spotting a blue _____ is a rare boon !
- The birds flew in the sky _____ .

forest

forest forest

Fill in the missing letters to write the word **forest**.

f		r	e		t
	o		e	s	
f	o				t
		r	e		t

probably

probably

Color each space red that has **probably**. Color the rest of your choice.

probably	energy	smart
ready	probably	color
super	probably	probably
probably	anyting	probably

legs

legs legs

Spot the word **legs**.

his	sat	legs	her	and
an	legs	off	all	legs
legs	the	him	legs	is
his	legs	and	sat	legs

sat

sat sat sat

Find your way through the maze. Color the word **sat** blue.

sat	sat	him	her	and
an	sat	sat	all	and
sat	the	sat	sat	is
the	sat	and	sat	sat

main

Trace the word.

main main

Color the initials of the words to get main.

m	a	n	g	o
a	d	v	e	n	t	u	r	e
i	n	d	u	s	t	r	y
n	e	s	t

winter

Trace the word.

winter winter

Color the code for each letter.

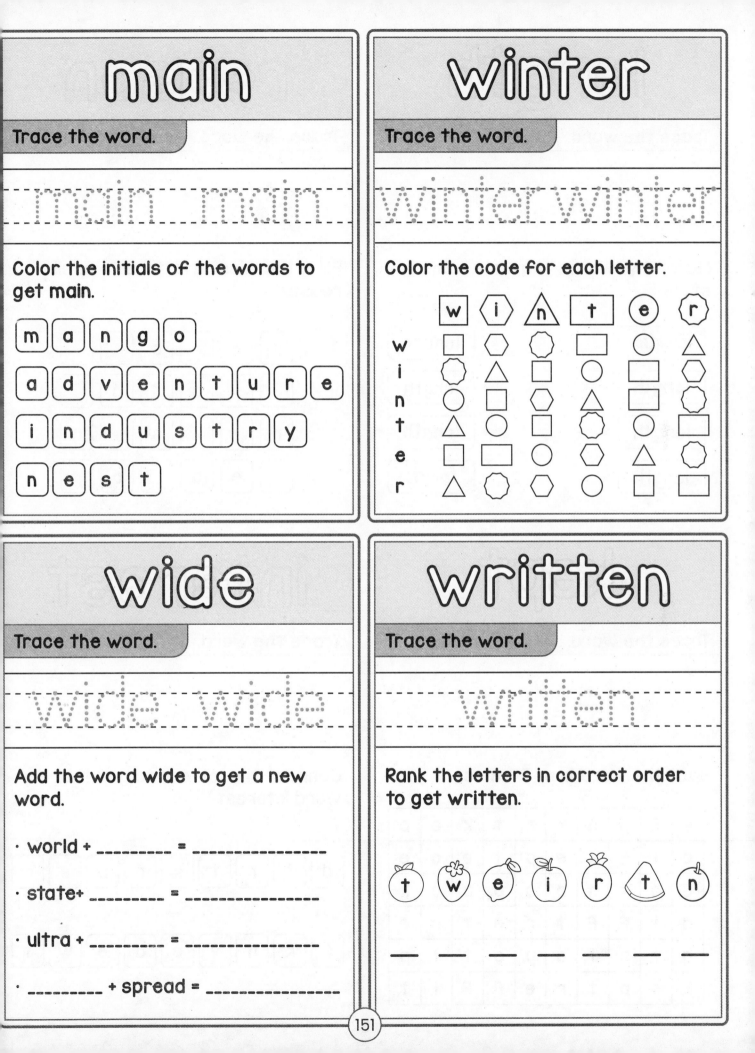

wide

Trace the word.

wide wide

Add the word wide to get a new word.

· world + _____ = _____

· state+ _____ = _____

· ultra + _____ = _____

· _____ + spread = _____

written

Trace the word.

written

Rank the letters in correct order to get written.

t w e i r t n

___ ___ ___ ___ ___ ___ ___

length

Trace the word.

length

Match the words that are same in style.

length •	• length
length •	• length
length •	• **length**
length •	• *length*

reason

Trace the word.

reason

Fill in the missing letters to spell reason.

r	e		s		
		a		o	
r			s		n
	e		a		o

kept

Trace the word.

kept kept

Spot the word kept 5 times.

s	f	p	a	k	n	t	k	o	p
d	i	f	k	e	p	t	e	c	e
u	o	t	n	p	a	p	p	c	k
d	i	f	f	t	r	e	t	c	e
q	t	n	i	a	p	o	t	l	p
k	e	p	t	r	e	f	f	i	t

interest

Trace the word.

interest

Connect the letters to get the word interest.

d	i	r	t	k	r	b	s	n

f	k	n	v	e	d	e	w	t

arms

Trace the word.

arms arms

Fill in the word **arms** to complete the sentences.

· She stood with her _____ outstretched.

· She cradled the child in her _____ .

· We welcome you with open _____ .

· The jacket is too tight in the _____ .

brother

Trace the word.

brother

Color the letters that spell brother.

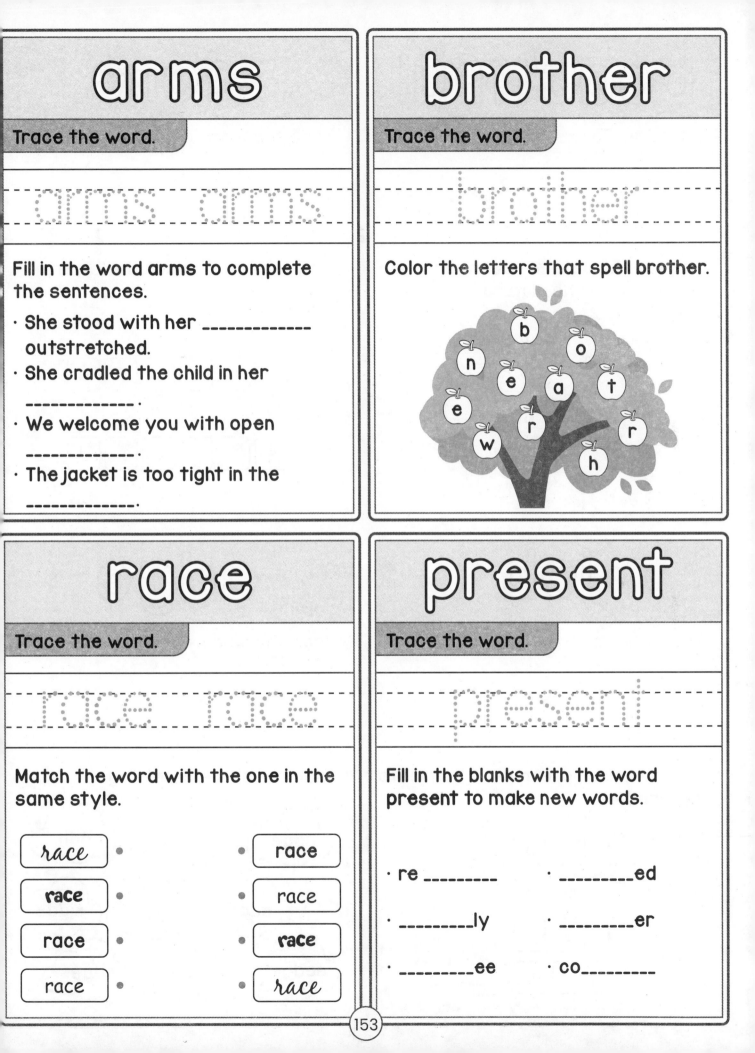

race

Trace the word.

race race

Match the word with the one in the same style.

race	·	·	race
race	·	·	race
race	·	·	**race**
race	·	·	*race*

present

Trace the word.

present

Fill in the blanks with the word **present** to make new words.

· re _____   · _____ed

· _____ly   · _____er

· _____ee   · co_____

beautiful

Trace the word.

beautiful

Connect the dots to spell beautiful and complete the picture.

e b a u t f u i

store

Trace the word.

store store

Draw lines to connect the letters and get the word store.

s d o m f e

s t p c r d

job

Trace the word.

job job job

Fill in the missing letters to complete the word job.

j		b
	o	b
j	o	
		b

edge

Trace the word.

edge edge

Color the correct spelling.

adge   egde   edjj

edge   edjj   eigde

eedge   egde   edgee

past

Trace the word.

past   past

Match each word that is same in style.

past •	• past
past •	• past
past •	• **past**
past •	• *past*

sign

Trace the word.

sign   sign

Color the fruits that spell sign.

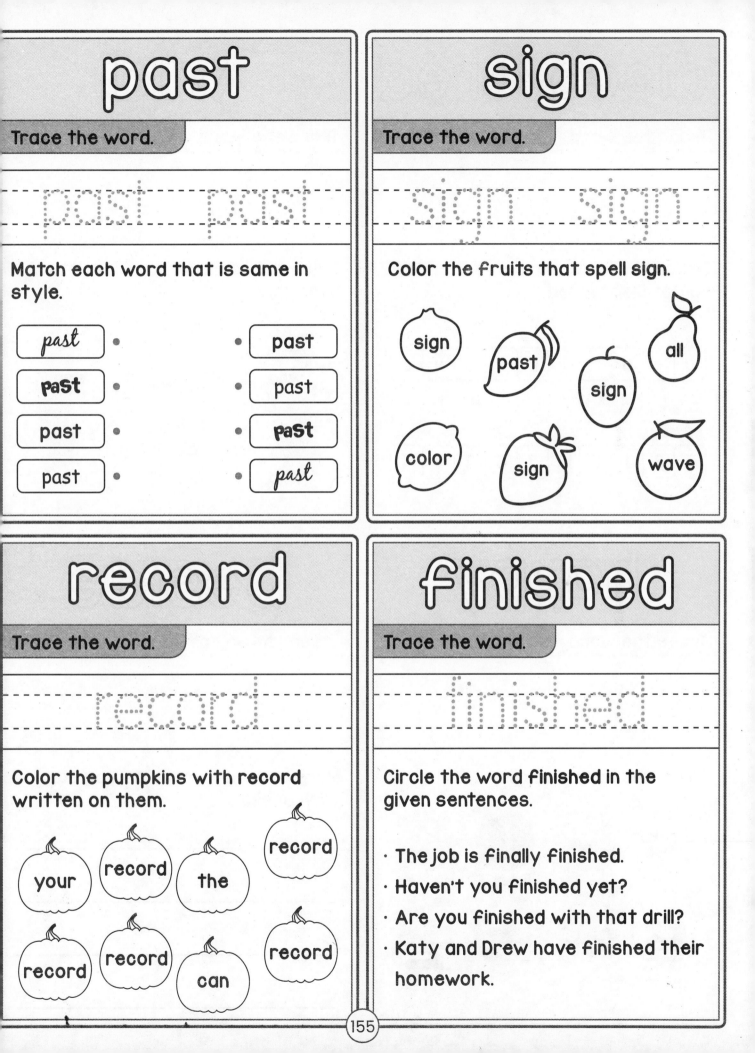

sign   past   all   sign   color   sign   wave

record

Trace the word.

record

Color the pumpkins with record written on them.

your   record   the   record   record   record   can   record

finished

Trace the word.

finished

Circle the word finished in the given sentences.

· The job is finally finished.
· Haven't you finished yet?
· Are you finished with that drill?
· Katy and Drew have finished their homework.

155

discovered

Trace the word.

discovered

Match the letters in correct order to get **discovered**.

d	e	d	r	i	s	e	c	v	o

7	8	1	3	10	2	6	9	5	4

wild

Trace the word.

wild   wild

Color the cards with **wild** written over them.

wild   wild   ear

wild   sky   wild

happy

Trace the word.

happy happy

Circle the happy emojis.

beside

Trace the word.

beside

Make as many words as you can with **beside**.

----

gone

gone gone

Read the statements and complete the questions.

· Where has Mady _____?
Mady has gone to Chile.

· Has he _____? He has_____.

· Have the Smiths _____ to Canada? Yes, the Smiths have gone to Canada.

sky

Trace the word.

sky sky sky

Help the bird find its way to its nest by following sky.

sky	here	single
sky	single	mouth
mouth	sky	sky	way
choose	blue	sky
touch	bird	gone

grass

Trace the word.

grass grass

Circle the rhyming pairs.

grass x brass   grass x mass

flask x grass   last x grass

pass x grass   cask x grass

million

Trace the word.

million million

Write the number names.

1,000,000 [   ]

12, 000, 000 [   ]

24, 000, 000 [   ]

15, 000, 000 [   ]

36, 000, 000 [   ]

west

Trace the word.

west west

Connect the dots to complete the picture.

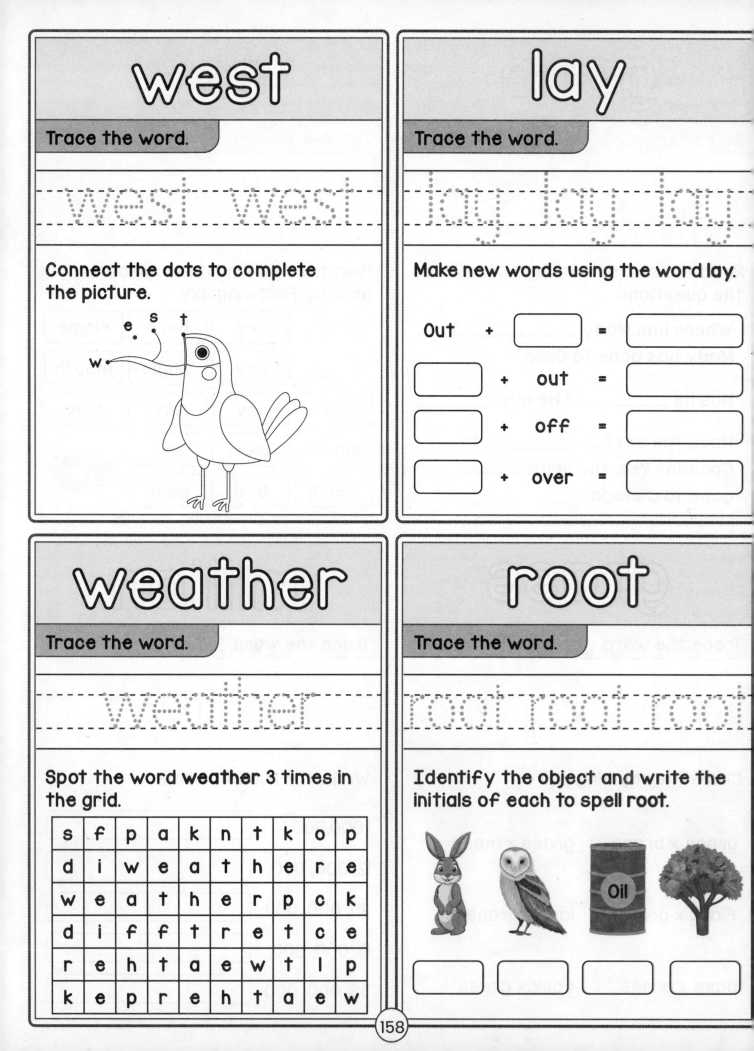

lay

Trace the word.

lay lay lay

Make new words using the word lay.

Out + _____ = _____

_____ + out = _____

_____ + off = _____

_____ + over = _____

weather

Trace the word.

weather

Spot the word weather 3 times in the grid.

s	f	p	a	k	n	t	k	o	p
d	i	w	e	a	t	h	e	r	e
w	e	a	t	h	e	r	p	c	k
d	i	f	f	t	r	e	t	c	e
r	e	h	t	a	e	w	t	l	p
k	e	p	r	e	h	t	a	e	w

root

Trace the word.

root root roo

Identify the object and write the initials of each to spell root.

_____ _____ _____

instruments

Trace the word.

instruments

Fill in the missing letters.

__ n __ t __ u __ e __ t __

__ __ s t __ __ m e __ __ s

i __ s __ r __ m __ n __ s

i n __ t __ __ m __ n t __

meet

Trace the word.

meet meet

Color the correct code for each letter.

m	e	e	t

m	□	⬡	⚙	▭
e	⚙	⬡	□	○
e	○	□	△	⚙
t	△	○	⚙	▭

third

Trace the word.

third third

How many times can you spot third?

third	how	third
who	third	witch
third	what	third
with	third	win

I spotted third ☐ times.

months

Trace the word.

months

Spot the word months in the grid.

s	f	p	m	k	n	t	k	o	m
d	i	m	o	n	t	h	s	r	o
w	e	a	n	h	e	r	p	c	n
d	i	f	t	t	r	e	t	c	t
r	e	h	h	a	e	w	t	l	h
k	e	p	s	e	h	t	a	e	s

paragraph

paragraph

Replace the underlined with 'graph' to form the word **paragraph**.

para<u>lle</u>l _____

para<u>digm</u> _____

para<u>dise</u> _____

para<u>noid</u> _____

para<u>site</u> _____

para<u>noia</u> _____

raised

Trace the word.

raised

Read the words and write **raised** next to each word that rhymes with it. Cross out that does not.

faced _____

plague _____

glazed _____

nasal _____

represent

Trace the word.

represent

Draw lines to connect the letters to spell **represent**.

| i | r | j | p | a | e | v | e | v | t |

| c | j | e | h | r | i | s | s | n | j |

soft

Trace the word.

soft soft soft

Identify the objects that are **soft** and put X that are not. Write **soft** below each.

_____ _____ _____ _____ _____

160

whether

whether

Fill in the blanks with the word whether.

· I really don't know _____ to meet him or not.

· _____ or not she tells him is the big question.

· I'm going _____ you like it or not.

clothes

clothes

Complete the spelling by filling in the missing letters.

c		o		e	
	l	t		e	s
	o		h		s
c	l	t	h		

flowers

flowers

Spot the word flowers 3 times in the puzzle.

s	f	l	o	w	e	r	s	o	p
d	i	w	e	a	t	h	e	r	e
f	l	o	w	e	r	s	p	c	k
d	i	f	f	t	r	e	t	c	e
r	e	h	t	a	e	w	t	l	p
k	e	f	l	o	w	e	r	s	w

shall

shall   shall

Match the same fonts.

shall ·   · shall

Shall ·   · shall

shall ·   · **Shall**

shall ·   · *shall*

teacher

Trace the word.

teacher

Circle the word **teacher** on the white board as many times as you see it.

teacher   logic   teacher
    then   teacher   catch
down   suit   trip   look
here   teacher   joker
   teacher   good   teacher

held

Trace the word.

held   held

Complete the spelling by filling in the missing letters.

		l	d
	e		d
h		l	
	e	l	

describe

Trace the word.

describe

Circle the word **describe** as many times you spot.

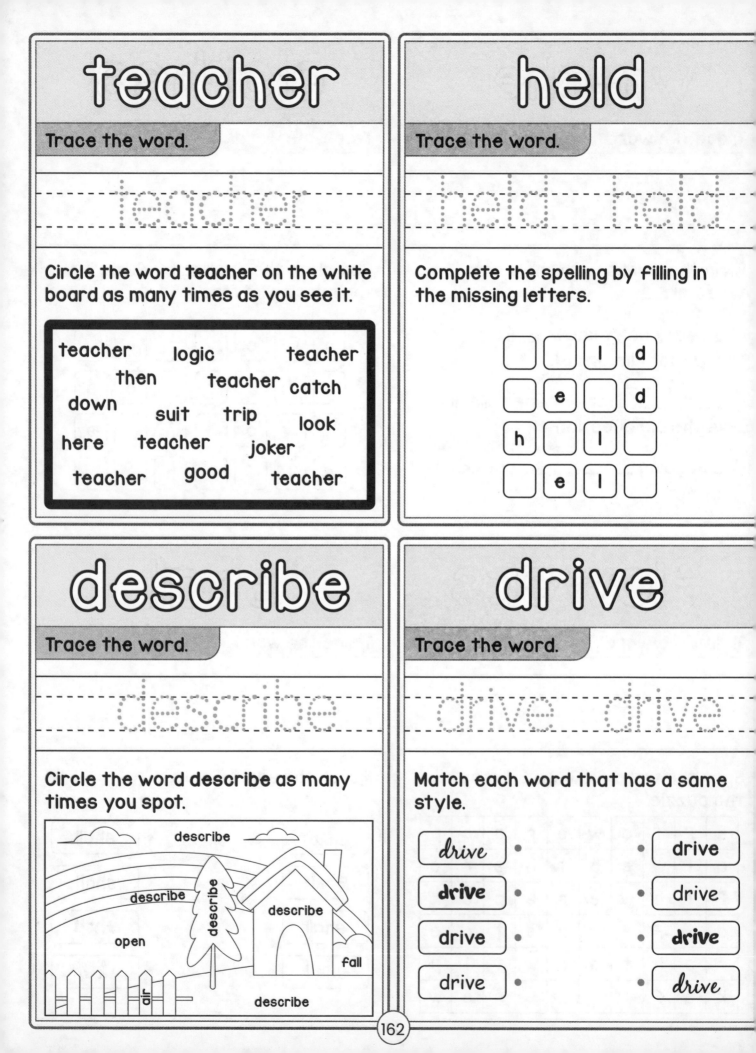

describe
describe
describe
describe
open
fall
air
describe

drive

Trace the word.

drive   drive

Match each word that has a same style.

drive   •   • drive

drive   •   • drive

drive   •   • **drive**

drive   •   • *drive*

162

let's revise!

1. Write the plurals.

singular	plural
flower	
leg	
arm	
instrument	
month	

2. Use the w-words correctly.

(whether, winter, wide, written, wild, west, weather)

· He opened his eyes _____ .

· _____ you drive fast or slow, please drive carefully.

· He has not _____ to them for a leave.

· The _____ today will be hot and dry.

· The Sun rises in the east and sets in the _____ .

· I want to see the _____ animals.

· In _____ the nights are long and cold.

3. Write the past tense of the given words.

· raise _____   lie _____

· develop _____   finish _____

· hold _____   sit _____

4. Underline the describing words in the sentences.

· A lion is a wild animal.

· Peter is a confident and happy child.

· It was a beautiful morning.

· Add enough milk to form a soft dough.

cross

Trace the word.

cross cross

Fill in the blanks with the word cross.

· Let us _____ the bridge.
· We used a plank to _____ the ditch.
· _____ with care at the traffic lights.
· You can _____ the river by ferry.
· _____ off any items we've already got.

speak

Trace the word.

speak speak

Color the words that end with -eak.
peak, beak, speak, leak, weak

s	f	p	e	a	k	t	k	o	w
l	e	a	k	n	t	h	s	r	e
w	e	a	n	h	e	r	p	c	a
d	i	f	t	t	r	e	e	c	k
r	b	e	a	k	e	w	a	l	h
k	e	p	s	e	h	t	k	e	s

solve

Trace the word.

solve solve

Draw lines to connect the letters of the word solve.

| h | e | o | a | v | w |

| l | s | t | l | j | e |

appear

Trace the word.

appear

Circle the word appear as many times you spot it.

· Where did he appear from?
· He will appear as a witness against the accused.
· The presidency is beginning to appear as a political irrelevance.
· He is anxious to appear a gentleman.

164

metal

Trace the word.

metal metal

Count and write the number of times you spot **metal**.

metal	here	right
when	metal	kite
fight	metal	play
metal	speak	metal

☐ times

son

Trace the word.

son son son

Underline the word **son** in the given words.

· person
· reason
· season
· prison
· lesson

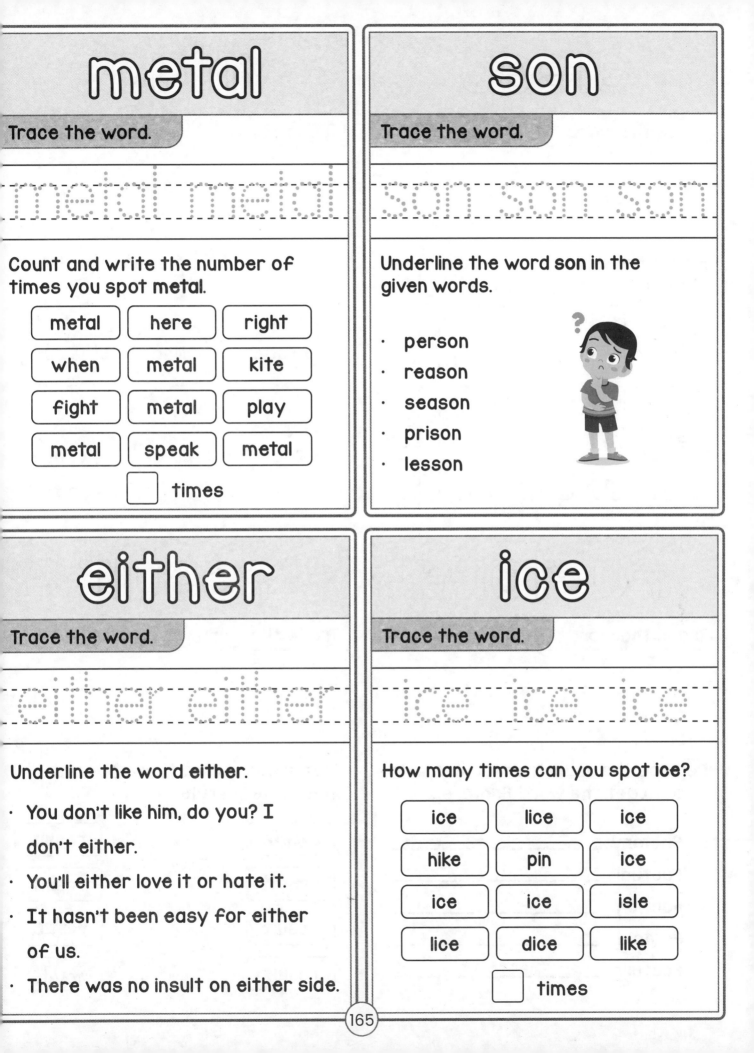

either

Trace the word.

either either

Underline the word **either**.

· You don't like him, do you? I don't either.
· You'll either love it or hate it.
· It hasn't been easy for either of us.
· There was no insult on either side.

ice

Trace the word.

ice ice ice

How many times can you spot **ice**?

ice	lice	ice
hike	pin	ice
ice	ice	isle
lice	dice	like

☐ times

sleep

Trace the word.

sleep sleep

Fill the boxes with the word **sleep** so that no letter is repeated.

s			s		s
	l	l		l	
e		e		e	
	e		e		e
p	p		p		

village

Trace the word.

village

Circle the correct spelling of the word.

veelage   village   vilage

village   villuge   village

factors

Trace the word.

factors

Replace the underlined letters with 'ors' to get the word **factors**.

· fact<u>ory</u> _____

· fact<u>ual</u> _____

· fact<u>ion</u> _____

· fact<u>oid</u> _____

· fact<u>ure</u> _____

result

Trace the word.

result result

Match each word that appears the same in style.

result	•	•	result
reSult	•	•	result
result	•	•	**reSult**
result	•	•	*result*

jumped

Trace the word.

jumped

Color the letters that spell jumped.

ABCDEFGH
IJKLMNO
PQRSTUVW
XYZ

snow

Trace the word.

snow snow

Color the space red with the word snow. Color the rest of the picture as per your choice.

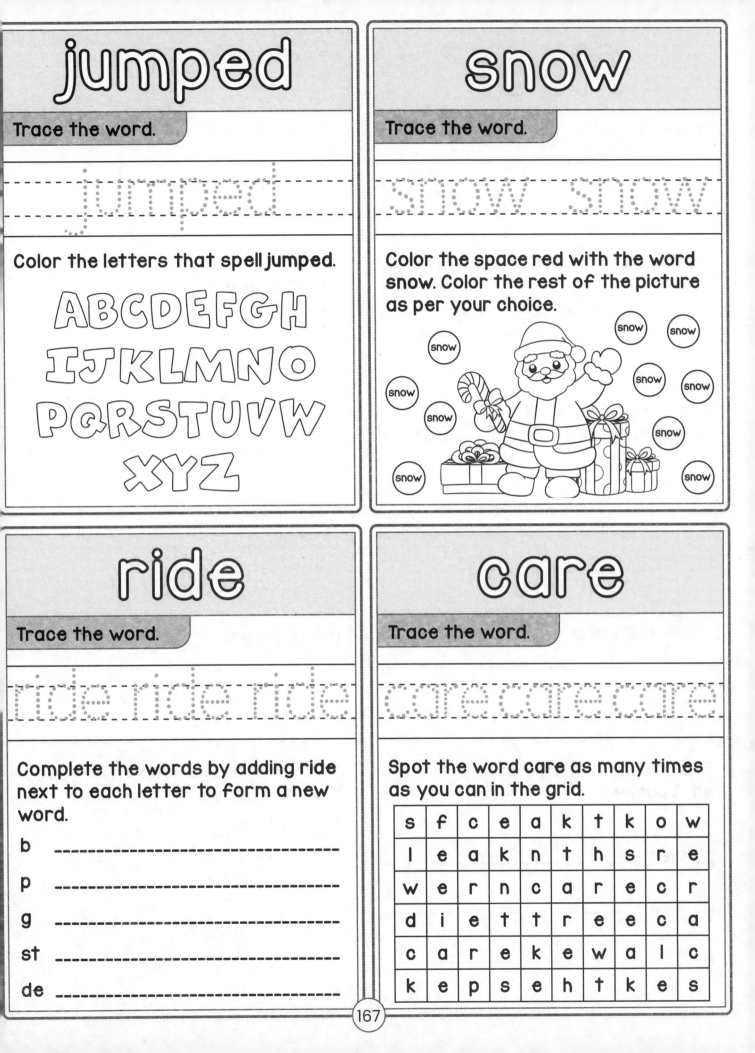

snow snow snow snow snow snow snow snow snow snow

ride

Trace the word.

ride ride ride

Complete the words by adding ride next to each letter to form a new word.

b _____

p _____

g _____

st _____

de _____

care

Trace the word.

care care care

Spot the word care as many times as you can in the grid.

s	f	c	e	a	k	t	k	o	w
l	e	a	k	n	t	h	s	r	e
w	e	r	n	c	a	r	e	c	r
d	i	e	t	t	r	e	e	c	a
c	a	r	e	k	e	w	a	l	c
k	e	p	s	e	h	t	k	e	s

floor

Trace the word.

floor floor

Color each tree with the word floor.

kite   floor   plain   floor

floor   seed   floor   bat

hill

Trace the word.

hill hill hill

Color the letters with your favorite colors to get the word hill.

a	r	q	c	p	e	l
s	h	g	f	l	d	o
t	u	j	i	k	m	n
v	y	b	w	x		

pushed

Trace the word.

pushed

Replace the last two letters to spell pushed.

pusher _____

pushup _____

pushes _____

baby

Trace the word.

baby baby

Color the spaces where you spot the word baby.

baby   baby   baby   baby

buy

Trace the word.

buy buy buy

Circle all the things which you can **buy**.

Shopping Bag

century

Trace the word.

century

Fill in the missing letters.

	e		t			y
		n	t		r	y
c	e	t	u		y
c			t		r	

outside

Trace the word.

outside

Replace the underlined with 'side' to get the word outside.

- out**come** _____
- out**look** _____
- out**door** _____
- out**line** _____
- out**rage** _____

everything

Trace the word.

everything

Fill in the blanks with the word **everything**.

- _____ is going fine with the house.
- Put _____ in tiptop order, Sally.
- Do _____ he says.
- _____ is going to be alright now.

tall

Trace the word.

tall tall tall

Circle the initials of the given words to get the word tall.

tiger   apple   leaf   lamp

-------- -------- -------- --------

already

Trace the word.

already

Read the sentences and underline the word already.

- We have already seen this method work.

- Hadn't she already forgotten?

- It was already past 4 o'clock.

- I've already had my breakfast.

instead

Trace the word.

instead

Connect the letters to spell the word instead.

| n | i | j | o | k | s | k | e | t | d |

| b | h | n | b | j | t | p | o | a | c |

phrase

Trace the word.

phrase

Let us learn what are phrases!

- A group of words that have a noun or pronoun is known as noun _____ .
- An adjective _____ is a group of words that consists of an adjective.
- A group of words that includes an adverb and other modifiers is an adverb _____ .

170

soil

Trace the word.

soil soil soil

Find the word soil 4 times in the given grid.

s	o	i	l	a	k	t	k	o	w
l	e	a	k	n	t	h	s	r	e
s	o	i	l	c	a	r	o	c	r
o	i	e	t	t	r	e	i	c	a
i	a	r	e	k	e	w	l	l	c
l	e	p	s	o	i	l	k	e	s

bed

Trace the word.

bed bed bed

Color the letters with your favorite colors to get the word bed.

a	r	q	c	p	e	z
s	h	g	f	l	d	o
t	u	j	i	k	m	n

v	y	b	w	x

copy

Trace the word.

copy copy

Add the word copy to make new words.

· _____ + right = _____

· _____ + read = _____

· multi + _____ = _____

· _____ + desk = _____

free

Trace the word.

free free free

Write the names of animals with the letters of the word free.

f _____

r _____

e _____

e _____

hope

hope hope

Fill in the blanks and complete the sentences with the word hope.

· Do you think it will rain? I _____ not.

· I will see you next week, I _____.

· Let us _____ we can find a parking space.

· We _____ to arrive around 2 o'clock.

spring

Trace the word.

spring spring

Complete the sentences.

Fun Facts about Spring.

· Tulips are one of the first flowers to bloom in _____.

· Honeybees swarm in _____.

· The Chinese New Year is a celebration of _____.

case

Trace the word.

case case

Match the words in same style.

Case	•	•	Case
CaSe	•	•	Case
Case	•	•	CaSe
Case	•	•	Case

laughed

Trace the word.

laughed

Replace the underlined with 'ed' to get laughed.

· laugh<u>ter</u>   _____

· laugh<u>ers</u>   _____

· laugh<u>ing</u>   _____

· laugh<u>able</u>   _____

nation

nation

Fill in the blanks with the word **nation**.

· They were representatives of the British _____ .

· The President will speak to the _____ tonight.

· The patriots stood up for the rights of their _____ .

quite

quite quite

Find the word **quite** by drawing lines.

| p | q | t | r | i | y | g | e |

| s | e | l | u | d | q | t | g |

type

type type

Fill in the words with **type**.

· Mexican is my favorite _____ of food.

· What _____ of music do you like?

· She continued to _____ while put in the call.

· I like to have simple _____ of breakfast.

themselves

themselves

Color the letters to spell word **themselves**.

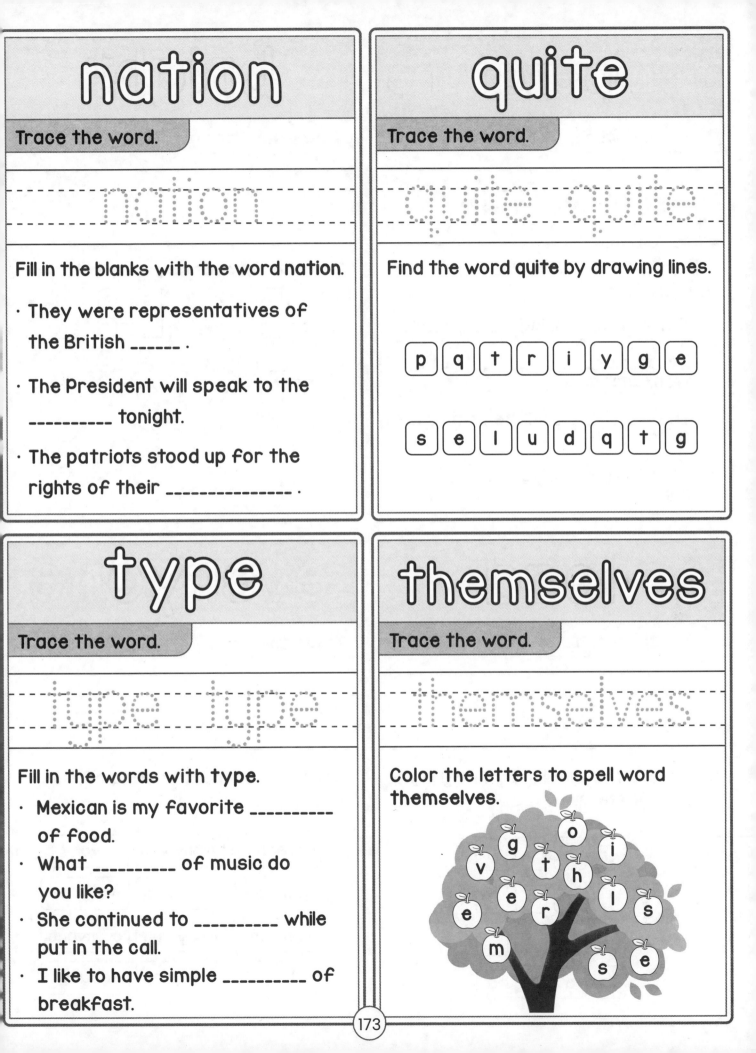

temperature

Trace the word.

temperature

Fill in the blanks with the word temperature.

· I think he's running a _____ .

· I took his _____ but it was normal.

· The _____ will be pretty high today.

· What's the average _____ here in Spain?

bright

Trace the word.

bright bright

Tick the correct code for bright.

	b	r	i	g	h	t
b	□	⬡	⚙	□	○	△
r	□	○	△	□	⬡	⚙
i	⚙	△	□	○	□	⬡
g	○	□	□	△	⬡	⚙
h	△	⚙	□	☆	○	□
t	□	□	□	○	⬡	△	⚙

lead

Trace the word.

lead lead

Complete the spelling by filling in the missing letters.

	e		d
l		a	d
	e		
l	e		d

everyone

Trace the word.

everyone

Color the correct spelling of the word.

eyeone	ivoryone	evary
everyone	everione	ivoryone
everyone	iverywon	everyone
evrywon	everyone	ebary

method

Trace the word.

method

Color the boxes with the word method on it.

method	bright	every
lead	method	type
method	iron	method
lake	method	section

section

Trace the word.

section

Make clouds around the word **section** as many times as you spot it.

section	after	aloof
hen	section	light
also	lake	section
watch	method	section

lake

Trace the word.

lake lake

Spot lake in the grid.

s	o	i	l	a	k	e	k	o	w
l	a	k	e	n	t	h	s	r	e
s	o	i	l	a	k	e	o	c	r
o	i	e	a	t	l	a	k	e	a
i	a	r	k	k	e	w	l	l	c
l	e	p	e	o	i	l	a	k	e

iron

Trace the word.

iron iron iron

Color in the letters to spell iron.

a	b	c	d	e	f	g
h	i	j	k	l	m	n
o	p	q	r	s	t	u
v	w	x	y	z		

let's revise!

1. Fill in the blanks with the appropriate words. (baby, pushed, lake, floor, laughed, everything, jumped, everyone, hope, spring, village, son, outside)

Carl was playing with his _____ and suddenly the baby _____ _____ kept on the _____ _____ the door. _____ _____at this. Carl's _____ went to the _____ with the _____ to enjoy the _____ season. He was elated and _____ in excitement to see the _____.

2. Underline the adverb in the sentences.
· He used a fork instead of chopsticks.
· My homework is already done.
· If you don't come, she won't come either.
· It's quite a small house.

3. Choose from the box the rhyming word for the given set of words.
 (tall, case, free, ride, bed)
· mall, ball, _____
· head, wed, _____
· race, face, _____
· tide, wide, _____
· tree, spree, _____
·
4. Remove the prefix to get the base word.
· unsolved
· reappear
· rebuy

within

within within

Fill in the blanks with the word within.

- It's a play _____ a play.
- Consume _____ two days of purchase.
- He repaid the loan _____ two years.
- The project was completed well _____ budget.

dictionary

dictionary

Unscramble the letters to find the word.

cditinoray   diairoycnt

_____   _____

odniacrtyi   idtcoianyr

_____   _____

hair

hair hair hair

Match the same font style for hair.

hair	•	•	hair
hair	•	•	hair
hair	•	•	hair
hair	•	•	hair

age

age age age

Let's learn phrases and their meanings! Fill in the blanks with age.

- coming of _____ - to reach adulthood.
- in this day and _____ - at the present time.
- act your _____ - to behave in accordance with one's maturity.

amount

Trace the word.

amount

Identify and write the first letter of each picture to find the hidden word.

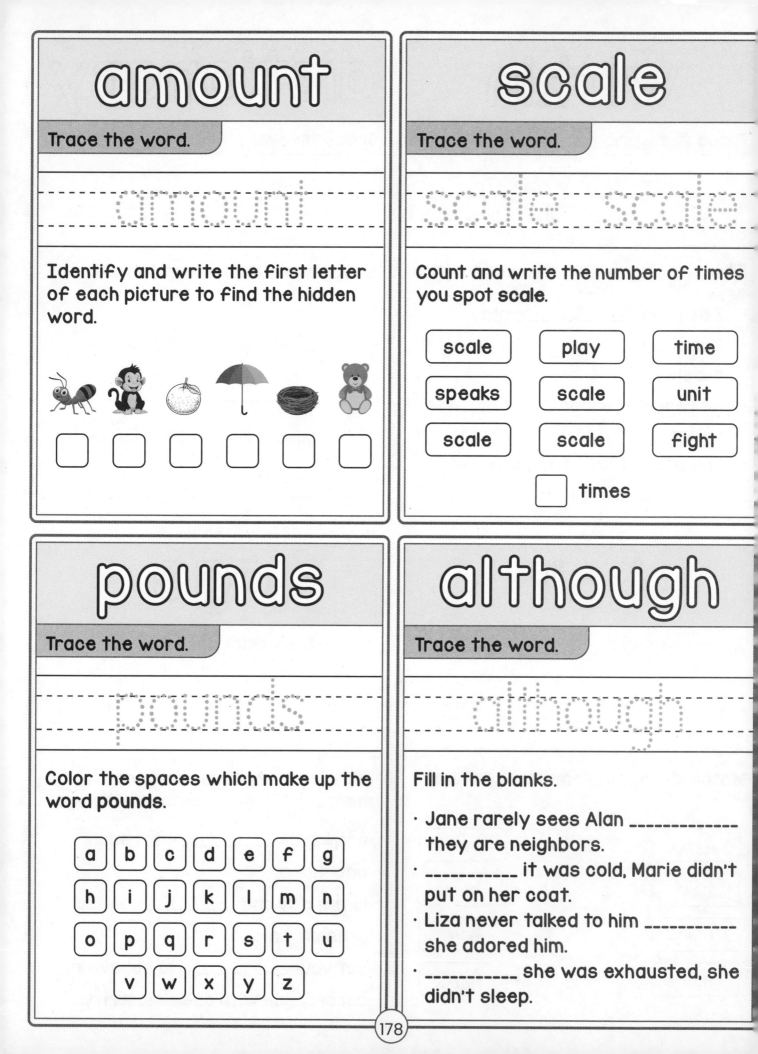

☐ ☐ ☐ ☐ ☐ ☐

scale

Trace the word.

scale   scale

Count and write the number of times you spot **scale**.

scale	play	time
speaks	scale	unit
scale	scale	fight

☐ times

pounds

Trace the word.

pounds

Color the spaces which make up the word **pounds**.

a	b	c	d	e	f	g
h	i	j	k	l	m	n
o	p	q	r	s	t	u
v	w	x	y	z

although

Trace the word.

although

Fill in the blanks.

· Jane rarely sees Alan _____ they are neighbors.

· _____ it was cold, Marie didn't put on her coat.

· Liza never talked to him _____ she adored him.

· _____ she was exhausted, she didn't sleep.

per

Trace the word.

per per per

Match each word that is the same in style.

per •	• per
per •	• per
per •	• **per**
per •	• *per*

broken

Trace the word.

broken broken

Join the dots to get **broken** and complete the picture.

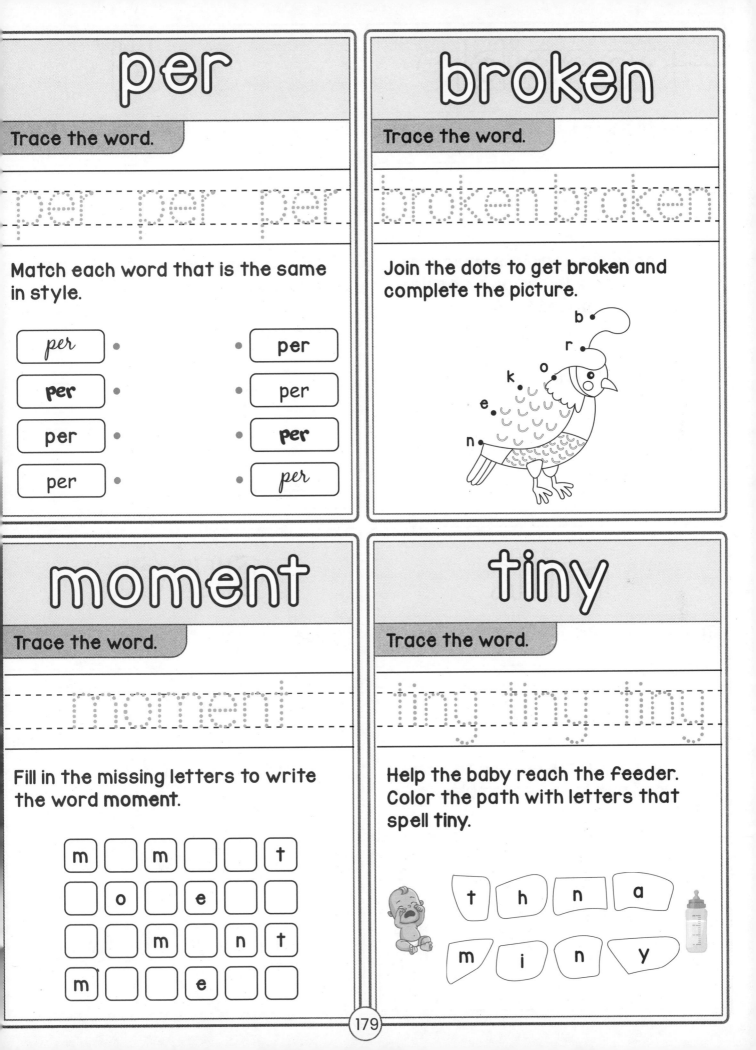

b
r
o
k
e
n

moment

Trace the word.

moment

Fill in the missing letters to write the word **moment**.

m		m			t
	o		e		
		m		n	t
m			e		

tiny

Trace the word.

tiny tiny tiny

Help the baby reach the feeder. Color the path with letters that spell **tiny**.

t	h	n	a
m	i	n	y

possible

Trace the word.

possible

Write possible against statements that are possible and put X beside the ones not possible.

· A peacock can dance. _____

· A nightingale can sing. _____

  Elephants can climb trees. _____

· Hippos can sleep underwater.

  _____

gold

Trace the word.

gold gold

Fill in the blanks with the word gold and make new words.

· _____ + finch = [ ]

· _____ + fish = [ ]

· _____ + eye = [ ]

· _____ + bug = [ ]

· _____ + field = [ ]

milk

Trace the word.

milk milk

Spot and color the letters to form the word milk in the scrambled letters.

y	n	b	g	m	i	l	k	q
y	e	k	c	d	m	i	l	k
i	n	m	i	l	k	t	y	u

quiet

Trace the word.

quiet quiet

Draw lines to get quiet.

| t | r | u | w | e | y |

| l | q | g | i | a | t |

natural

Trace the word.

natural

Color the resources that are natural. Put a X on the man-made resources.

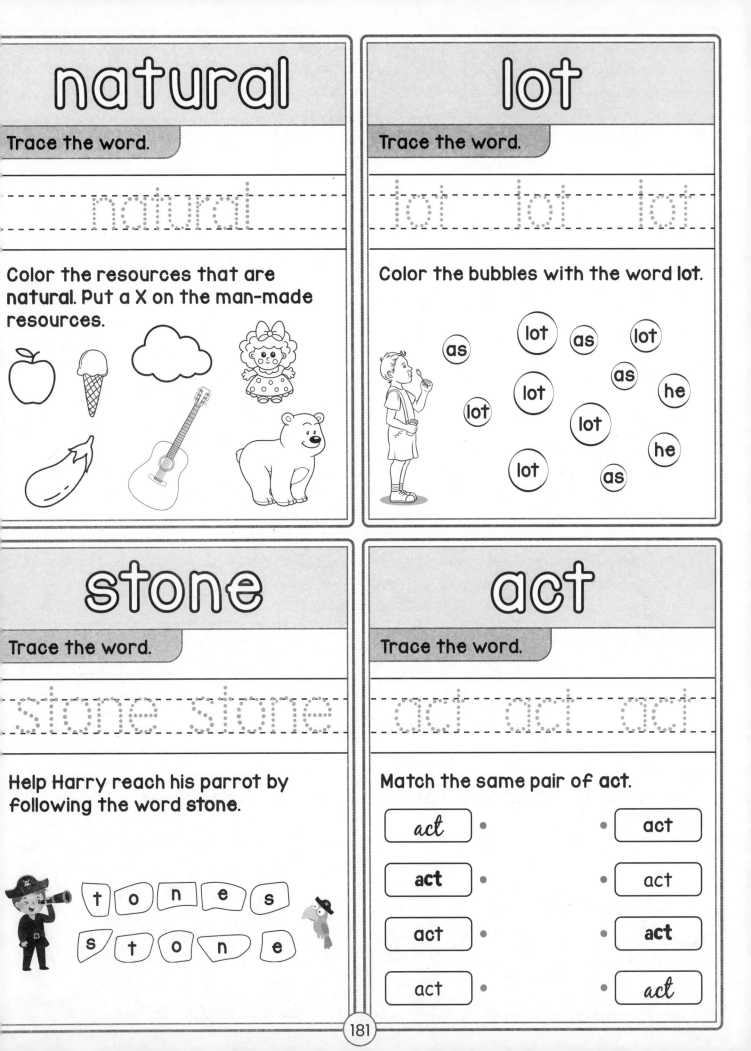

lot

Trace the word.

lot   lot   lot

Color the bubbles with the word lot.

as   lot   as   lot
lot   as   he
lot
lot   lot
he
lot   as

stone

Trace the word.

stone stone

Help Harry reach his parrot by following the word stone.

t o n e s
s t o n e

act

Trace the word.

act   act   act

Match the same pair of act.

act	act
act	act
act	act
act	act

build

Trace the word.

build build

Fill in the blanks with the word **build** and get a new word.

· _____ + er = builder

· _____ + ing = building

· _____ + s = builds

· re + _____ = rebuild

· over + _____ = overbuild

middle

Trace the word.

middle

Fill in the missing letters.

m		d		e
	i	d		
m		d		e
m			d	l

speed

Trace the word.

speed speed

Help the Car reach its destination. Color the path with letters that spell **speed**.

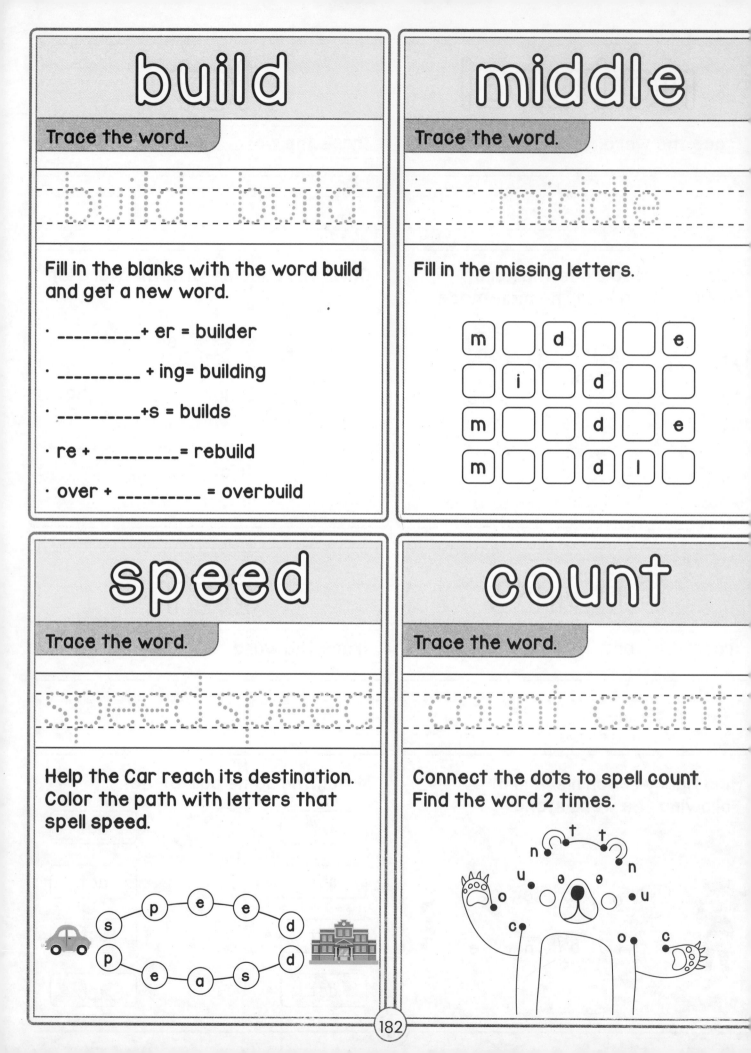

count

Trace the word.

count count

Connect the dots to spell count. Find the word 2 times.

consonant

Trace the word.

consonant

Let's color the consonants! Count the alphabets you colored.

a	r	n	c	p	e	z
s	h	g	f	n	d	o
t	u	j	i	k	m	n
	v	o	b	w	a	

someone

Trace the word.

someone

Replace the underlined word with 'one' to get **someone**.

· some<u>how</u> _____
· some<u>day</u> _____
· some<u>way</u> _____
· some<u>what</u> _____
· some<u>time</u> _____

sail

Trace the word.

sail sail sail

Write sail below the things that can sail.

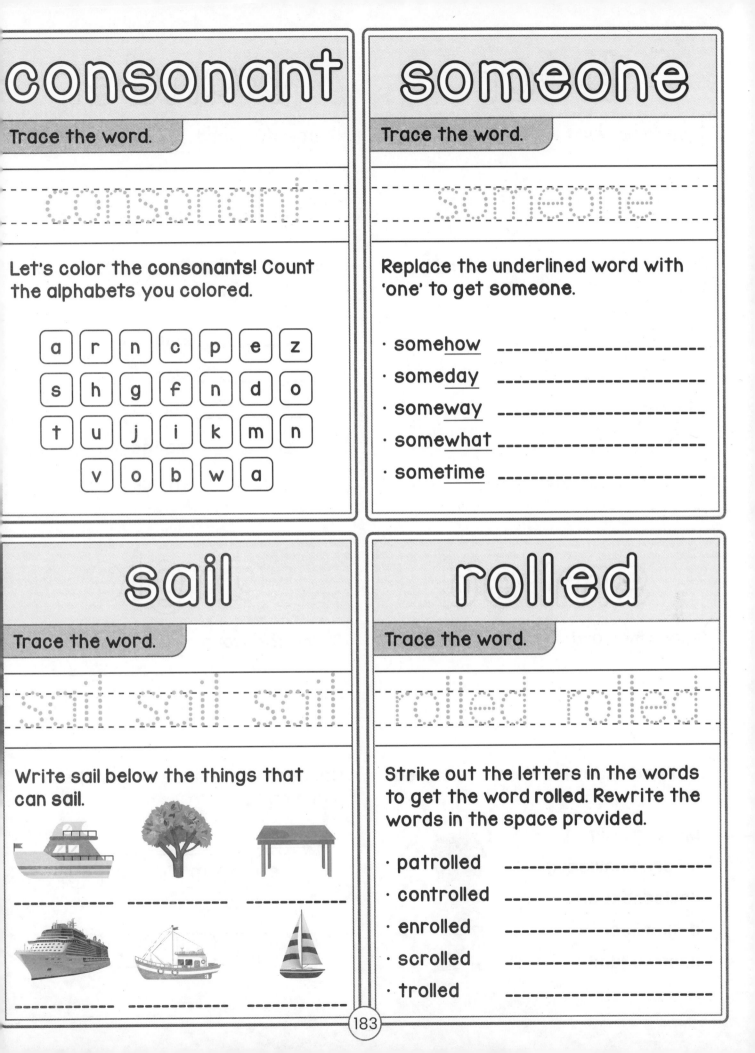

_____ _____ _____

_____ _____ _____

rolled

Trace the word.

rolled rolled

Strike out the letters in the words to get the word **rolled**. Rewrite the words in the space provided.

· patrolled _____
· controlled _____
· enrolled _____
· scrolled _____
· trolled _____

bear

bear bear

Fill in the blanks with the word **bear** to get a new word.

· Polar _____

· Gummy _____

· Teddy _____

· _____ grass

· _____ berry

wonder

wonder

Add the word **wonder** to the given words and get the new word.

· _____ land

· _____ work

· _____ ful

· _____ monger

· _____ struck

smiled

smiled smiled

Spot and underline the word **smiled**.

· bjfrjsmiledm

· sfjorjfnsmiledvg

· smilednbkbog

· dfgsmiledrty

· dssmileddcf

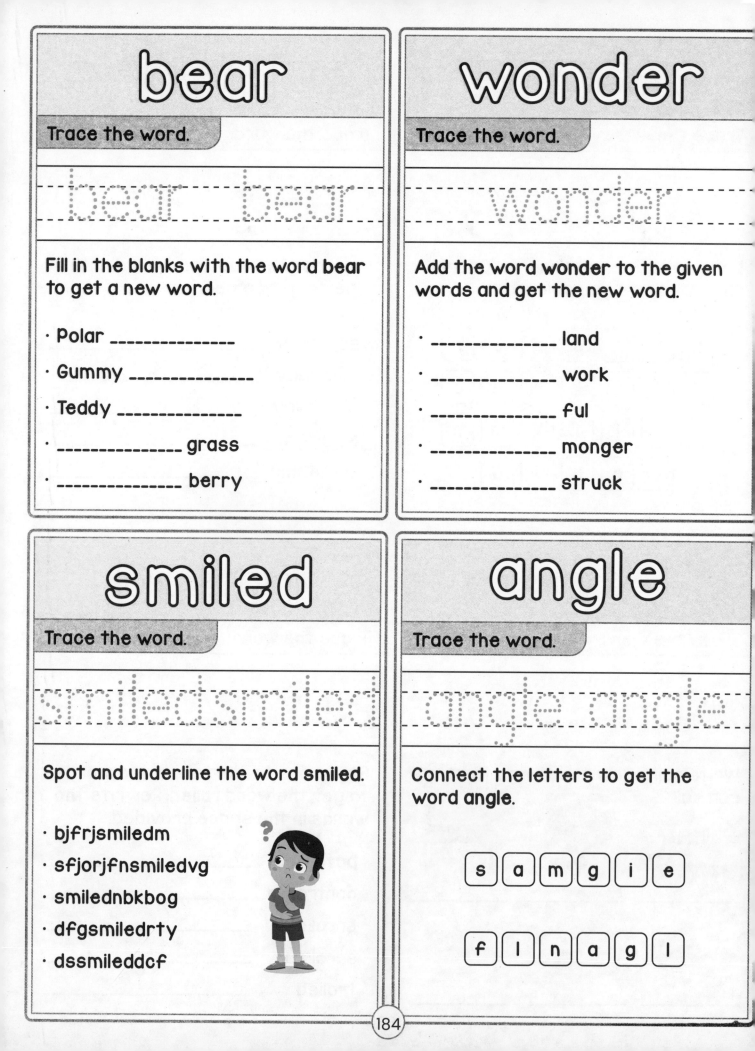

angle

angle angle

Connect the letters to get the word **angle**.

| s | a | m | g | i | e |

| f | l | n | a | g | l |

fraction

fraction

Circle the word fraction in the given picture.

fraction   the   fraction   her
believe   the   fraction   this   time
fraction   his
fraction   her   fraction
fraction   her   Fraction   fraction

Africa

Trace the word.

Africa Africa

Draw lines to connect the letters to form the word Africa.

a   f   i
c
a   r

☐ ☐ ☐ ☐ ☐ ☐

killed

Trace the word.

killed killed

Fill in the missing letters to get the word killed.

	i			e	
k		l		e	
k		l	l		d
	i			l	e

melody

Trace the word.

melody

Write the initials of the given words to spell melody.

☐ atter   ☐ ngine   ☐ eopard

☐ strich   ☐ enmark   ☐ acht

bottom

bottom

Identify and write **bottom** for the appropriate pictures.

_____   _____

_____   _____

trip

Trace the word.

trip trip trip

Fill in the blanks with the word **trip**.

· We went out on a day _____ on Thursday.
· The camping _____ was spoiled by bad weather.
· He is going on a road _____ across the country.
· Hoping you will have a pleasant _____!

hole

Trace the word.

hole hole hole

Add the word **hole** to make new words.

· loop   _____
· sink   _____
· pot   _____
· worm   _____
· peep   _____

poor

Trace the word.

poor poor

Replace the underlined letters with p. Rewrite the words in the space provided.

· <u>m</u>oor   _____
· <u>d</u>oor   _____
· <u>b</u>oor   _____
· <u>fl</u>oor   _____
· <u>in</u>door _____

let's

let's   let's

Complete the sentences.

- _____ go to Anna's house.
- _____ go out and eat dinner.
- _____ help the poor man.
- _____ go for a drive.

fight

fightfightfight

Match the same font style for fight.

fight •   • fight

fight •   • fight

fight •   • fight

fight •   • fight

surprise

Trace the word.

surprise

Complete the spelling by filling in the missing letters.

	u		r	i		e
s		p			s	
	r		r		s	e
s		r	p		i	e

French

Trace the word.

French

Find the word French by connecting the letters.

s a f g e e c e

f l n r g n g h

187

died

Trace the word.

died   died

Help the lion reach the zebra. Color the path with letters that spell died.

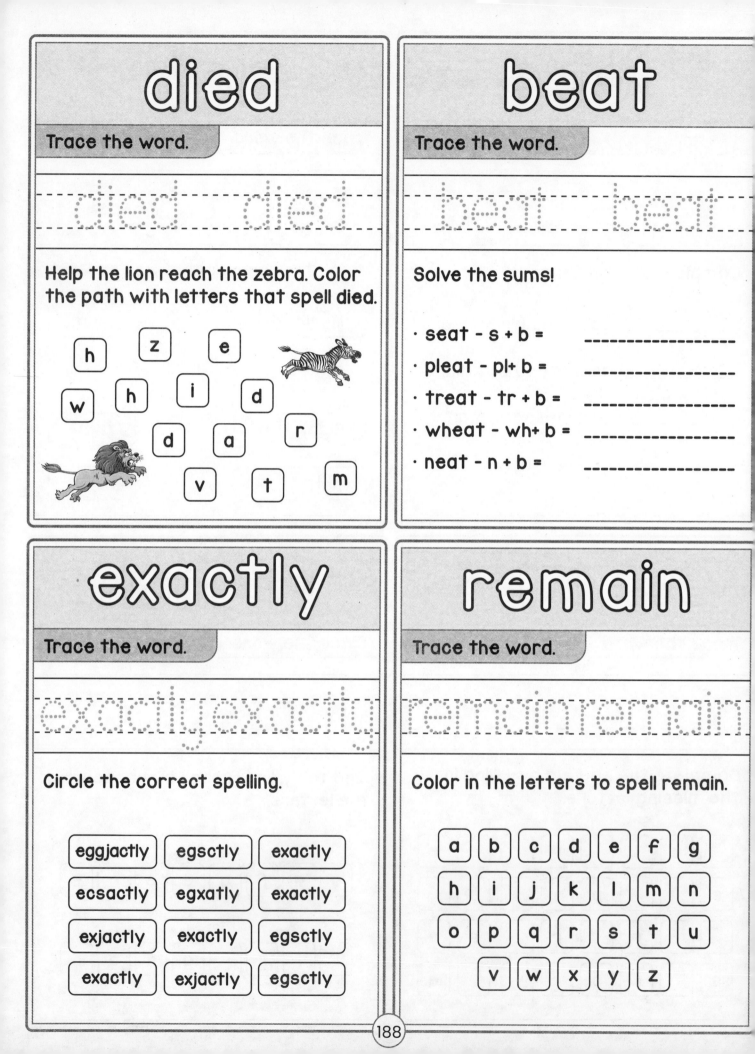

h   z   e

w   h   i   d

d   a   r

v   t   m

beat

Trace the word.

beat   beat

Solve the sums!

- seat – s + b = _____
- pleat – pl+ b = _____
- treat – tr + b = _____
- wheat – wh+ b = _____
- neat – n + b = _____

exactly

Trace the word.

exactly exactly

Circle the correct spelling.

eggjactly	egsctly	exactly
ecsactly	egxatly	exactly
exjactly	exactly	egsctly
exactly	exjactly	egsctly

remain

Trace the word.

remainremain

Color in the letters to spell remain.

a	b	c	d	e	f	g
h	i	j	k	l	m	n
o	p	q	r	s	t	u
v	w	x	y	z		

dress

Trace the word.

dress dress

Spot the word dress in the grid.

s	o	i	l	d	r	e	s	s	w
l	a	k	d	n	t	h	s	r	e
s	o	d	r	e	s	s	o	c	r
o	i	e	e	t	l	a	k	e	a
i	a	r	s	k	d	r	e	s	s
l	e	p	s	o	i	l	a	k	e

cat

Trace the word.

cat cat cat

Color each space that has the word cat.

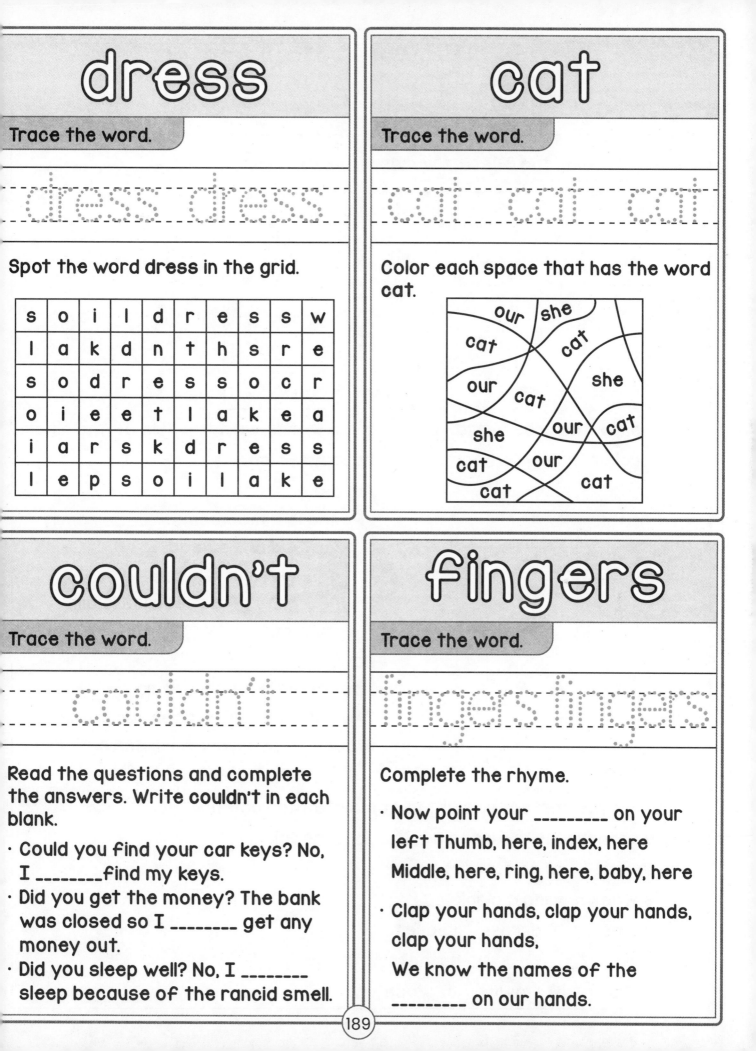

couldn't

Trace the word.

couldn't

Read the questions and complete the answers. Write **couldn't** in each blank.

· Could you find your car keys? No, I _____ find my keys.
· Did you get the money? The bank was closed so I _____ get any money out.
· Did you sleep well? No, I _____ sleep because of the rancid smell.

fingers

Trace the word.

fingers fingers

Complete the rhyme.

· Now point your _____ on your left Thumb, here, index, here Middle, here, ring, here, baby, here

· Clap your hands, clap your hands, clap your hands,
We know the names of the _____ on our hands.

let's revise!

1. Spot and color the 3-letter words in the picture.

2. Complete the crossword for the given words with the help of the clues.
(hair, broken, tiny, milk, bear, count, natural, Africa)

Across

1. Panda is a member of _____ family
3. grows on one's head
4. a cow gives us _____
6. what type of a resource is air?
7. very small

Down

1. past participle of break
2. world's second-largest continent
5. don't _____ your chickens before they hatch

3. Choose the correct spelling to complete the sentence.

· The winner was awarded a _____ medal.

   a) goled   b) gold   c) gould

· She was wearing a black _____.

   a) drees   b) drress   c) dress

· A rolling _____ gathers no moss.

   a) stone   b) stown   c) stoon

row

row row row

Write the first things that come to your mind with the letters of the word row.

r _____

o _____

w _____

least

Trace the word.

least   least

Underline the word least in the given words.

· leastwise   _____

· oleasters   _____

· atleast   _____

· leastways   _____

catch

Trace the word.

catch   catch

Replace the first letter with c.

· watch   _____

· patch   _____

· match   _____

· batch   _____

· hatch   _____

climbed

Trace the word.

climbed

Fill in the blanks to complete the sentences.

· The plane _____ quickly to a height of 30,000 feet.

· The higher we _____, the steeper became the mountain.

· Have you ever _____ Mount Everest?

· He _____ down from the cab.

wrote

Trace the word.

wrote wrote

Match each word that looks the same.

wrote •	• wrote
wrote •	• wrote
wrote •	• **wrote**
wrote •	• *wrote*

shouted

Trace the word.

shouted

Write the initials to get **shouted**.

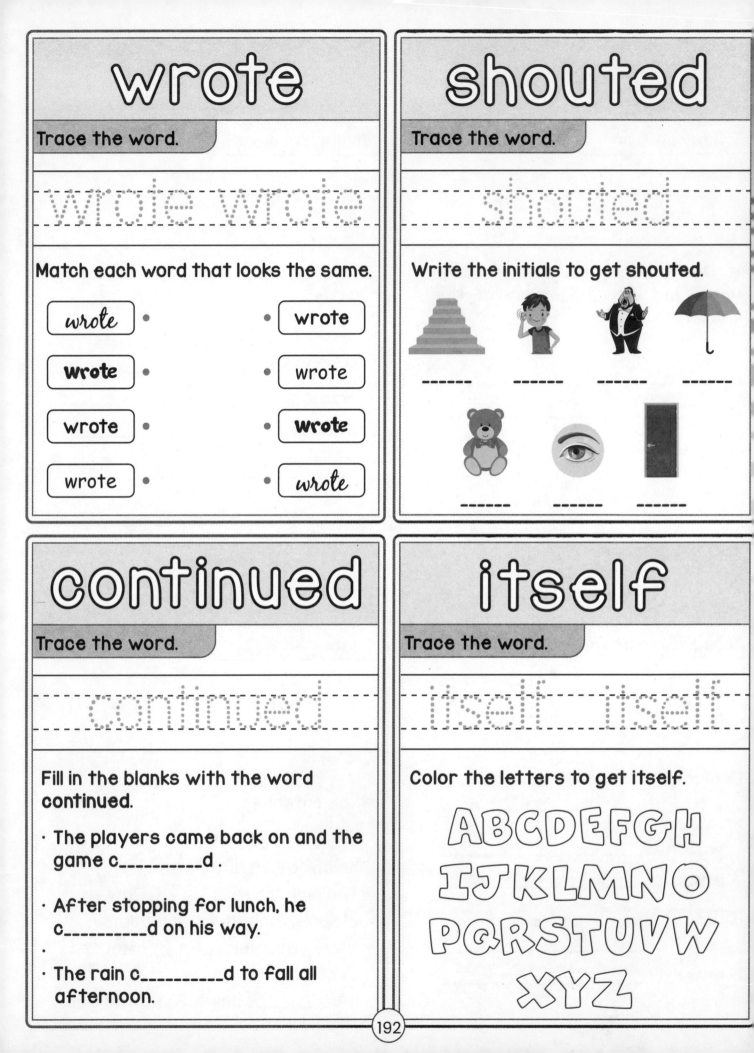

- - - - -   - - - - -   - - - - -   - - - -

- - - - -   - - - - -   - - - - -

continued

Trace the word.

continued

Fill in the blanks with the word **continued**.

· The players came back on and the game c_____d .

· After stopping for lunch, he c_____d on his way.

·

· The rain c_____d to fall all afternoon.

itself

Trace the word.

itself   itself

Color the letters to get **itself**.

ABCDEFGH
IJKLMNO
PQRSTUVW
XYZ

else

Trace the word.

else else else

Connect the dots to spell else. Find the word 2 times.

plains

Trace the word.

plains plains

Find the word plains 3 times in the grid.

s	o	i	l	d	r	e	s	s	w
p	l	a	i	n	s	h	s	r	e
s	o	d	r	e	s	s	o	c	r
o	i	p	l	a	i	n	s	e	a
i	a	r	s	k	d	r	e	s	s
l	e	p	l	a	i	n	s	k	e

gas

Trace the word.

gas gas gas

Color the correct code for each letter.

England

Trace the word.

England

Fill in the missing letters.

	n	g		a	n	
E			l	a		d
E	n				n	d
	n		l		n	
	g			a	n	

burning

Trace the word.

burning

Connect the letters in the correct order to get the word **burning**.

n	r	n	b	i	u	g
1	4	2	5	3	6	7

design

Trace the word.

design design

Color the letters of the word **design** in your favorite colors and read aloud.

DESIGN
DESIGN

joined

Trace the word.

joined joined

Add **joined** to the prefixes to make a new word.

· con _____

· dis _____

· re _____

· mis _____

· sub _____

foot

Trace the word.

foot foot foot

Make clouds around the word **foot** as many times as you spot it.

foot   bed
          twins
rain
          foot
     tomato
          red
foot   nails

194

law

Trace the word.

law law law

Add the word law to these letters to make a new word.

b	y			
c				s
			n	y
f				s

ears

Trace the word.

ears ears ears

Match the word with the one in the same style.

ears •   • ears

earS •   • ears

ears •   • **earS**

ears •   • *ears*

glass

Trace the word.

glass glass

Write glass next to objects that are made up of glass.

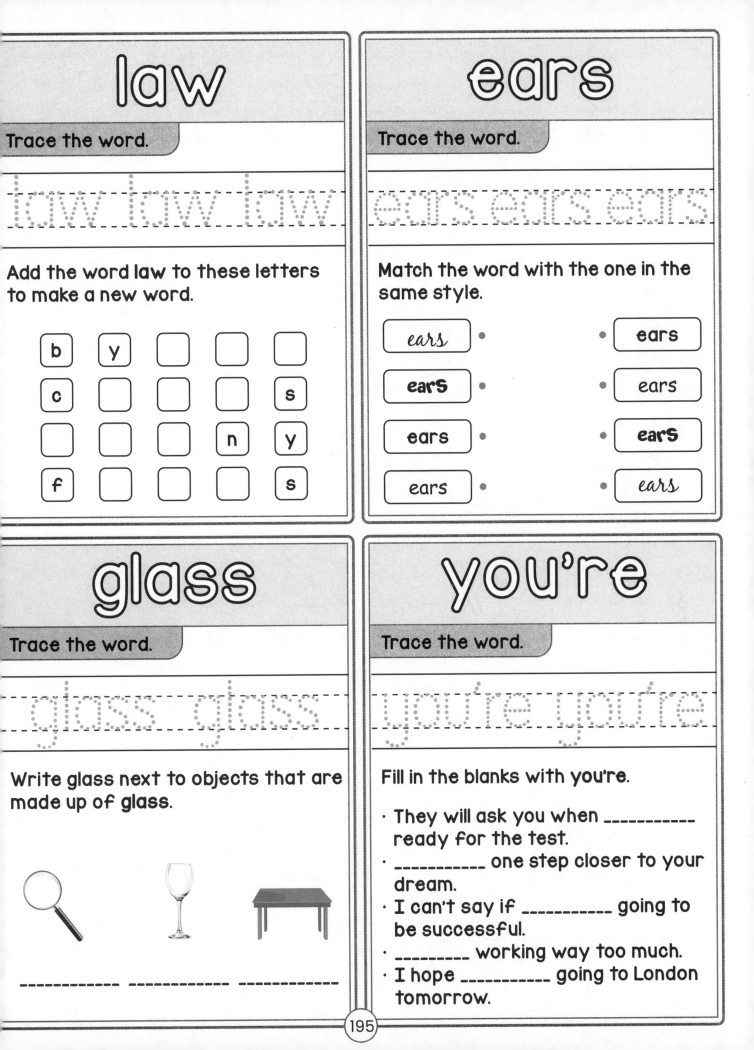

_____   _____   _____

you're

Trace the word.

youre youre

Fill in the blanks with **you're**.

· They will ask you when _____ ready for the test.
· _____ one step closer to your dream.
· I can't say if _____ going to be successful.
· _____ working way too much.
· I hope _____ going to London tomorrow.

grew

grew grew

Find the word grew 3 times in the word search.

g	o	i	l	d	r	e	s	s	w
r	l	a	i	n	g	r	e	w	e
e	o	d	r	e	s	s	o	c	r
w	i	p	l	g	r	e	w	e	a
i	a	r	s	k	d	r	e	s	s
l	e	p	l	a	i	n	s	k	e

skin

Trace the word.

skin skin skin

Connect the letters to spell skin.

t s o u i w k e

i h k d s n t h

valley

Trace the word.

valley valley

Spell the word valley.

cents

Trace the word.

cents cents

Circle the words containing cents.

underline   crescents   exposure

scents   cook   underwater

lesson   adolescents   innocents

percents   founder

key

key key key

Add the word key to the given words. Now read aloud the words formed.

_____ word

_____ note

_____ hole

_____ pads

_____ set

president

Trace the word.

president

Find the word president 2 times.

g	o	i	l	d	r	e	s	s	w
p	r	e	s	i	d	e	n	t	e
e	o	d	r	e	s	s	o	c	r
w	p	r	e	s	i	d	e	n	t
i	a	r	s	k	d	r	e	s	s
l	e	p	l	a	i	n	s	k	e

brown

Trace the word.

brown brown

Circle the objects that are brown in color.

trouble

Trace the word.

trouble

Color in the letters to spell trouble.

a	b	c	d	e	f	g
h	i	j	k	l	m	n
o	p	q	r	s	t	u
	v	w	x	y	z	

cool

Trace the word.

cool cool

Fill in the blanks to spell cool.

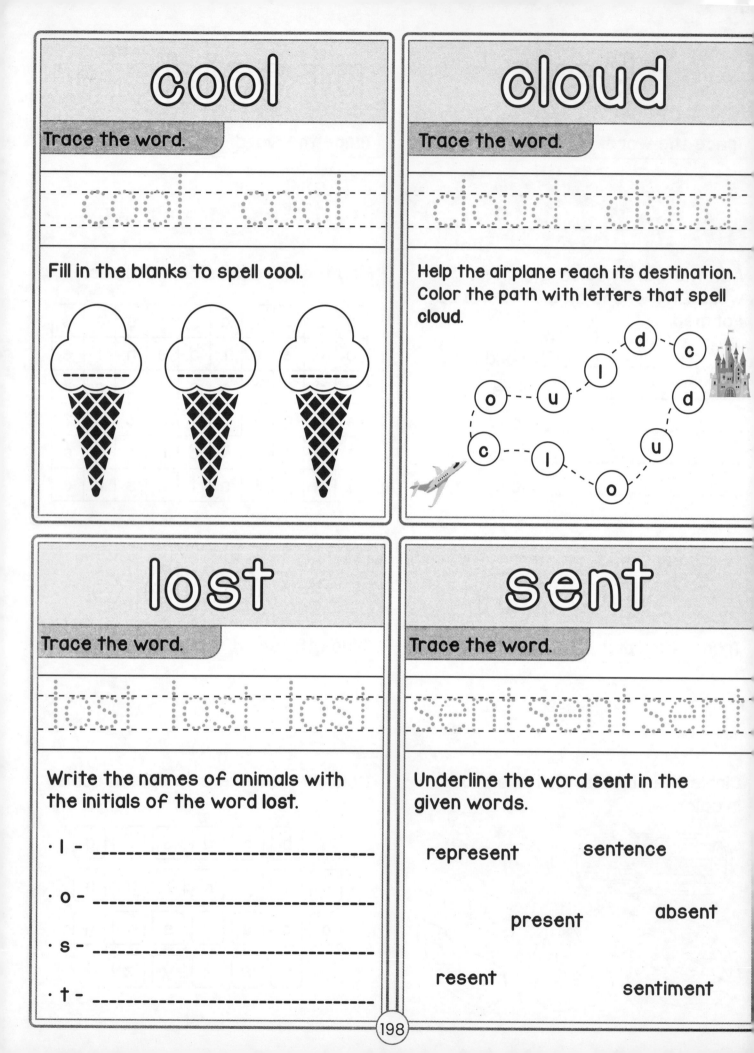

cloud

Trace the word.

cloud cloud

Help the airplane reach its destination. Color the path with letters that spell cloud.

lost

Trace the word.

lost lost lost

Write the names of animals with the initials of the word lost.

· l - _____

· o - _____

· s - _____

· t - _____

sent

Trace the word.

sent sent sent

Underline the word sent in the given words.

represent   sentence

            present   absent

resent

            sentiment

symbols

Trace the word.

symbols

Connect the dots to spell **symbols**.

s
l
o
b
m
y
s

wear

Trace the word.

wear wear

Replace the underlined letters to get **wear**.

· <u>t</u>ear _____

· <u>n</u>ear _____

· <u>h</u>ear _____

· <u>f</u>ear _____

· <u>d</u>ear _____

bad

Trace the word.

bad bad bad

Match the words in same style.

bad	·	·	bad
bad	·	·	bad
bad	·	·	**bad**
bad	·	·	bad

save

Trace the word.

save save

Help the frog reach the pond by following **save**.

s   a   p

e   o   v   e

r   m   t

experiment

Trace the word.

experiment

Rank the letters in the correct order to get experiment.

| e | n | t | x | p | e | i | m | r | e |

☐ ☐ ☐ ☐ ☐ ☐ ☐ ☐ ☐ ☐

engine

Trace the word.

engine

Form the word engine.

e
e n
e n g
e n g i
e n g i n
e n g i n e

alone

Trace the word.

alone alone

Color the letters with your favorite colors to get the word alone.

a	b	c	d	e	f	g
h	i	j	k	l	m	n
o	p	q	r	s	t	u
	v	w	x	y	z	

drawing

Trace the word.

drawing

Fill in the missing letters to spell drawing.

d		a			g
d			i	n	
d	r	w			g
		a		i	g

east

east   east

Underline the word **east** in the given words.

yeast   eastern

beasts   feast

easter

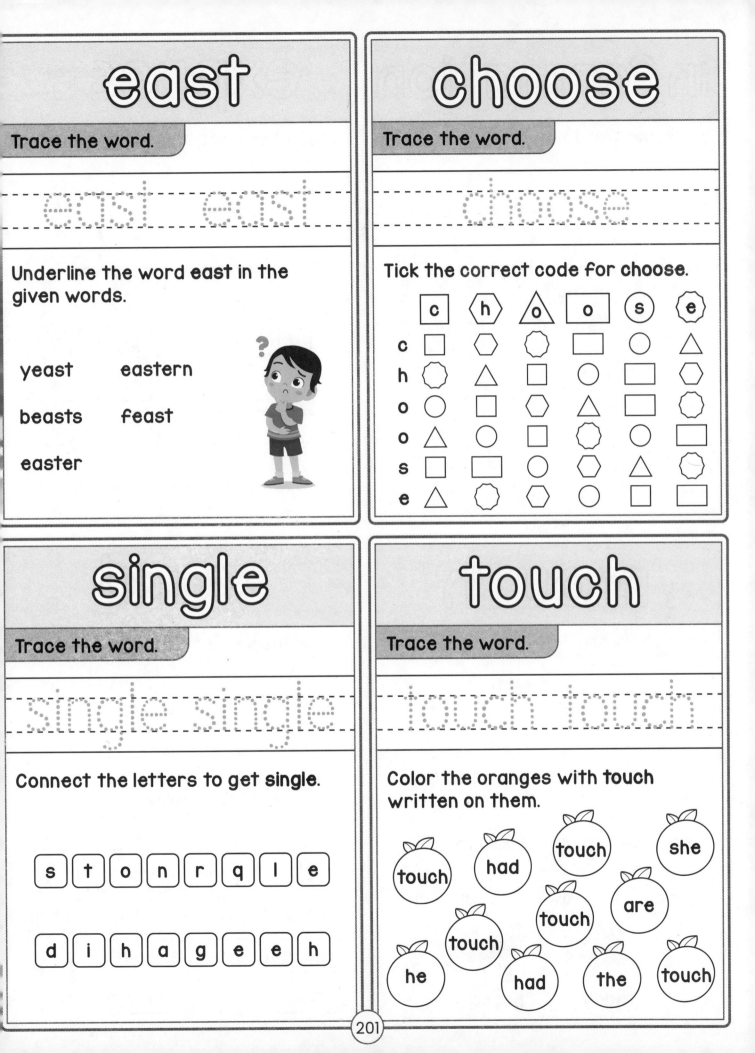

choose

Trace the word.

choose

Tick the correct code for **choose**.

	c	h	o	o	s	e
c	□	⬡	✿	▭	○	△
h	✿	△	□	○	▭	⬡
o	○	□	⬡	△	▭	✿
o	△	○	□	✿	○	▭
s	□	▭	○	⬡	△	✿
e	△	✿	⬡	○	▭	▭

single

Trace the word.

single single

Connect the letters to get **single**.

s	t	o	n	r	q	l	e

d	i	h	a	g	e	e	h

touch

Trace the word.

touch touch

Color the oranges with **touch** written on them.

touch   had   touch   she

touch   touch   are

he   touch   had   the   touch

201

information

Trace the word.

information

Unscramble the letters to spell the word information.

o f i r o
t
a n i e n m

_____

express

Trace the word.

express

Color the letters to get express.

a	r	n	c	p	e	z
s	h	g	f	n	d	o
t	x	j	i	k	m	s
	v	o	b	e	a	

mouth

Trace the word.

mouth mouth

Circle initials of the words to get mouth.

map   owl   unicorn

teddy   horse

yard

Trace the word.

yard yard

Help the farmer reach the fields. Follow the word yard.

yard	yard	single
single	yard	mouth
mouth	east	yard	yard
choose	next	east
touch	single	mouth

let's revise!

1. Write the simple past of the action words.

simple present	simple past
climb	
send	
lose	
grow	
join	
shout	
write	

2. Complete the sentences. (mouth, foot, skin, ears)

- Rayna injured her _____ .
- Moby is having her _____ pierced.
- Laila has a sensitive _____ .
- We should keep our _____ closed when chewing.

3. Find the 4-letter words. (east, wear, cool, lost, sent, yard)

e	a	s	t	d	r	e	s	s	s
c	r	e	s	i	w	e	a	r	e
o	y	a	r	d	p	o	r	t	n
o	p	r	e	s	i	d	e	n	t
l	a	r	e	l	o	s	t	s	s

4. Unscramble the letters to find the word.

- ymsobsl – _____
- truelob – _____
- eginen – _____

203

equal

Trace the word.

equal equal

Complete the spelling by filling in the missing letters.

	q		a	
e		u		l
		a	l	
e	q	u		

decimal

Trace the word.

decimal

Connect the dots to spell decimal.

l
a
m i c e d

yourself

Trace the word.

yourself

Replace the underlined letters with the word your to get yourself.

· himself : _____

· herself : _____

· oneself : _____

· thyself : _____

· ourself : _____

control

Trace the word.

control control

Tick the correct code for control.

c	o	n	t	r	o	l

204

practice

Trace the word.

practice

How many times can you spot practice? Count and write.

practice	slow	here
speaks	practice	practice
down	scale	practice

☐ times

report

Trace the word.

report report

Spot report in the grid 3 times.

r	o	i	l	d	r	e	s	s	w
e	r	e	s	i	d	e	n	t	e
p	o	d	r	e	p	o	r	t	r
o	p	r	e	s	i	d	e	n	t
r	a	r	e	p	o	r	t	s	s
t	e	p	l	a	i	n	s	k	e

straight

Trace the word.

straight

Spot and circle the straight lines.

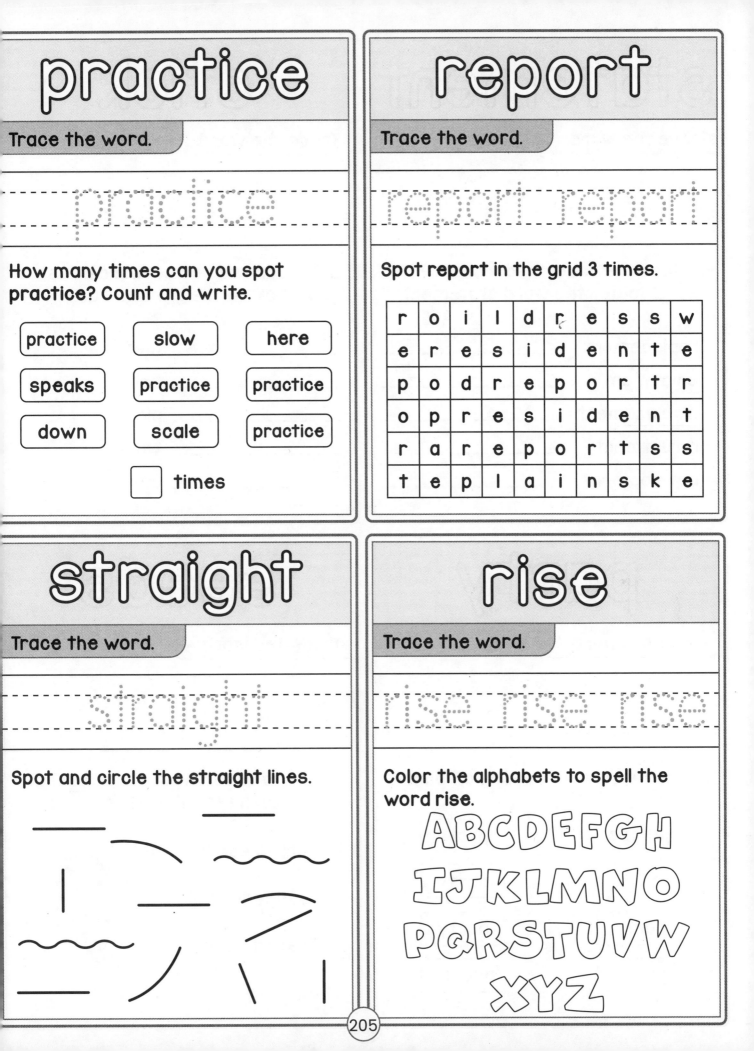

rise

Trace the word.

rise rise rise

Color the alphabets to spell the word rise.

ABCDEFGH
IJKLMNO
PQRSTUVW
XYZ

statement

Trace the word.

statement

Replace the underlined words with 'state' to get the word statement.

· <u>replace</u>ment : _____
· <u>enjoy</u>ment : _____
· <u>displace</u>ment : _____
· <u>adjust</u>ment : _____
· <u>develop</u>ment : _____

stick

Trace the word.

stick stick stick

Let's learn some new words. Just add 'stick' to the given words.

_____ men
_____ ball
_____ pin
_____ work
_____ out

party

Trace the word.

party party

Color the correct spelling of party.

partee	party
parti	party
party	purty
party	paerty

seeds

Trace the word.

seeds seeds

Spot and underline the word seeds in the given set of letters.

· dehihgrseeds
· sssseedshifbj
· dfseedsopyu
· duviseedsjoy

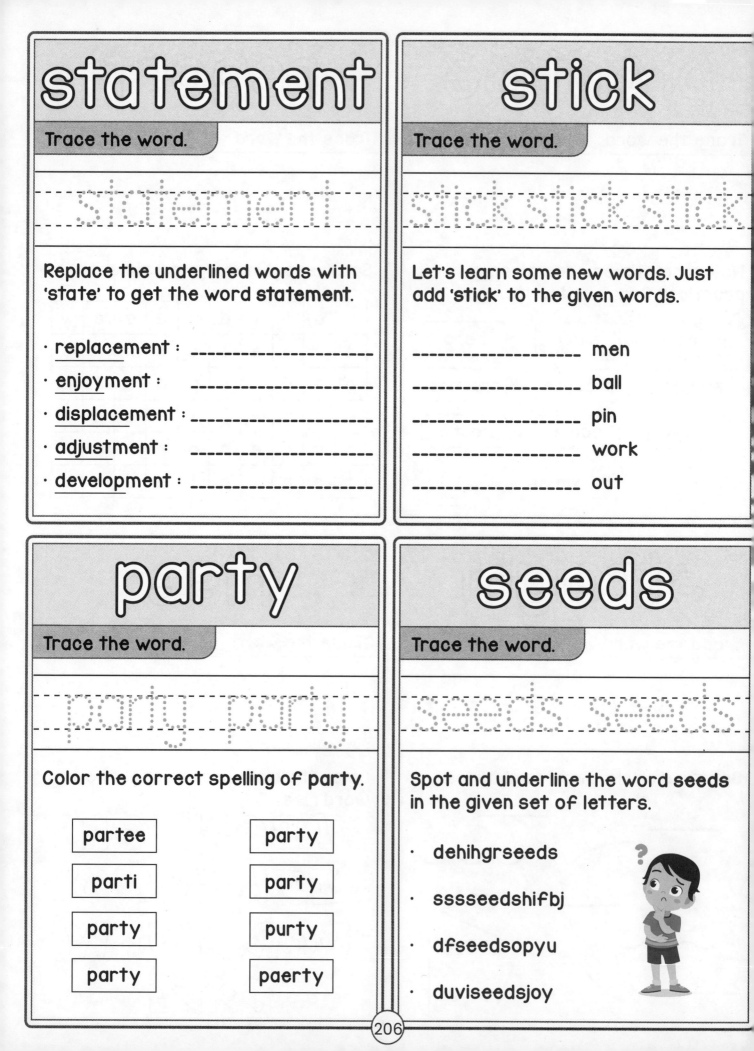

suppose

Trace the word.

suppose

Draw line to connect the letters to spell suppose.

s   e   p   s

u   p   o

☐ ☐ ☐ ☐ ☐ ☐ ☐

woman

Trace the word.

woman

Fill in the blanks with **woman**.

· You are the most beautiful _____.
· She grew up to become a confident _____.
· You're a brave _____.
· The young _____ got into a car accident.
· The tired old _____ was unable to go any further.

coast

Trace the word.

coast coast

Help the elephant reach the apple.

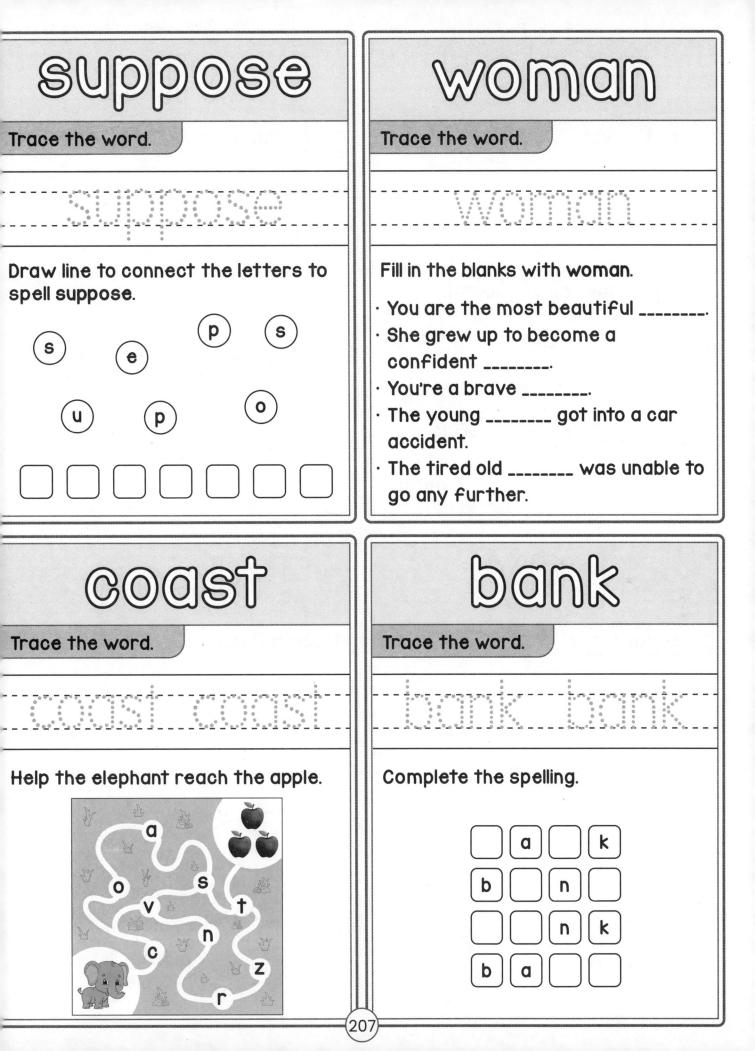

bank

Trace the word.

bank bank

Complete the spelling.

	a		k
b		n	
		n	k
b	a		

period

Trace the word.

period period

Make a box around the word **period** as many times as you spot it.

period   aloof   period

     after   hen   also

sky   period   period

               als

     watch   period

wire

Trace the word.

wire wire wire

Connect the letters to find the **wire**.

| c | w | o | n | r | q | l | e |

| d | i | h | i | g | e | e | h |

pay

Trace the word.

pay pay pay

Fill in the blanks with the word **pay** to make new words.

· over _____
· pre _____
· re _____
· _____ out
· _____ day
· _____ roll

clean

Trace the word.

clean clean

Spot and color the word **clean**.

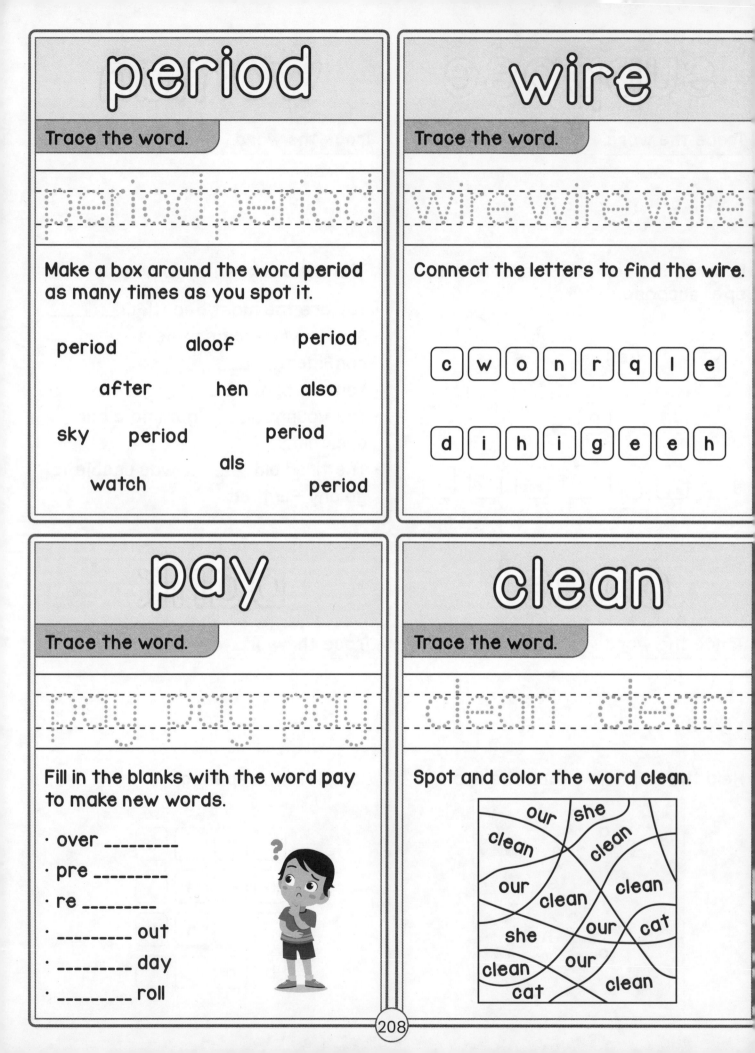

our   she
clean   clean
our   clean
     clean
she   our   cat
clean   our
     cat   clean

visit

Trace the word.

visit visit visit

Help Charlie get his files. Color the path with letters that spell visit.

his	card	clean	him
clean	visit	visit	
him	visit	yard	his
visit	visit	card	him

bit

Trace the word.

bit bit bit

Match each word that is the same style.

bit • • bit

bit • • bit

bit • • **bit**

bit • • bit

whose

Trace the word.

whose whose

Match lines to get **whose**.

| w | s | o | u | i | e | k | e |

| i | h | k | d | s | n | t | h |

received

Trace the word.

received

Color the object with correct spelling.

received	reskeeved
received	received
received	received
reeseved	received
received	received

209

garden

Trace the word.

garden

Color the spaces that has the word garden.

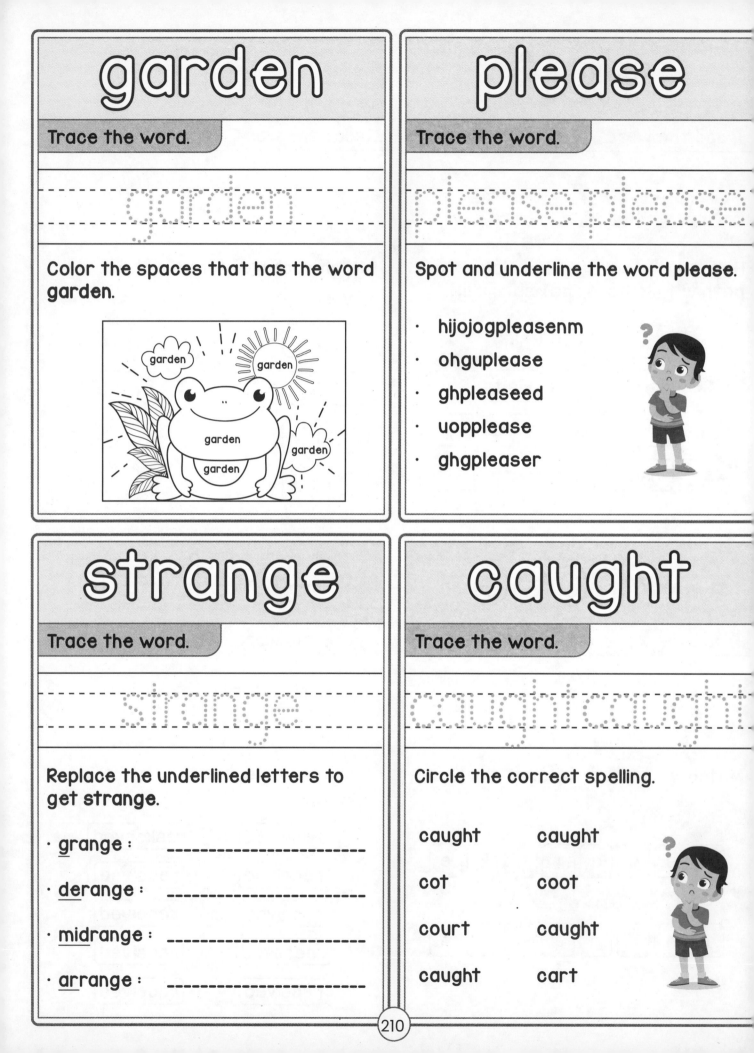

please

Trace the word.

please please

Spot and underline the word please.

- hijojogpleasenm
- ohguplease
- ghpleaseed
- uopplease
- ghgpleaser

strange

Trace the word.

strange

Replace the underlined letters to get strange.

- <u>g</u>range : _____
- <u>d</u>erange : _____
- <u>mid</u>range : _____
- <u>a</u>rrange : _____

caught

Trace the word.

caughtcaught

Circle the correct spelling.

caught	caught
cot	coot
court	caught
caught	cart

fell

Trace the word.

fell fell fell

Join the dots to spell fell.

f •   • l

e •   • l

team

Trace the word.

team team

Replace the underlined letters to form team.

· dream   _____
· beam   _____
· scream   _____
· cream   _____
· stream   _____

god

Trace the word.

god god god

Connect the dots to spell god.

| a | s | g | u | i | d | k | e |

| i | l | k | d | o | n | t | r |

captain

Trace the word.

captain

Find the word captain 2 times.

r	o	i	l	d	r	e	s	s	w
e	r	e	s	i	d	e	n	t	e
p	o	c	a	p	t	a	i	n	r
o	p	r	e	s	i	d	e	n	t
r	a	r	c	a	p	t	a	i	n
t	e	p	l	a	i	n	s	k	e

direct

Trace the word.

direct direct

Fill in the missing letters.

	i	r		c	
d			e		t
d	i			c	t
		r		c	

ring

Trace the word.

ring ring ring

Color each space using the correct color code.

ring	*ring* – red
ring	ring – yellow
ring	**ring** – green
ring	ring – blue

serve

Trace the word.

serve serve

Find the word serve in the grid 4 times.

r	s	e	r	v	e	e	s	s	w
e	r	e	s	e	r	v	e	t	e
p	o	c	a	p	t	a	i	n	r
o	p	r	e	s	e	r	v	e	t
r	a	r	c	a	p	t	a	i	n
s	e	r	v	e	i	n	s	k	e

child

Trace the word.

child child

How many times can you spot the word child? Count and write.

child	here	every
four	ring	captain
child	team	child
king	child	time

[ ] times

212

desert

Trace the word.

desert desert

Join the dots to get **desert** and color the picture.

increase

Trace the word.

increase

Identify the pictures and write its first letter to find the hidden word.

------- ------- ------- -------

------- ------- ------- -------

history

Trace the word.

history history

Color the letters to get **history**.

a	b	c	d	e	f	g
h	i	j	k	l	m	n
o	p	q	r	s	t	u
v	w	x	y	z		

cost

Trace the word.

cost cost cost

Complete the spelling.

	o		t
c		s	
		s	t
c	o		

maybe

Trace the word.

maybemaybe

Join the dots to get maybe.

m g i y u e t

t a k n b m h

business

Trace the word.

business

Fill in the missing letters.

b	u			n	e		
		s	i			s	s
		u		i		e	s
b		s		n			s
		u	s			e	s

separate

Trace the word.

separate

Connect the letters to find the word separate.

s w p n r q t c

d e h a g a e e

break

Trace the word.

break break

Trace the letters to get break.

ABCDEFGH
IJKLMNO
PQRSTUVW
XYZ

uncle

Trace the word.

uncle uncle

Tick the box with correct spelling of uncle.

- uncal ☐
- uncle ☐
- uncle ☐
- ankle ☐

- ungkal ☐
- uncle ☐
- unckle ☐
- uncle ☐

hunting

Trace the word.

hunting

Match the numbers to the letters in correct order to get hunting.

n	g	i	h	u	n	t

4	5	1	6	2	7	3

flow

Trace the word.

flow flow flow

Color each space in the picture with its designated color.

Flow	*Flow* – **Red**
Flow	Flow – **Yellow**
Flow	**Flow** – **Green**
Flow	Flow – **Blue**

lady

Trace the word.

lady lady lady

How many times can you spot the word lady? Count and write.

child	lady	lady
four	lady	captain
lady	lady	child
king	child	lady

I spotted lady ☐ times.

students

Trace the word.

students

Complete the spelling.

s	t			e	n	
		u	d		t	s
	t		d		n	t
s		u		e		s
	t	u			e	t

human

Trace the word.

human

Tick the correct code for the word human.

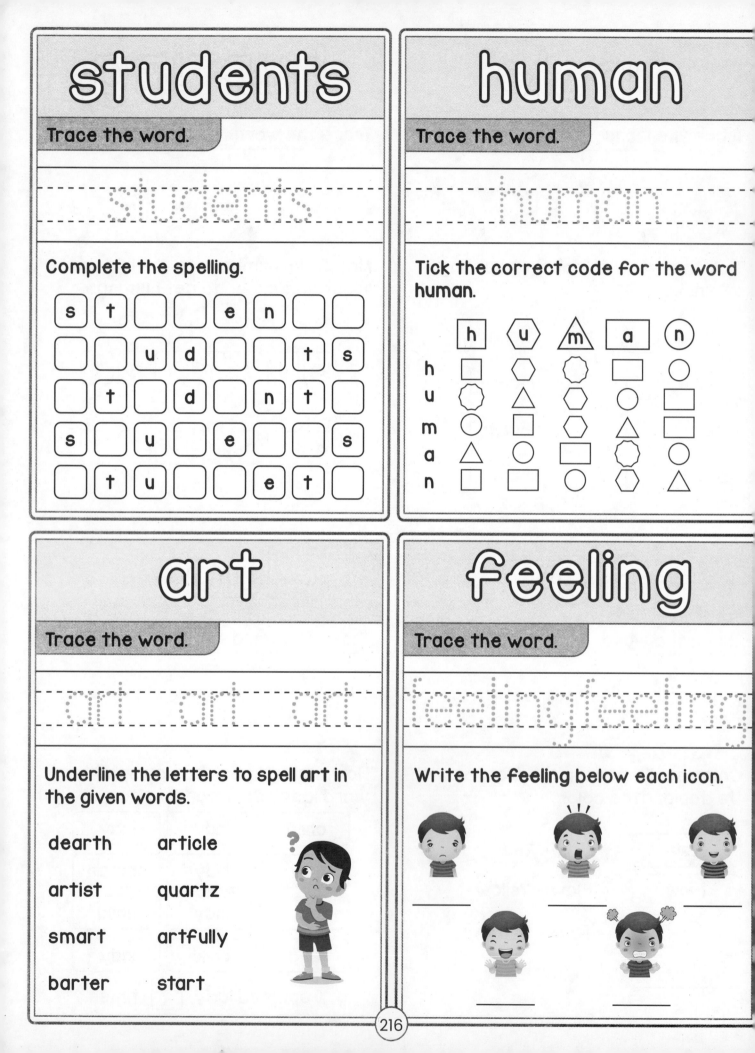

art

Trace the word.

art art art

Underline the letters to spell art in the given words.

dearth   article

artist   quartz

smart   artfully

barter   start

feeling

Trace the word.

feelingfeeling

Write the feeling below each icon.

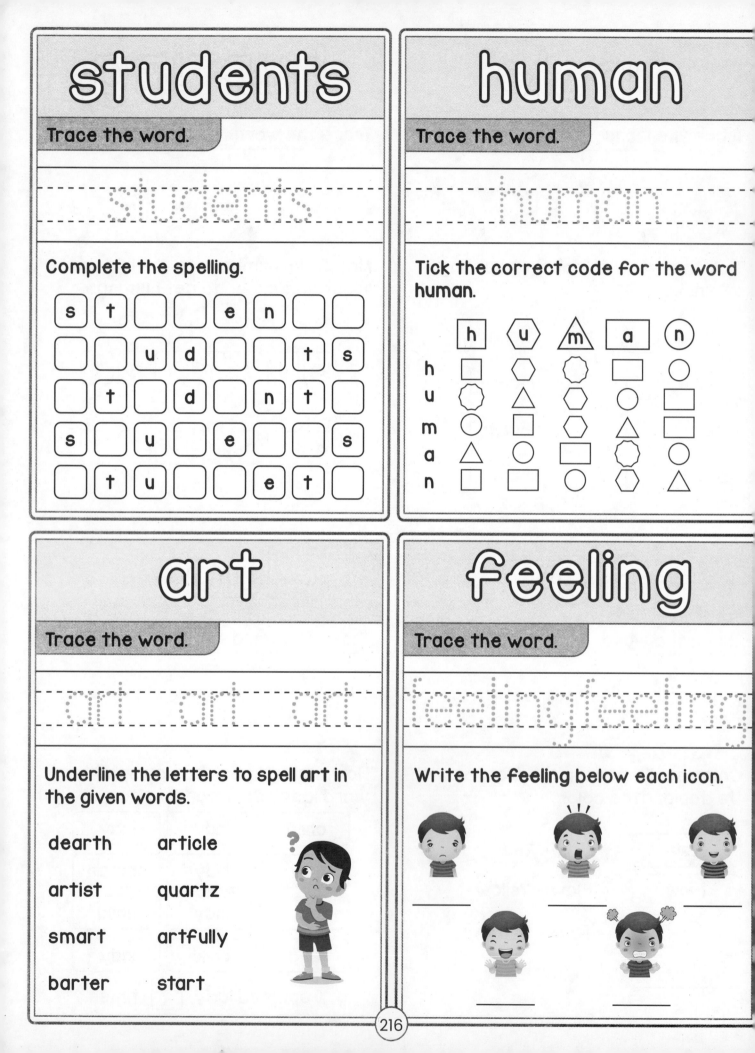

_____   _____

let's revise!

1. Circle the given words in the picture. (period, wire, whose, direct, desert, report, straight, garden, business, separate, hunting)

super   period   hunting   straight   separate   direct

report   night   business   whose   day   garden

cloud   desert   saw   here   wire   slow

2. Unscramble the letters to find the word.

u h a n m	
t o n c r o l	
w m a o n	
m e c a d i l	
v e s r e	

3. Rearrange the jumbled words to form meaningful sentences.

· Martha/ a / player / is / team   ------------------------------

· aunt /visit / I / week / my / every   ------------------------------

· house/ I / have / to / clean / the /   ------------------------------

· you / share / could / bowl / please / the ------------------------------

· Carl / off / bike / fell / his   ------------------------------

4. Underline the naming words in the given sentences.

· My uncle bought me this book.

· He helped an old lady cross the street.

· The students are working hard.

· We got a loan from the bank.

supply

Trace the word.

supply

Identify the object and write the first letter of each to find the hidden word.

_____ _____ _____

_____ _____ _____

corner

Trace the word.

corner corner

Color the objects that are at the 4 corners of each box. Trace the letters to get corner.

c c c c c
o o o o o
r r r r r
n n n n n
e e e e e
r r r r r

electric

Trace the word.

electric

Circle the objects that run on electricity.

insects

Trace the word.

insects

Color only the group of insects. Also, write the name of the group.

_____ _____

_____ _____

crops

Trace the word.

crops crops

Replace the underlined letters with 'c' to spell crops.

· <u>p</u>rops : _____

· <u>d</u>rops : _____

· <u>st</u>rops : _____

tone

Trace the word.

tone tone

Color the correct code for each letter.

	t	o	n	e
t	□	⬡	◯	▢
o	□	⬡	◯	▢
n	□	⬡	◯	▢
e	□	⬡	◯	▢

hit

Trace the word.

hit hit hit

Color each space in the picture by sorting the right color.

hit	hit – red
hit	hit – yellow
hit	**hit** – green
hit	hit – blue

sand

Trace the word.

sand sand

Complete the word with sand to get a new word.

_____ + storm = _____

_____ + man = _____

_____ + paper = _____

_____ + stone = _____

doctor

doctor doctor

Complete the spelling.

d		c		o	
	o		t		r
d	o			o	r
d				o	r
		c	t		r

provide

Trace the word.

provide

Complete the sentences with the word provide.

· The NGO's goal is to _____ shelter to people.
· The school will not _____ any stationery.
· Nature does not _____ everything we want.
· He is unable to _____ for his family.

thus

Trace the word.

thus thus thus

Match the words in same style.

thus	•	•	thus
thus	•	•	thus
thus	•	•	**thus**
thus	•	•	*thus*

won't

Trace the word.

won't won't

Complete the answers to the questions with won't.

· Q –Will the government provide shelter?
Ans: They _____ .
· Q –Will he go to school tomorrow?
Ans: No, he _____ .
· Q –It seems it will rain tomorrow.
Ans: No, it _____ rain.

cook

Trace the word.

cook cook

Replace the underlined letters to form the word cook.

· look _____
· book _____
· took _____
· hook _____
· nook _____

bones

Trace the word.

bones bones

Find the word bones in the grid 3 times.

r	o	i	l	d	r	e	s	s	b
e	r	b	o	n	e	s	n	t	o
p	o	c	a	p	t	a	i	n	n
b	o	n	e	s	i	d	e	n	e
r	a	r	c	a	p	t	a	i	s
t	e	p	l	a	i	n	s	k	e

mall

Trace the word.

mall mall mall

Join the dots to spell the word mall 2 times.

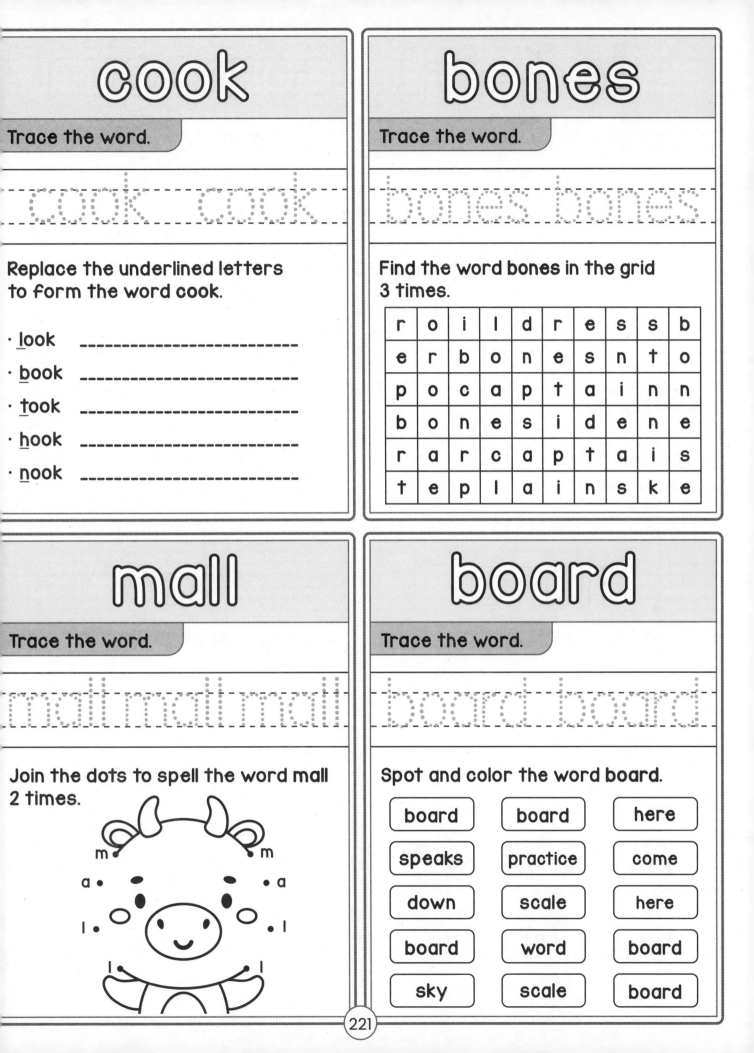

m   m
a   a
l   l

board

Trace the word.

board board

Spot and color the word board.

board	board	here
speaks	practice	come
down	scale	here
board	word	board
sky	scale	board

modern

Trace the word.

modern

Complete the sentences with modern.

· It is a wonder of the _____ world.

· Noise is a curse of _____ city life.

· The house has _____ kitchen appliances.

compound

Trace the word.

compound

Replace the last 4 letters of the given words with 'ound' and write the word you get.

· composer _____

· compiled _____

· computed _____

· computer _____

· compress _____

mine

Trace the word.

mine   mine

Connect the letters to spell mine.

| w | s | m | u | n | n | t |

| i | h | k | d | i | c | e |

wasn't

Trace the word.

wasn't wasn't

Circle the correct spelling of the word.

· was'nt   · wasn't

· wasn't   · wasnt

· wasn't   · wa'snt

fit

Trace the word.

fit   fit   fit

Match the same font for **fit**.

fit •   • fit
fit •   • fit
fit •   • **fit**
fit •   • fit

addition

Trace the word.

addition

Circle the letters to spell **addition** in the jumbled letters.

- d, a, k, o, d, d, f, i, w, q, t, i, p, o, n
- a, f, f, d, k, j, d, i, w, o, t, y, i, o, n
- a, g, d, s, d, e, i, a, t, c, i, l, o, f, n
- v, a, b, d, d, o, i, a, p, t, l, r, h, i, o, n

belong

Trace the word.

belong

Tick the correct color code for belong.

| b | e | l | o | n | g |

safe

Trace the word.

safe   safe

Write safe below the things which are safe to do.

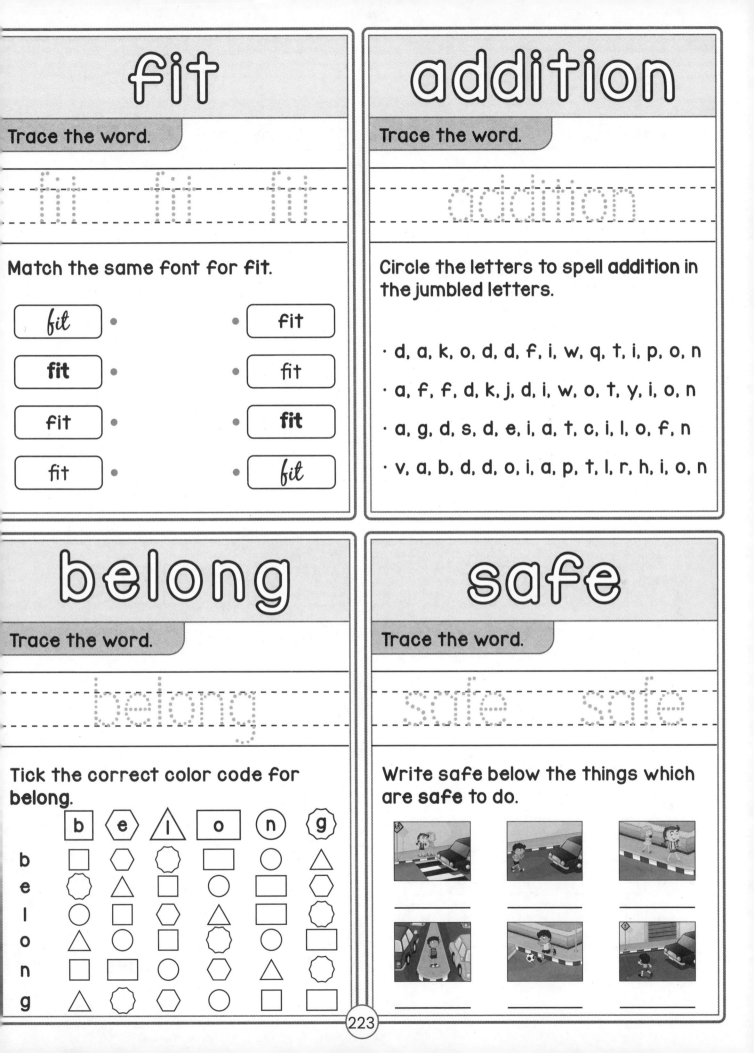

soldiers

soldiers

Underline the correct spelling of the word soldiers.

soldiers   soldiers

solders   soljers

soldrer   solderirs

soldiers

guess

guess guess

Join the dots to spell guess.

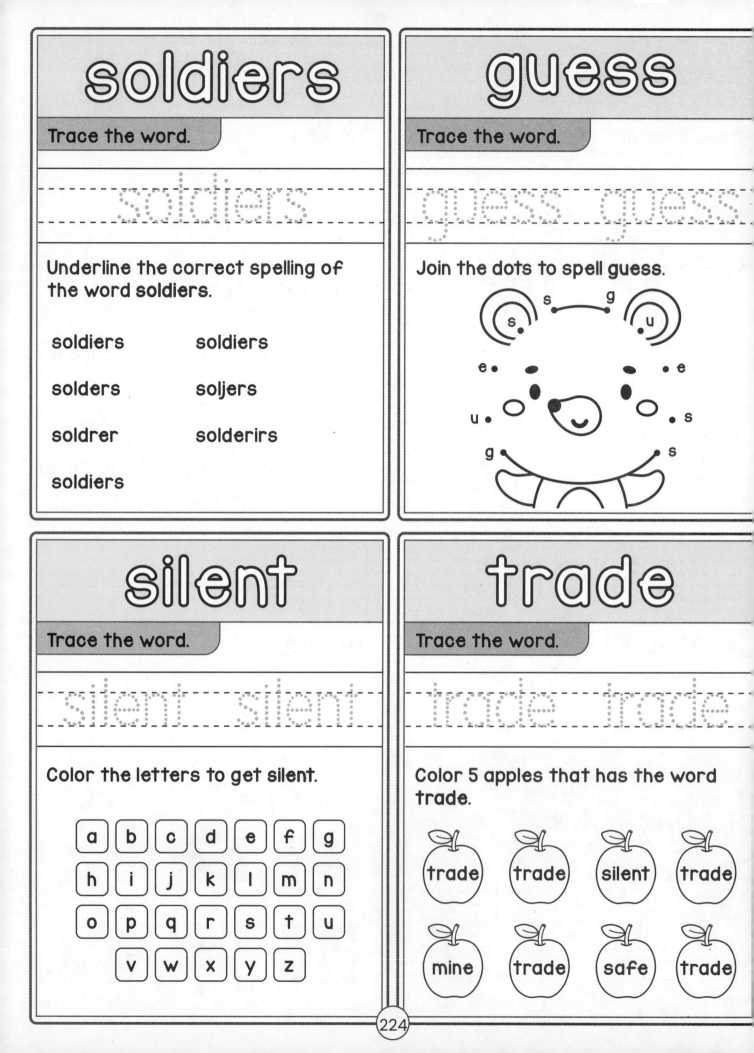

silent

silent   silent

Color the letters to get silent.

a	b	c	d	e	f	g
h	i	j	k	l	m	n
o	p	q	r	s	t	u
	v	w	x	y	z	

trade

trade trade

Color 5 apples that has the word trade.

trade   trade   silent   trade

mine   trade   safe   trade

rather

rather rather

Identify the pictures and write the first letter of each to find the hidden word.

------   ------   ------

------   ------

compare

compare

Color the letters to get **compare**.

a	b	c	d	e	f	g
h	i	j	k	l	m	n
o	p	q	r	s	t	u
v	w	x	y	z		

crowd

crowd crowd

Write where you spot the crowd.

----------   ----------

poem

poem poem

Underline the word **poem** every time you spot it.

A shape poem is a poem that takes on the shape of the thing you're writing about. So, if you wanted to write a poem about an apple, you could write it inside of the outline of an apple, or you could write a short poem and make the words the outline of the apple.

enjoy

enjoy enjoy

Circle the initials to get **enjoy**.

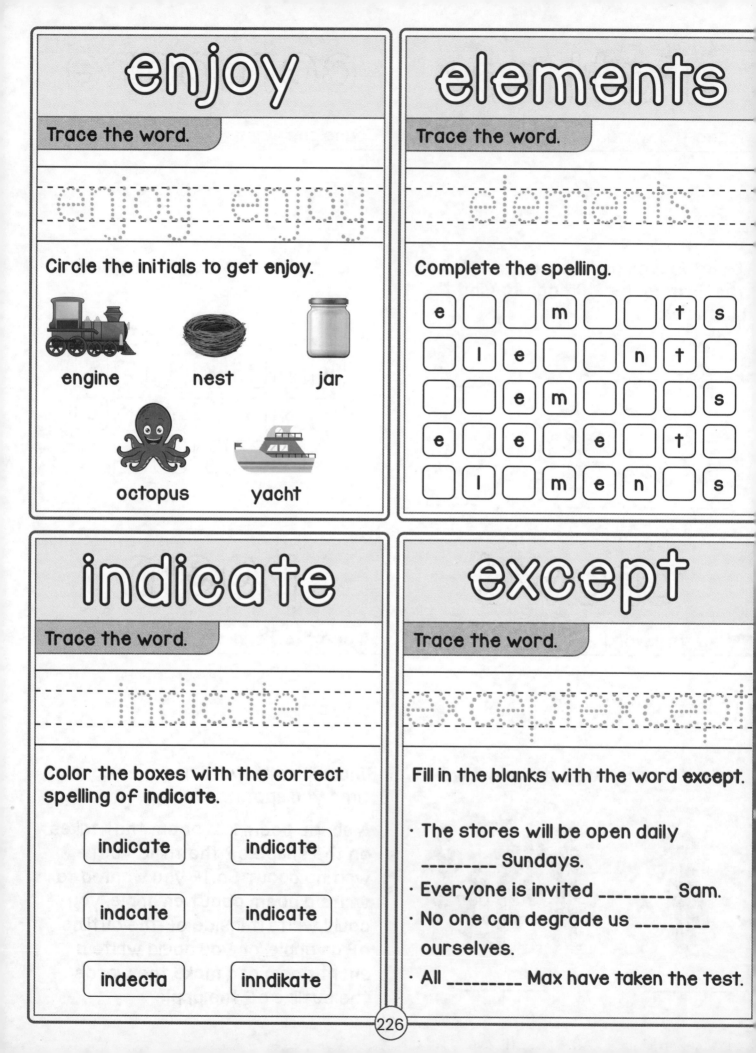

engine   nest   jar

octopus   yacht

elements

Trace the word.

elements

Complete the spelling.

e			m			t	s
	l	e			n	t	
		e	m				s
e		e		e		t	
	l		m	e	n		s

indicate

Trace the word.

indicate

Color the boxes with the correct spelling of **indicate**.

indicate	indicate
indcate	indicate
indecta	inndikate

except

Trace the word.

exceptexcept

Fill in the blanks with the word **except**.

· The stores will be open daily
  _____ Sundays.
· Everyone is invited _____ Sam.
· No one can degrade us _____
  ourselves.
· All _____ Max have taken the test.

226

expect

expect expect

Tick the correct color code for expect.

	e	x	p	e	c	t
e	□	⬡	○	□	○	△
x	⚙	△	□	○	□	⬡
p	○	□	⬡	△	□	⚙
e	△	○	□	⚙	○	□
c	□	□	○	◇	△	⚙
t	△	⚙	⬡	○	□	□

---

flat

Trace the word.

flat flat flat

Complete the given sums to get the word flat.

- **flask - sk + t =** _____
- **flap - p + t =** _____
- **fly - y + at =** _____
- **flip - ip + at =** _____
- **flow - ow + at =** _____

---

seven

Trace the word.

seven seven

Replace the underlined with 's' to get seven.

- <u>e</u>leven _____
- <u>un</u>even _____
- <u>sw</u>even _____

---

interesting

Trace the word.

interesting

Spot and underline the word interesting in the given set of letters

- yhinterestinguiop
- interestingopo
- uiinterestingghi
- iointerestingop
- interestingghu

227

sense

Trace the word.

sense sense

Circle the initials to get **sense**.

sand   egypt   nails

ship   engine

string

Trace the word.

string string

Connect the letters to get the word string.

| w | s | m | r | n | a | t |

| i | h | t | d | i | n | g |

blow

Trace the word.

blow blow

Color the letters to get blow.

a	b	c	d	e	f	g
h	i	j	k	l	m	n
o	p	q	r	s	t	u
v	w	x	y	z

famous

Trace the word.

famous

Connect the numbers with the letters to rank the word.

| u | f | s | o | m | a |

| 6 | 1 | 3 | 2 | 5 | 4 |

value

Trace the word.

value   value

Underline **value** in the following words.

- revalued
- overvalue
- valueless
- transvalue
- eigenvalue

wings

Trace the word.

wings   wings

Color the things with **wings**.

movement

Trace the word.

movement

Replace the highlighted words with 'move'. Write the new word in the blank space.

- <u>aba</u>sement   _____
- <u>amend</u>ment   _____
- <u>achieve</u>ment   _____
- <u>allot</u>ment   _____
- <u>align</u>ment   _____

pole

Trace the word.

polepolepole

Join the dots to spell **pole**. Spot the word 2 times.

e   e

l   l

o   o

p   p

exciting

exciting

Fill in the missing letters.

e	x		i		i		
		c	i			n	
e		c		t			g
	x			t		n	
e	x				i		

branches

Trace the word.

branches

Unscramble the word branches from the jumbled letters. Circle the right letters.

· r, s, b, d, f, r, c, k, a, g, n, l, c, h, e, s

· c, b, r, e, a, h, l, n, c, y, h, h, e, d, s, p

· b, r, j, m, e, a, b, c, n, c, e, h, x, e, s, i

· b, r, q, l, e, s, a, f, h, n, j, c, w, h, e, s

thick

Trace the word.

thick   thick

Circle the things that are thick. Strike off the thin things.

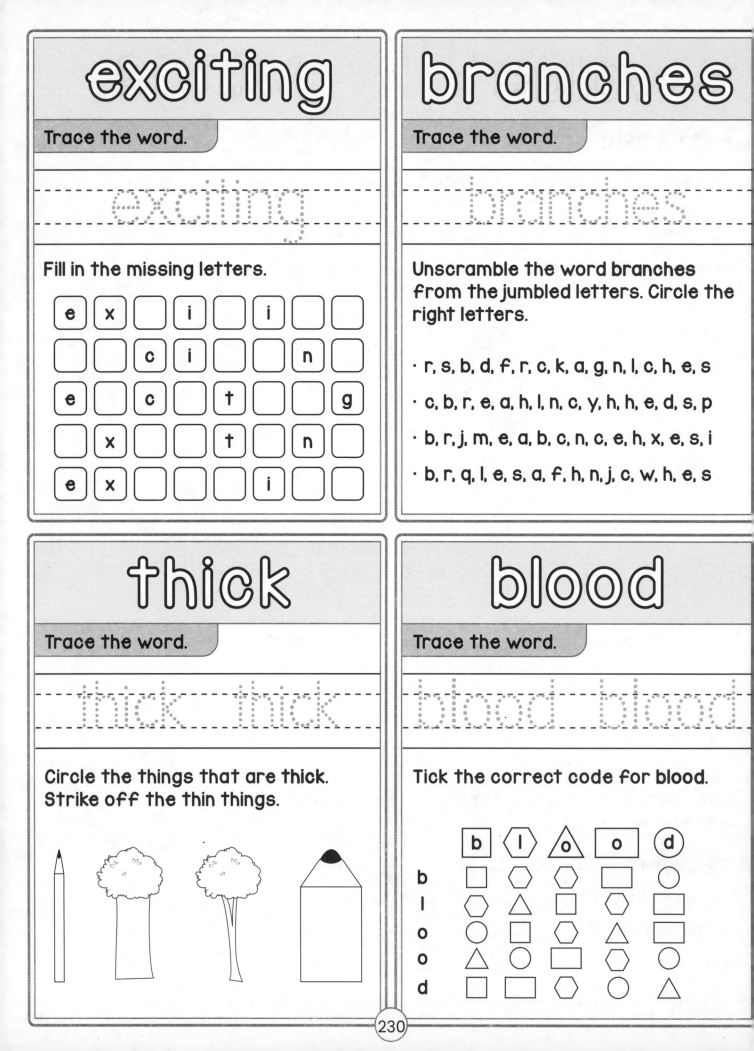

blood

Trace the word.

blood   blood

Tick the correct code for blood.

230

let's revise!

1. Fill in the blanks with the appropriate words. (wings, sense, electric, wasn't, board)

- A lot of _____ lamps illuminated the stage.
- He tried to _____ a plane at Nice airport.
- There _____ anything to worry about.
- Her _____ of smell is wonderful.
- The bird spread its _____ .

2. Add 's' to write the plurals.

- insect _____
- crop _____
- bone _____
- soldier _____
- element _____

3. Circle the describing words in the sentences.

- He wore glasses with thick rims.
- The film had an exciting plot.
- He was a serious, silent man.
- Sandra sounds like a really interesting person.

4. Spot the words. (crowd, poem, enjoy, string, safe)

e	a	s	t	d	e	n	j	o	y
c	r	o	w	d	w	e	a	r	e
o	y	a	r	d	p	o	r	t	n
o	p	o	e	m	i	d	e	n	t
s	t	r	i	n	g	s	a	f	e

lie

Trace the word.

lie lie lie

Color the shapes that spell lie.

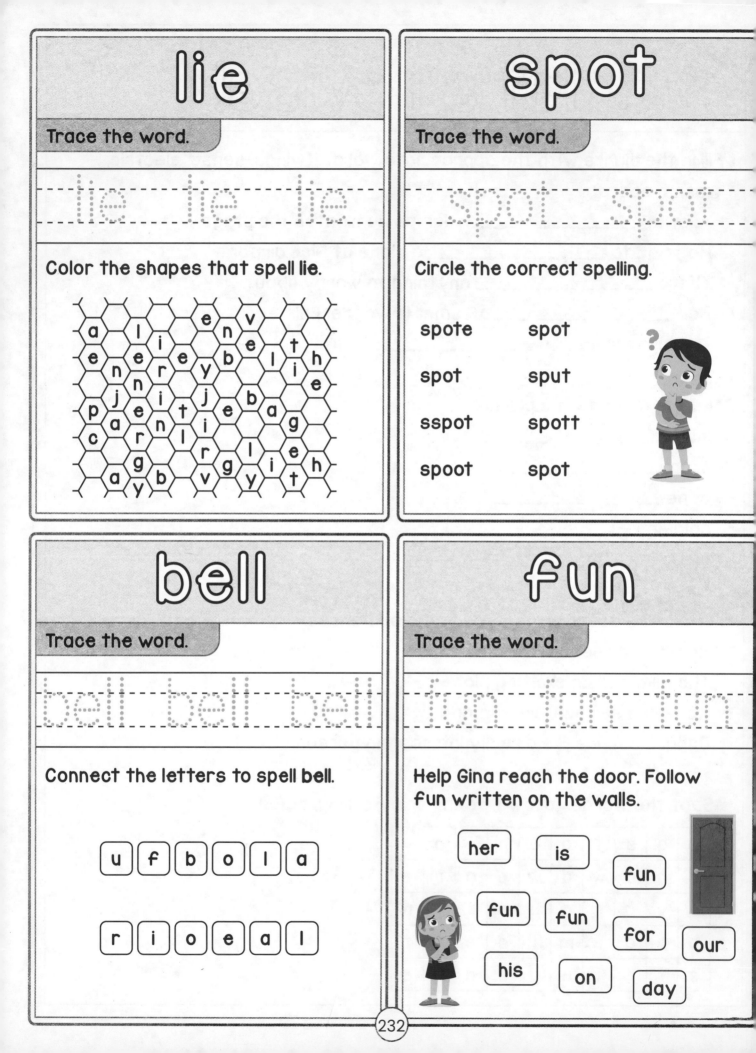

spot

Trace the word.

spot spot

Circle the correct spelling.

spote   spot

spot   sput

sspot   spott

spoot   spot

bell

Trace the word.

bell bell bell

Connect the letters to spell bell.

u f b o l a

r i o e a l

fun

Trace the word.

fun fun fun

Help Gina reach the door. Follow fun written on the walls.

her   is

fun

fun   fun

for

his   on   our

day

loud

Trace the word.

loud   loud

Connect the dots to get loud and finish the picture.

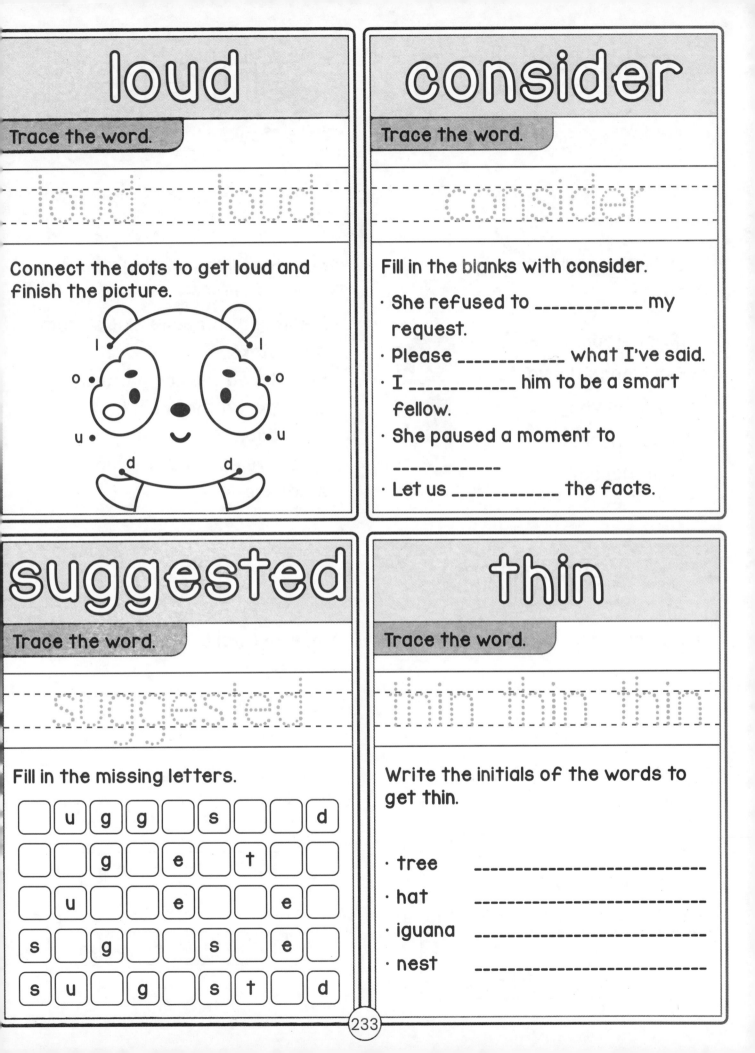

consider

Trace the word.

consider

Fill in the blanks with **consider**.

· She refused to _____ my request.
· Please _____ what I've said.
· I _____ him to be a smart fellow.
· She paused a moment to _____
· Let us _____ the facts.

suggested

Trace the word.

suggested

Fill in the missing letters.

	u	g	g		s		d
		g		e		t	
	u			e			e
s		g			s		e
s	u		g		s	t	d

thin

Trace the word.

thin thin thin

Write the initials of the words to get thin.

· tree   _____
· hat   _____
· iguana   _____
· nest   _____

position

Trace the word.

position

Spot and underline the word position.

- bjfrjpositionm
- sfjorjfnpositionvg
- positionnbkbog
- dfgpositionrty
- dspositiondcf

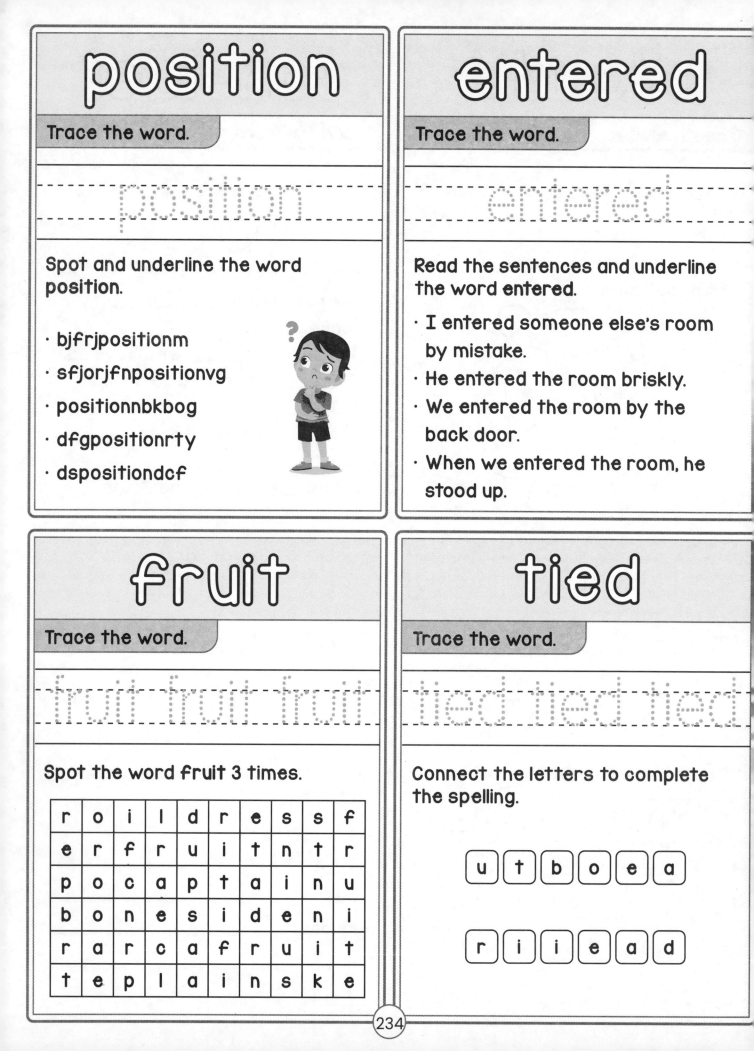

entered

Trace the word.

entered

Read the sentences and underline the word **entered**.

- I entered someone else's room by mistake.
- He entered the room briskly.
- We entered the room by the back door.
- When we entered the room, he stood up.

fruit

Trace the word.

fruit fruit fruit

Spot the word fruit 3 times.

r	o	i	l	d	r	e	s	s	f
e	r	f	r	u	i	t	n	t	r
p	o	c	a	p	t	a	i	n	u
b	o	n	e	s	i	d	e	n	i
r	a	r	c	a	f	r	u	i	t
t	e	p	l	a	i	n	s	k	e

tied

Trace the word.

tied tied tied

Connect the letters to complete the spelling.

u t b o e a

r i i e a d

chief

Trace the word.

chief   chief

Color the word chief.

ABCDEFGH
IJKLMNO
PQRSTUVW
XYZ

Japanese

Trace the word.

Japanese

Circle the initials to get the word Japanese.

· jug   · nest

· apple   · engine

· piano   · sun

· ant   · eskimo

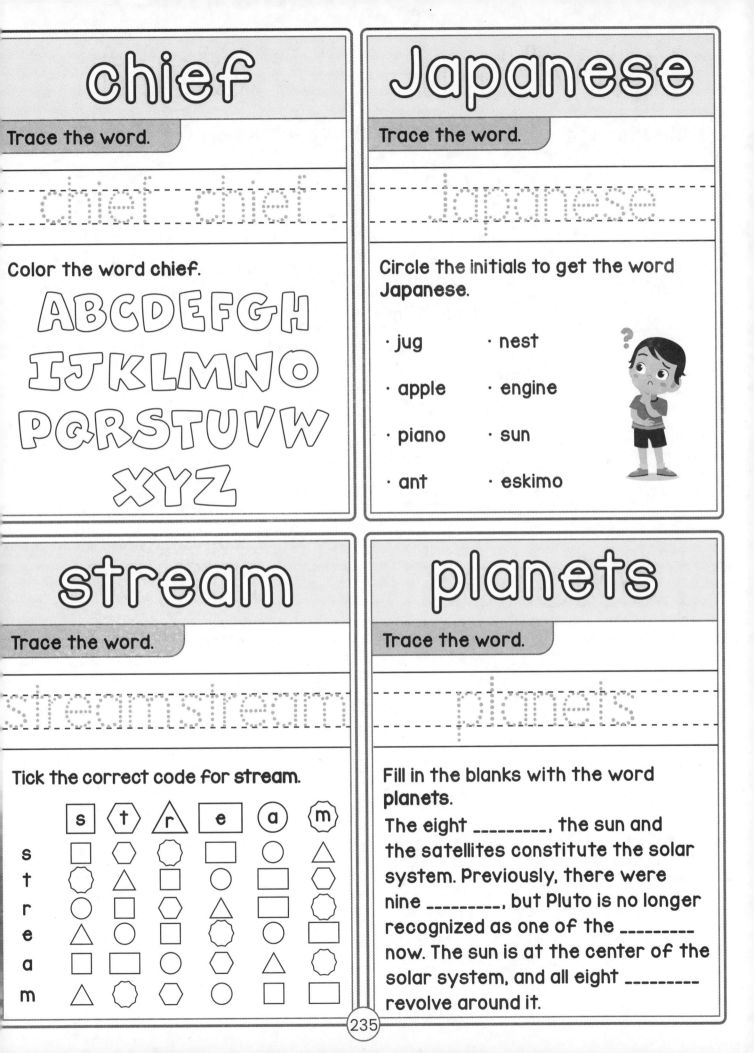

stream

Trace the word.

stream stream

Tick the correct code for stream.

	s	t	r	e	a	m
s	□	⬡	⬡	▭	○	△
t	⬡	△	□	○	▭	⬡
r	○	□	⬡	△	○	⬡
e	△	○	□	⬡	○	▭
a	□	▭	○	⬡	△	⬡
m	△	⬡	⬡	○	□	□

planets

Trace the word.

planets

Fill in the blanks with the word planets.

The eight _____, the sun and the satellites constitute the solar system. Previously, there were nine _____, but Pluto is no longer recognized as one of the _____ now. The sun is at the center of the solar system, and all eight _____ revolve around it.

rhythm

Trace the word.

rhythm rhythm

Color the correct code for each letter.

	r	h	y	t	h	m
r	□	⬡	✿	□	○	△
h	✿	△	□	○	□	⬡
y	○	△	⬡	△	□	✿
t	△	○	□	✿	○	□
h	□	□	○	⬡	△	✿
m	△	✿	⬡	○	□	□

eight

Trace the word.

eight eight

Count and color **eight** balls.

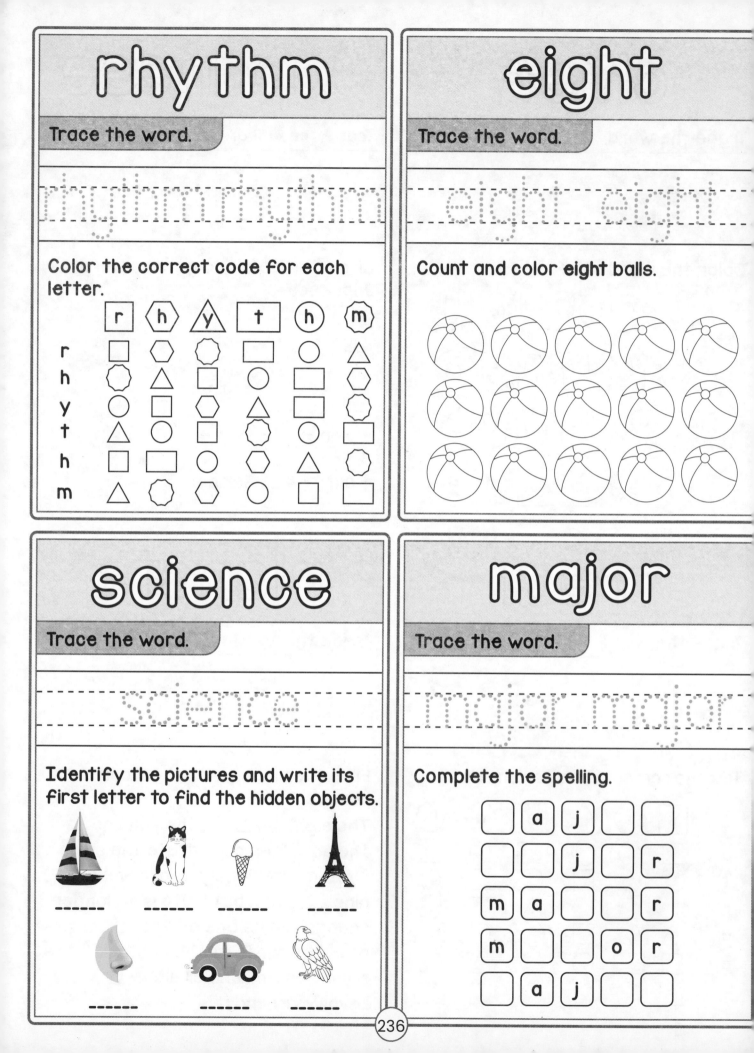

science

Trace the word.

science

Identify the pictures and write its first letter to find the hidden objects.

------   ------   ------   ------

------   ------   ------

major

Trace the word.

major major

Complete the spelling.

	a	j		
		j		r
m	a			r
m			o	r
		a	j	

observe

Trace the word.

observe

Find the word **observe** 3 times.

r	o	b	s	e	r	v	e	s	f
e	r	f	r	u	i	t	n	t	r
p	o	c	a	p	t	a	i	n	u
b	o	b	s	e	r	v	e	n	i
r	a	r	c	a	f	r	u	i	t
t	o	b	s	e	r	v	e	k	e

tube

Trace the word.

tube tube tube

Complete the spelling.

t		b	
	u		e
t			e
t		b	
	u		e

necessary

Trace the word.

necessary

Color the letters that spell the word **necessary**.

l   e   c   s
a   o   y
n   e   t   s   r

----

weight

Trace the word.

weight weight

Underline **weight** in the given words.

weiht   weight

weight   waeyt

waiit   wayt

weiggt   weight

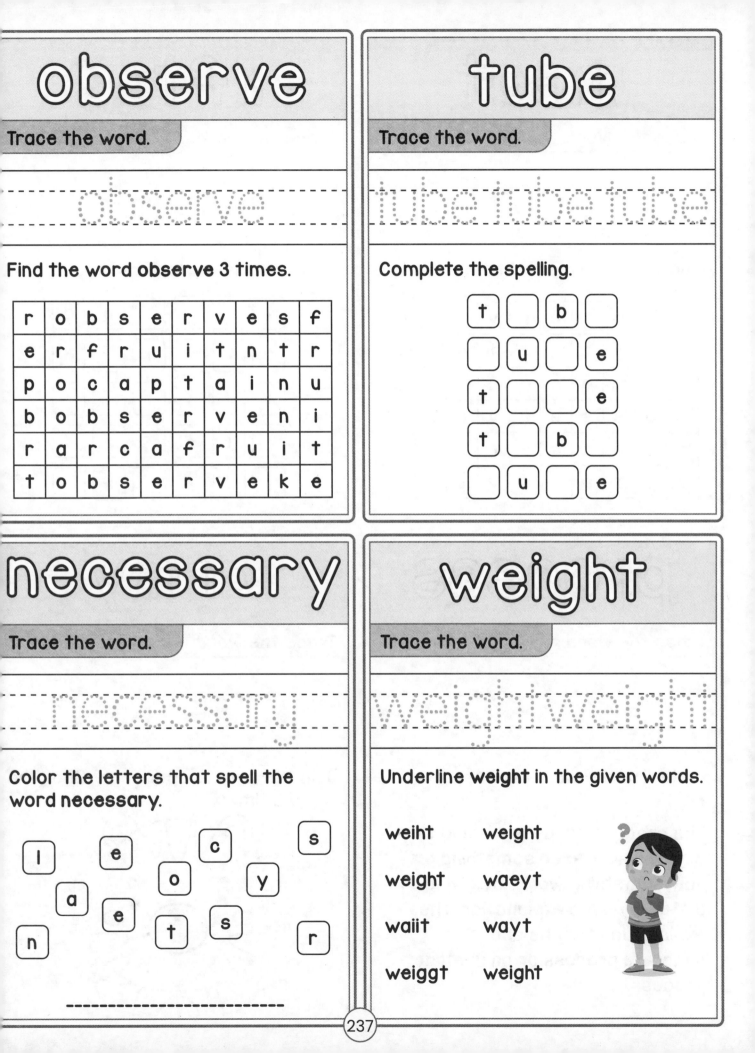

237

meat

Trace the word.

meat meat

Find the word meat 4 times.

m	e	a	t	e	r	v	e	s	m
e	r	f	r	u	i	t	n	t	e
p	o	m	e	a	t	a	i	n	a
b	o	e	s	e	r	v	e	n	t
r	a	a	c	a	f	r	u	i	t
t	o	t	s	e	r	v	e	k	e

lifted

Trace the word.

lifted lifted

Fill in the missing letters.

l	i			e	d
			t		d
l				t	
	i	f			d
l		f		e	

process

Trace the word.

process

Underline the word process.

The process essay is writing that explains how to do something or how something works by giving a step-by-step explanation. The explanation may be about a concrete process or an abstract process.

army

Trace the word.

army army

Join the dots to spell army. Spot the word 2 times.

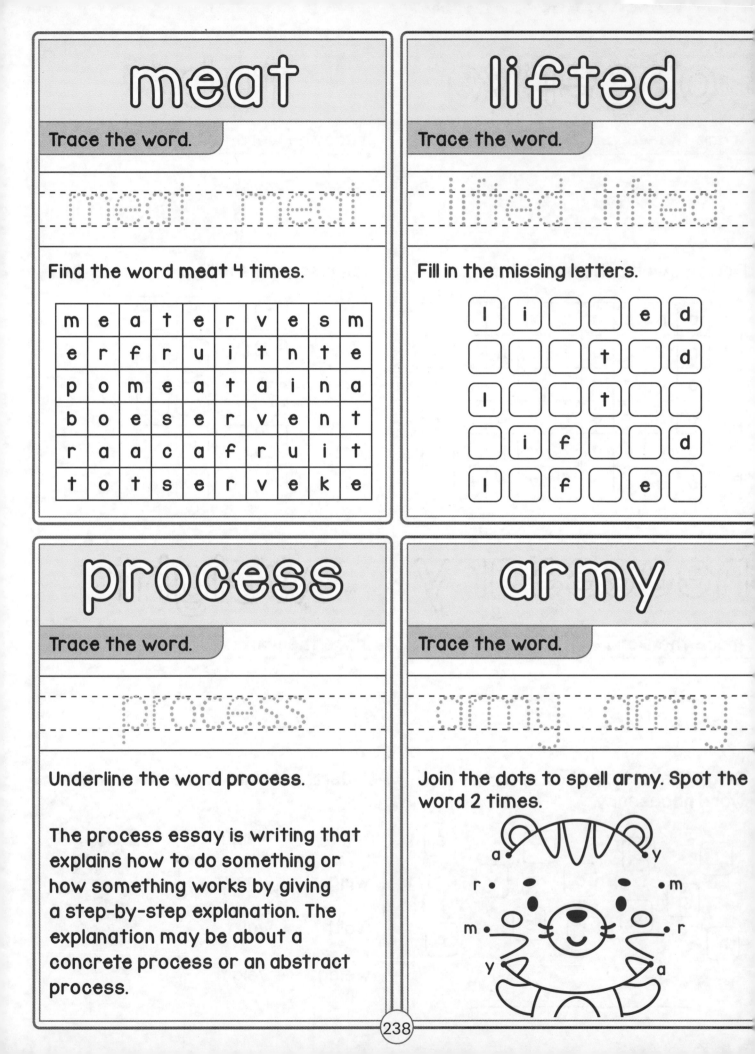

hat

Trace the word.

hat hat hat

Connect the letters to spell hat.

| p | q | h | r | i | y | t |

| s | e | l | u | a | q | t |

property

Trace the word.

property

Rank the letters in the correct order to get the word property.

| p | e | y | p | r | t | o | r |

| 7 | 1 | 6 | 2 | 4 | 8 | 5 | 3 |

particular

Trace the word.

particular

Find the word particular 2 times in the word search puzzle.

p	a	r	t	i	c	u	l	a	r
e	r	f	r	u	i	t	n	t	e
p	o	m	e	a	t	a	i	n	a
p	a	r	t	i	c	u	l	a	r
r	a	a	c	a	f	r	u	i	t
t	o	t	s	e	r	v	e	k	e

swim

Trace the word.

swim swim

Spot the word 3 times.

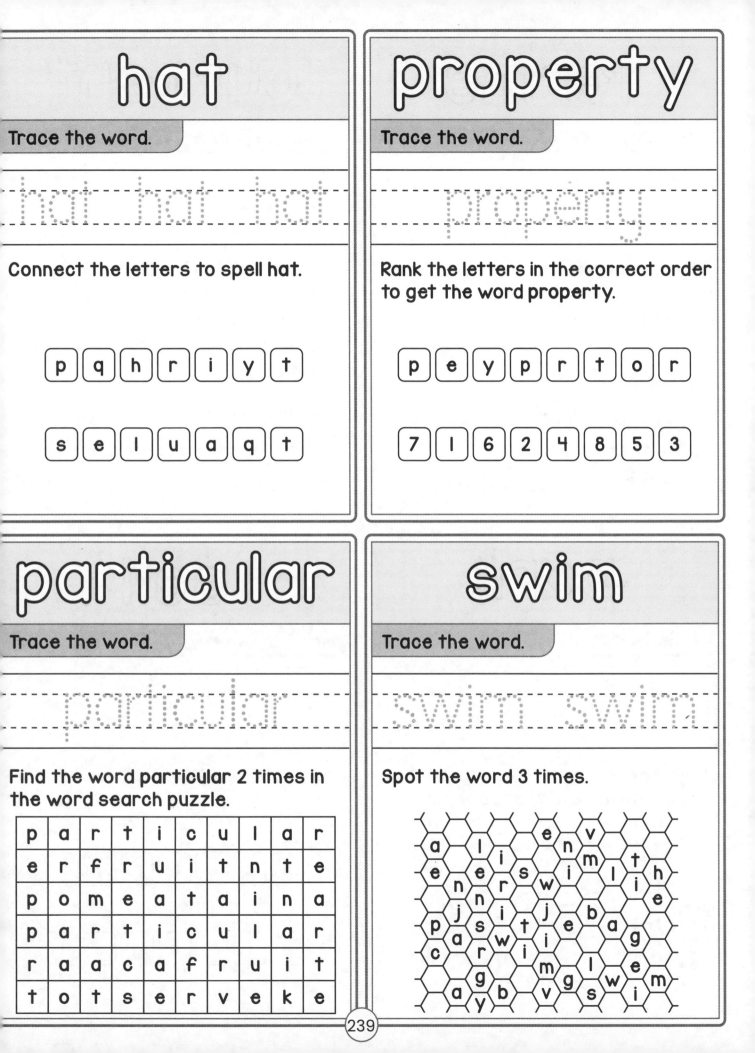

239

terms

terms terms

Fill in the blanks.

· I agree to your _____ .
· The _____ of their deal were over.
· They are on good _____ with their neighbors.
· Are the _____ fulfilled?

current

current current

Add **current** to the given words to make new words.

· under + _____ = _____
· cross + _____ = _____
· super + _____ = _____
· inter + _____ = _____
· photo + _____ = _____

park

park park park

Help Rick reach the swing. Color the path with letters that spell park.

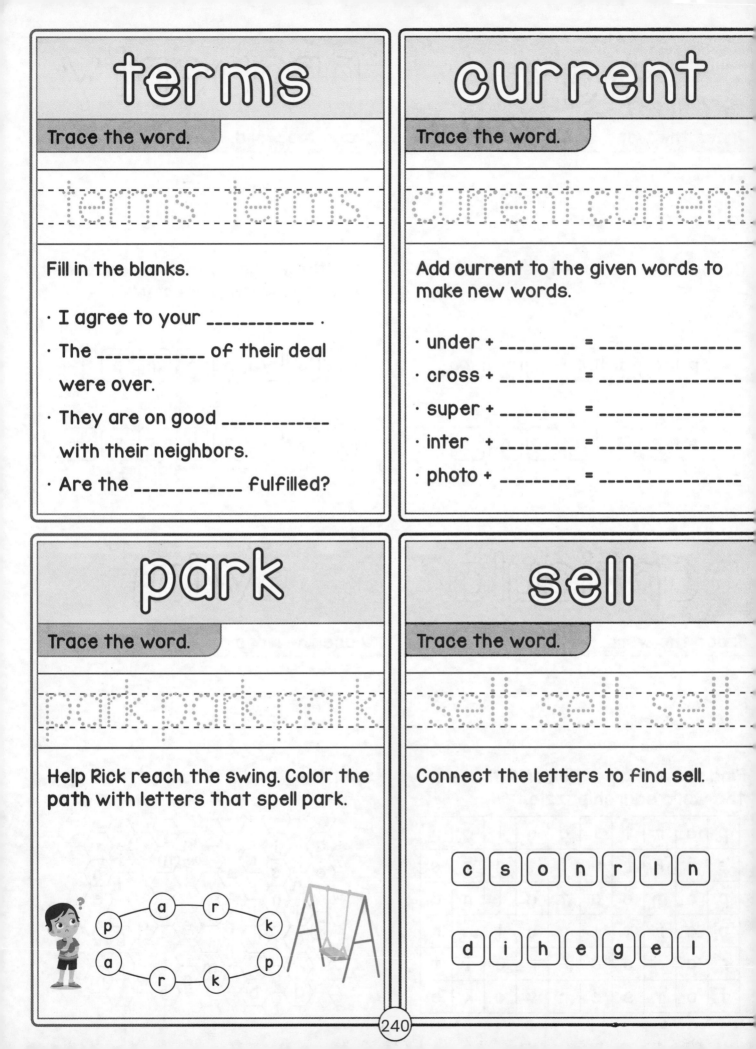

sell

sell sell sell

Connect the letters to find **sell**.

| c | s | o | n | r | l | n |

| d | i | h | e | g | e | l |

shoulder

Trace the word.

shoulder

Fill in the blanks with the word shoulder.

· He rested the baby's head on his

_____ .

· She carried a backpack on one

_____ .

· Ryan glanced over his _____ .

· Put your _____ to the wheel.

industry

Trace the word.

industry

Replace the underlined letters with 'indus'. Write the new word in the blanks.

· ministry   _____

· infantry   _____

· forestry   _____

· registry   _____

· tapestry   _____

wash

Trace the word.

wash wash

Color the letters to get wash.

a	b	c	d	e	f	g
h	i	j	k	l	m	n
o	p	q	r	s	t	u
	v	w	x	y	z	

block

Trace the word.

block block

Join the dots to form the word block.

spread

Trace the word.

spread spread

Tick the correct code for spread.

	s	p	r	e	a	d
s						
p						
r						
e						
a						
d						

cattle

Trace the word.

cattle   cattle

Replace the first letter with 'c' to get the word cattle.

· battle   _____

· rattle   _____

· tattle   _____

· wattle   _____

wife

Trace the word.

wife wife wife

Connect the letters to get wife.

w t o f r q n

d i h a g e l

sharp

Trace the word.

sharp   sharp

Write the names of animals with the letters of the word sharp.

s _____

h _____

a _____

r _____

p _____

company

Trace the word.

company

Spot and find the word company.

m	e	a	c	o	p	a	n	y	c
e	r	f	r	u	i	t	n	t	p
c	o	m	p	a	n	y	i	n	p
b	o	e	s	e	r	v	e	n	t
c	o	m	p	a	n	y	u	i	t
t	o	t	s	e	r	v	e	k	e

radio

Trace the word.

radio   radio

Circle the letters to get the word radio.

fbrjoaoegdjbibgo

bbrbjkajjdjjiblon

bfkrdhaifdohifbo

qwrhajdkvibjbo

we'll

Trace the word.

we'llwe'llwe'll

Fill in the blanks with we'll.

· _____ go there tomorrow.
· _____ have our dinner in some time.
· _____ win the soccer match.
· _____ complete our tasks in time.
· _____ share the presentation with him soon.

action

Trace the word.

action action

Join the dots to spell action. Find the word 2 times.

let's revise!

1. Write words that sound the same.

· meet _____

· wait _____

· ate _____

2. Add –ed to the words to get the past form.

· enter _____

· suggest _____

· lift _____

3. What are the opposites of the given words?

· fat _____

· blunt _____

· receive _____

· poor _____

· boredom _____

4. Find and circle the hidden words.

hat

tube

science

planets

dollars

army

capital

capital capital

Replace the underlined with 'ital'.
Rewrite the words in the space
provided.

- cap**able** - _____
- cap**tion** - _____
- cap**ture** - _____
- cap**tain** - _____
- cap**sule** - _____

factories

Trace the word.

factories

Spot and underline the word
factories.

hfgnfactoriesmoi

ffrfactoriessssdfp

bfhrefactoriesrfgj

gkbnffactoriessfer

obrnofactoriesjlkp

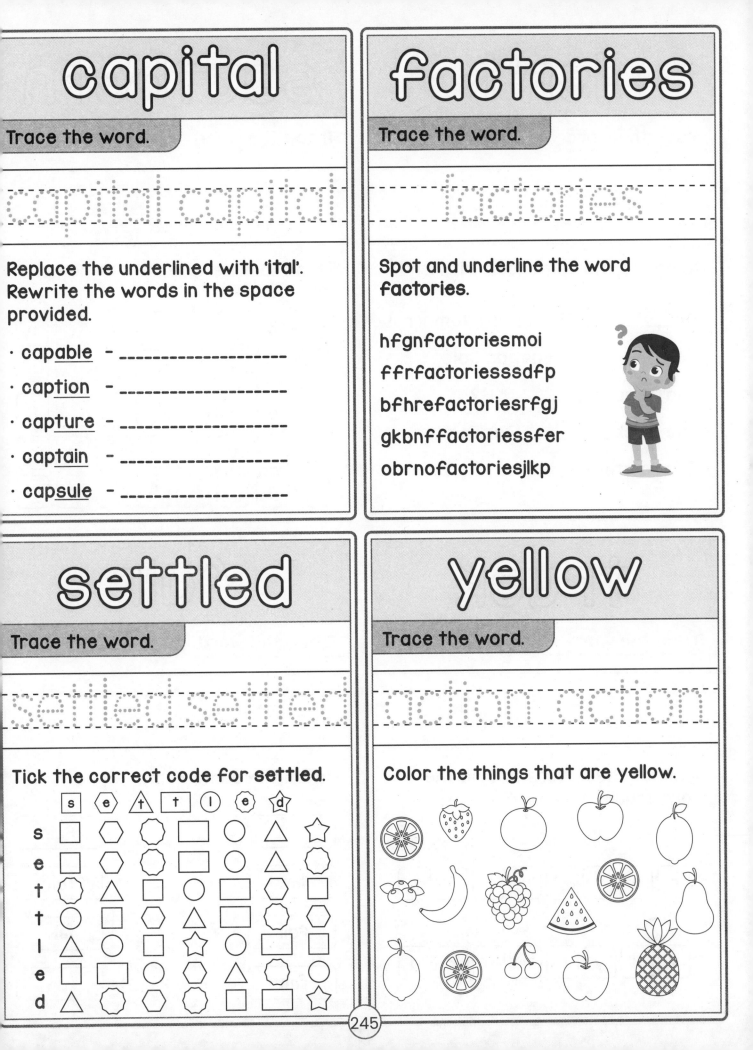

settled

Trace the word.

settled settled

Tick the correct code for settled.

	s	e	t	t	l	e	d
s							
e							
t							
t							
l							
e							
d							

yellow

Trace the word.

action action

Color the things that are yellow.

isn't

isn't isn't isn't

Complete the sentences with isn't.

· He _____ coming until tomorrow.

· He _____ as fast as Cole.

· That's good, _____ it?

· The clock _____ working.

· I am a student, but he _____

southern

southern

Fill in the missing letters to complete the spelling.

s	o			h	e		n
s		u	t			r	
	o		t		e		n
		u	t			r	n
	o			h		r	

truck

truck   truck

Connect the letters to find the word truck.

r	c	t	y	u	h	j	k

v	u	y	r	n	c	k	d

fair

fair fair fair

Match the same font.

fair	•	•	fair
fair	•	•	fair
fair	•	•	fair
fair	•	•	fair

printed

Trace the word.

printed

Circle the correct spelling of the word printed.

printted   printed

printed   prrinted

preented   prented

printeed   printed

wouldn't

Trace the word.

wouldn't

Fill in the blanks to complete the sentence.

· I _____ be able to come today.

· He _____ bring his laptop.

· _____ you like to join us?

· She _____ take her coat off.

· Charles _____ eat all that junk food.

ahead

Trace the word.

ahead ahead

How many times can you spot the word **ahead**? Count and write.

reel	state	ahead
speaks	ahead	unit
scale	ahead	fight

☐ times

chance

Trace the word.

chance

Find the word chance 3 times.

m	e	a	c	o	p	a	n	y	c
e	r	f	r	u	i	t	n	t	h
c	h	a	n	c	e	y	i	n	a
b	o	e	s	e	r	v	e	n	n
c	h	a	n	c	e	y	u	i	c
t	o	t	s	e	r	v	e	k	e

born

Trace the word.

born   born

Connect the letters to get the word born.

w b m u r k j k

i h k o i e n d

level

Trace the word.

level level level

Rank the letters in the correct order to get level. Write in correct order in the space provided.

l e v e l

1 4 2 5 3

☐ ☐ ☐ ☐ ☐

triangle

Trace the word.

triangle triangle

Fill in the boxes with correct letters to get the word triangle.

☐	i	a	☐	e
t	☐	a	n	l
r	i	☐	g	e
t	r	☐	n	g

molecules

Trace the word.

molecules

Draw a line to connect the letters to spell molecules. Then write it in the box.

m   e   u   e
              s

o   l   c   l

☐ ☐ ☐ ☐ ☐ ☐ ☐ ☐

France

Trace the word.

France France

Help Jim reach **France**. Color the stars to spell **France**.

f r a k

r s n c

o a x e

repeated

Trace the word.

repeated

Fill in the missing letters.

r	e		e		t		d
		p	e				d
r			e	a		e	
	e	p			t		d
r	e				t		

column

Trace the word.

column column

Circle the right letters to spell **column**.

· r, c, d, f, r, o, k, a, l, n, l, u, h, m, s, n

· c, c, o, e, l, h, l, u, c, k, m, h, n, e, o, s

· z, c, g, r, o, m, e, l, b, c, u, m, e, n, x

· c, n, b, r, q, l, o, s, l, o, u, l, j, m, w, n

western

Trace the word.

western

Strike off the underlined letters and replace with 'west' to form **western**.

· <u>con</u>cern _____

· <u>ea</u>stern _____

· <u>pat</u>tern _____

· <u>dis</u>cern _____

· <u>lan</u>tern _____

church

Trace the word.

church church

Help Max reach the church.

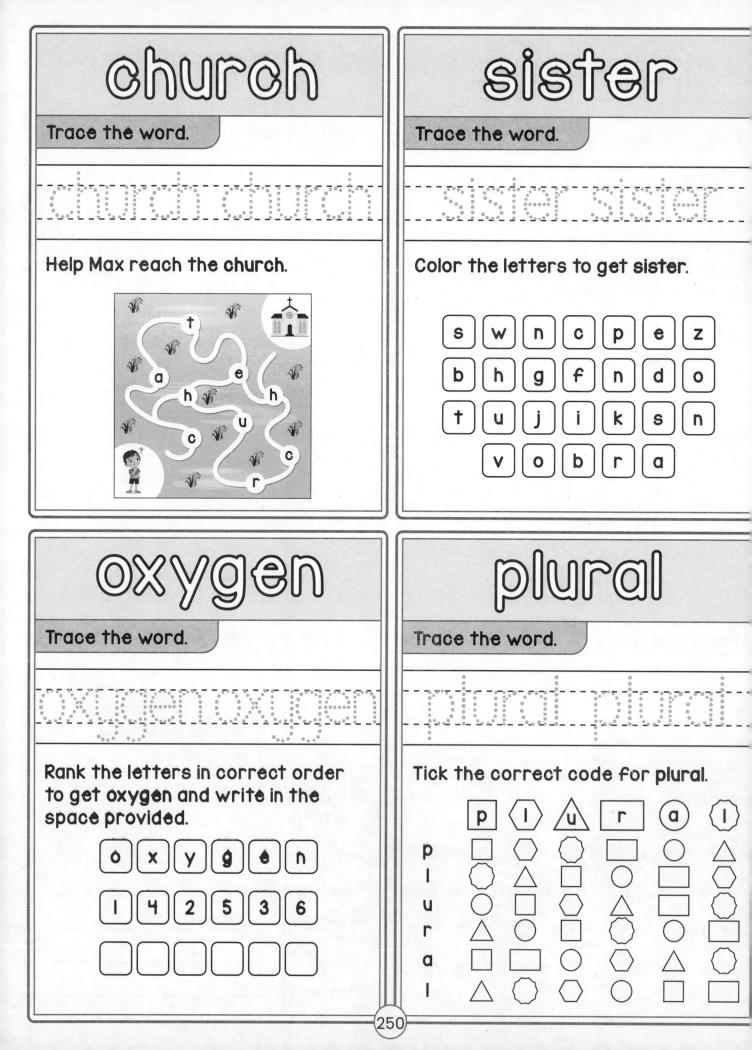

sister

Trace the word.

sister sister

Color the letters to get sister.

s	w	n	c	p	e	z
b	h	g	f	n	d	o
t	u	j	i	k	s	n
v	o	b	r	a		

oxygen

Trace the word.

oxygen oxygen

Rank the letters in correct order to get oxygen and write in the space provided.

o	x	y	g	e	n
1	4	2	5	3	6

plural

Trace the word.

plural plural

Tick the correct code for plural.

various

various various

Underline the word various in the following sentences.

- Briana stared at the various flavors of chips.
- There are various other options.
- Alex and I talked about various things.
- Steve collected various information.
- The gardener had tulips of various kinds.

agreed

Trace the word.

agreed agreed

Circle the correct spelling.

agreed	ugrid
agrid	agreed
agrhid	acred
agreed	agreed

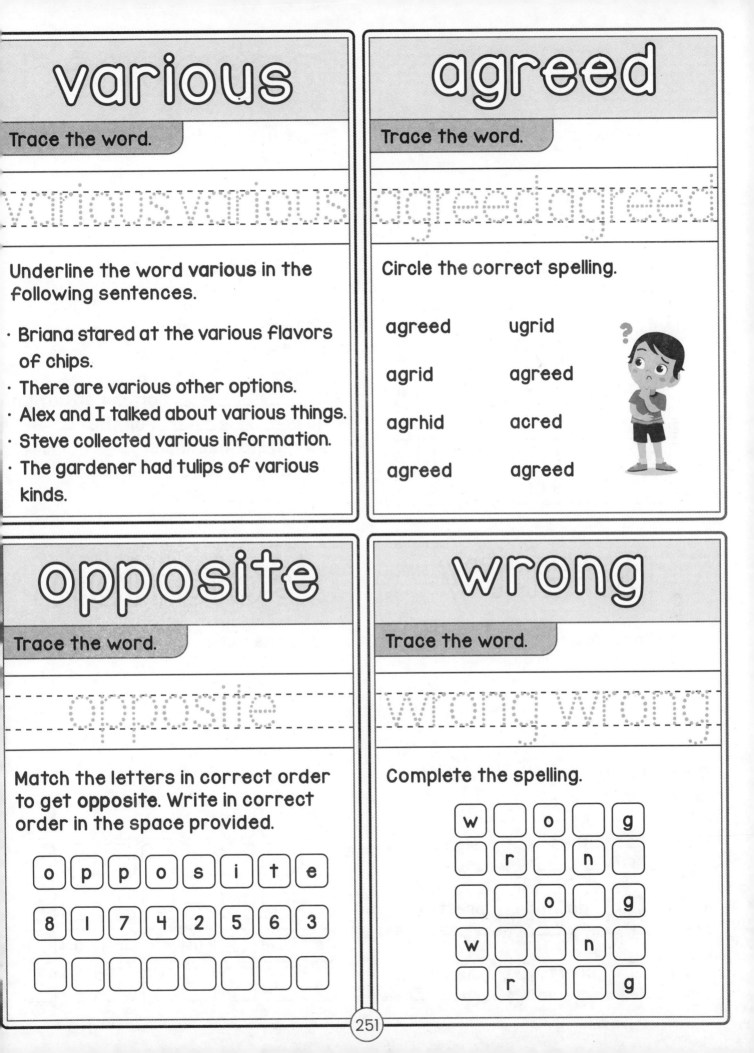

opposite

Trace the word.

opposite

Match the letters in correct order to get opposite. Write in correct order in the space provided.

o	p	p	o	s	i	t	e
8	1	7	4	2	5	6	3

wrong

Trace the word.

wrong wrong

Complete the spelling.

w		o		g
	r		n	
		o		g
w			n	
	r		g	

251

chart

Trace the word.

chartchartchart

Find the word **chart** 3 times in the grid.

m	e	a	c	o	p	a	n	y	c
e	r	f	r	u	i	t	n	t	h
c	h	a	r	t	e	y	i	n	a
b	o	e	s	e	r	v	e	n	r
c	h	a	r	t	e	y	u	i	t
t	o	t	s	e	r	v	e	k	e

prepared

Trace the word.

prepared

Fill in the blanks.

· The nurses _____ the patient for surgery.
· The teacher _____ the students for the test.
· I'm _____ for any situation.
· He is _____ for the swimming lessons.
· The store sells a selection of _____ foods.

pretty

Trace the word.

pretty   pretty

Color the objects with the word **pretty** on it.

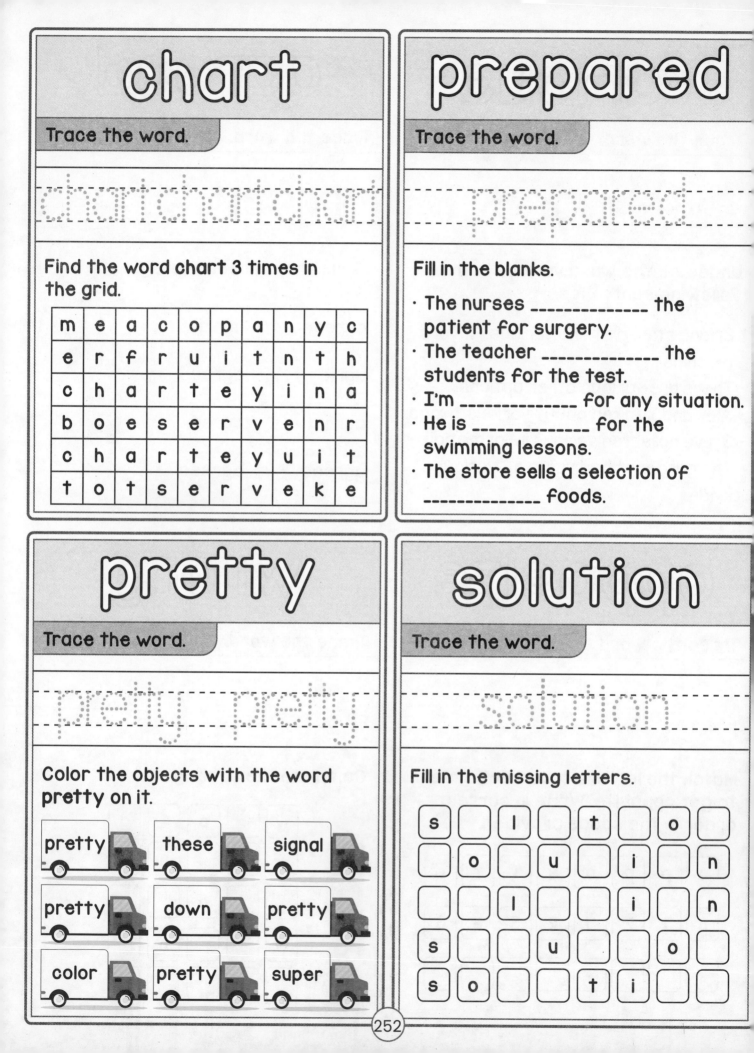

pretty   these   signal

pretty   down   pretty

color   pretty   super

solution

Trace the word.

solution

Fill in the missing letters.

s		l		t		o	
	o		u		i		n
		l				i		n
s			u			o	
s		o			t		i	

fresh

Trace the word.

fresh   fresh

Connect the letters to spell fresh.

| c | f | g | e | i | o | k | h |

| v | h | r | l | j | k | s | j |

shop

Trace the word.

shop shop shop

Tick the correct code for shop.

	s	h	o	p
	□	⬡	△	□
s	□	⬡	⬡	□
h	⬡	⬡	△	○
o	○	□	△	△
p	□	○	□	⬡

suffix

Trace the word.

suffix suffix

Spot and highlight the word suffix 3 times.

s	u	f	f	i	x	a	n	y	c
e	r	f	r	u	i	t	n	t	h
c	h	a	r	t	e	y	i	n	a
b	o	e	s	u	f	f	i	x	r
c	h	a	r	t	e	y	u	i	t
t	o	t	s	u	f	f	i	x	e

especially

Trace the word.

especially

Fill in the missing letters.

e		p		c		a		l	
e			e					l		y
		s			c	i				y
			p		c		a	l		
e			e			i		l	l	
			p		c		a	l		y

253

shoes

Trace the word.

shoes shoes

Color the boxes with correct spelling of shoes.

shoos

shooz

shoes

shoez

shows

shoes

shoes

shuz

actually

Trace the word.

actually

Replace the underlined letters to spell actually.

· <u>es</u>pecially _____

· <u>even</u>tually _____

· <u>origin</u>ally _____

· <u>person</u>ally _____

· <u>materi</u>ally _____

nose

Trace the word.

nosenosenose

Join the dots to spell nose. Spot the word 2 times.

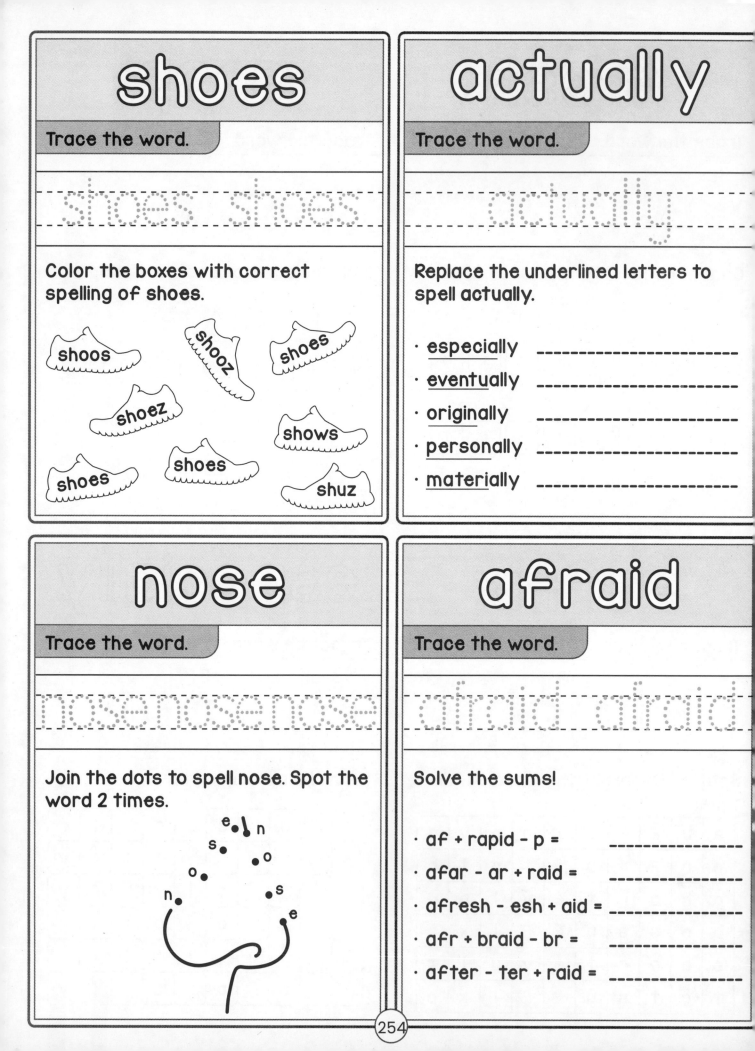

afraid

Trace the word.

afraid afraid

Solve the sums!

· af + rapid – p = _____

· afar – ar + raid = _____

· afresh – esh + aid = _____

· afr + braid – br = _____

· after – ter + raid = _____

254

dead

Trace the word.

dead dead

Read the given words and replace the underlined letters with 'd' to spell **dead**.

· <u>h</u>ead _____

· <u>l</u>ead _____

· <u>r</u>ead _____

· <u>b</u>ead _____

· <u>br</u>ead _____

sugar

Trace the word.

sugar sugar

Help the farmer reach the sugarcane fields. Color the path with letters that spell **sugar**.

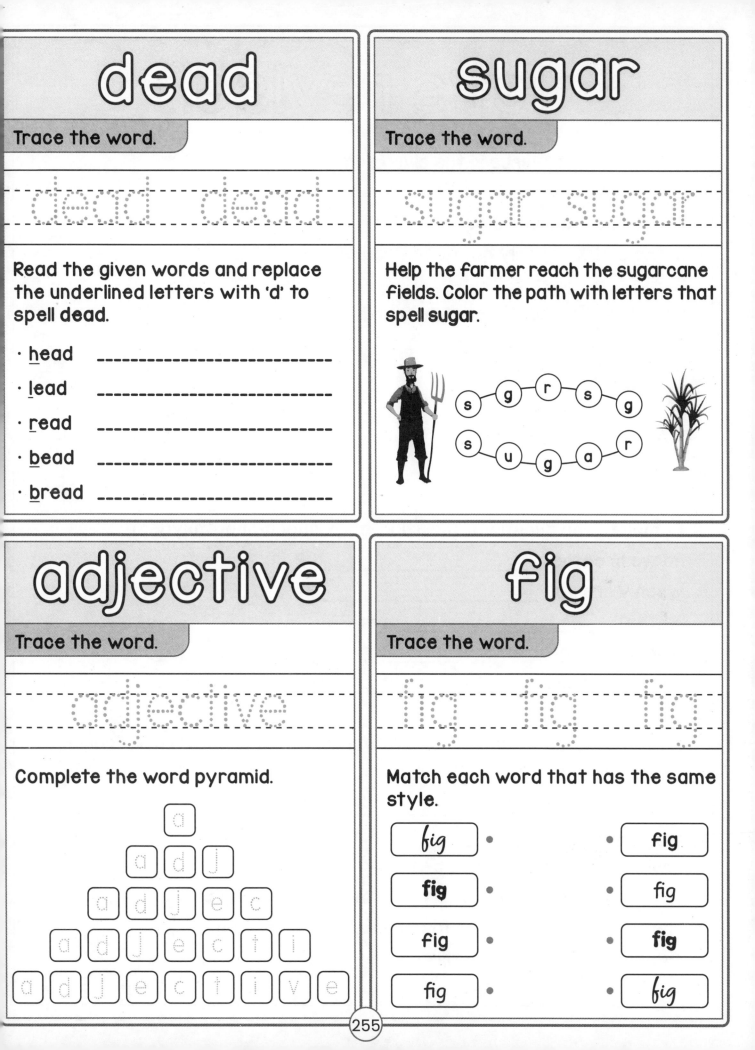

adjective

Trace the word.

adjective

Complete the word pyramid.

```
          a
       a  d  j
    a  d  j  e  c
 a  d  j  e  c  t  i
a  d  j  e  c  t  i  v  e
```

fig

Trace the word.

fig   fig   fig

Match each word that has the same style.

fig	·	·	fig
fig	·	·	fig
fig	·	·	**fig**
fig	·	·	*fig*

let's revise!

1. Underline the adverbs in the given sentences.

· I love animals, especially dogs.

· The road ahead was blocked.

· In the end, I actually got quite fond of him.

2. Fill in the blanks with the right words.

· _____ + ly = freshly

· _____ + ly = deadly

· _____ + ly = wrongly

· _____ + ly = sisterly

· _____ + ly = fairly

3. Complete the questions. (solution, born, sugar, shop, oxygen)

· Do we breathe in _____ ?

· When were you _____ ?

· Is the _____ open ?

· What is this problem's _____ ?

· Can I get some _____ with my tea?

4. Fill in the blanks with appropriate words. (pretty, level, truck, France, chart, agreed)

· She nearly got hit by a _____ today.

· She rose to the _____ of manager.

· How many times have you been to _____ ?

· The teacher showed the children how to create a pie _____.

· They _____ not to oppose her nomination.

· I feel _____ in this dress.

office

Trace the word.

office   office

How many times do you see the word **office**? Count and write.

believe OFFICE believe her
        the   this OFFICE
office office office
        his OFFICE office
office
her OFFICE this believe

☐ times

huge

Trace the word.

huge   huge

Spot and highlight the word **huge** 3 times.

s	u	f	h	u	g	e	n	y	c
e	r	f	r	u	i	t	n	t	h
c	h	u	g	e	e	y	i	n	u
b	o	e	s	u	f	f	i	x	g
c	h	a	r	t	e	y	u	i	e
t	o	t	s	u	f	f	i	x	e

gun

Trace the word.

gun gun gun

Color each object red that has the word **gun**. Color the rest of your choice.

gun   him   no   gun   go

go   gun   him   go   gun

gun   him   gun   go   gun

similar

Trace the word.

similar similar

Write the first letter of each picture and find the hidden word.

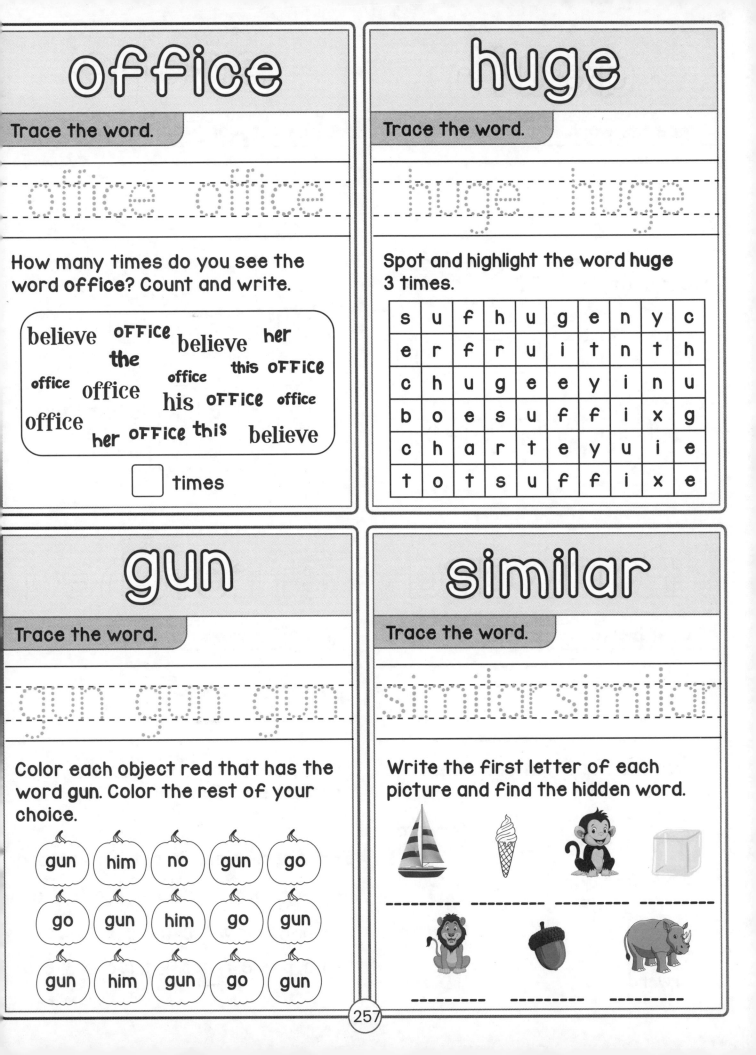

_____ _____ _____ _____

_____ _____ _____

death

Trace the word.

death death

Connect the letters to spell the word **death**.

d w p a r q t h

d e h a g t e g

score

Trace the word.

score score

Color in the letters to spell score.

a b c d e f g
h i j k l m n
o p q r s t u
v w x y z

forward

Trace the word.

forwardforward

Match the word that are same in style.

forward •   • forward

forward •   • forward

forward •   • **forward**

forward •   • forward

stretched

Trace the word.

stretched

Circle the letters that spell stretched in each set.

· s, z, t, r, w, e, q, e, s, t, c, l, h, e, o, d
· p, s, m, t, t, r, k, e, x, t, e, c, h, e, d
· s h, t, e, r, c, e, r, t, n, c, e, h, s, e, d
· t s, p, t, e, r, d, e, t, t, r, c, e, h, e, d

experience

Trace the word.

experience

Fill in the missing letters.

	x		e		i		n		e
e		p		r		e	c		
e	x			r			n		e
		p		e		e			e
	x	p				i		e	e
e				r			e	c	

rose

Trace the word.

rose   rose

Help the frog reach the pond. Color the leaves with the word **rose**.

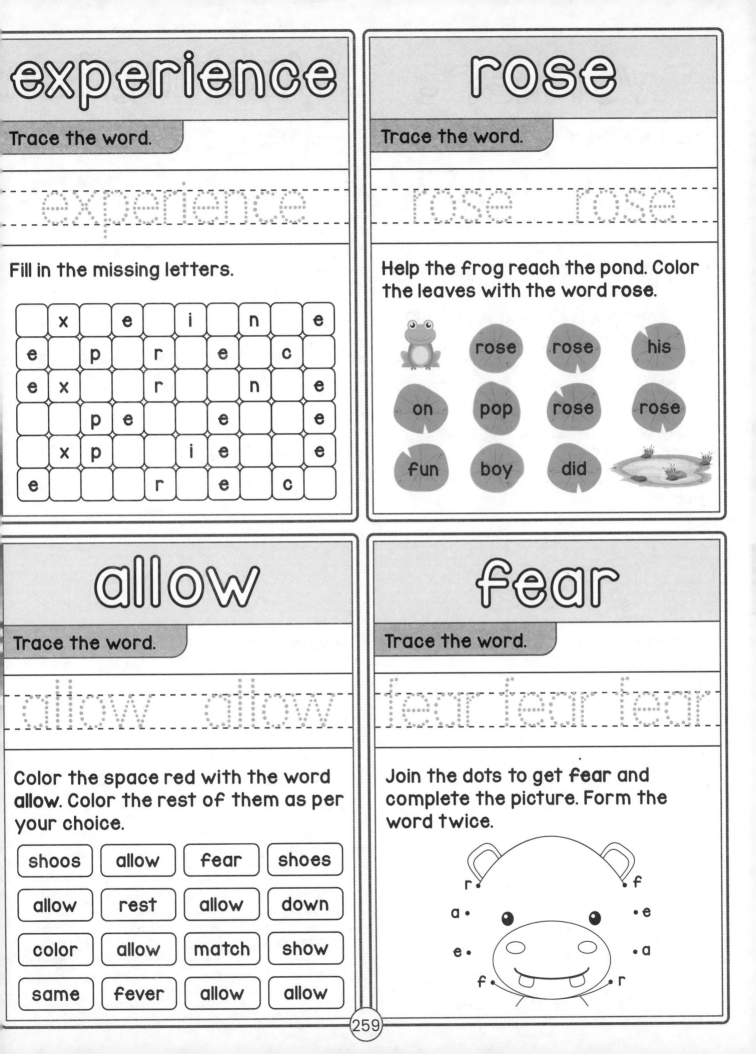

rose rose his

on pop rose rose

fun boy did

allow

Trace the word.

allow   allow

Color the space red with the word **allow**. Color the rest of them as per your choice.

shoos	allow	fear	shoes
allow	rest	allow	down
color	allow	match	show
same	fever	allow	allow

fear

Trace the word.

fear fear fear

Join the dots to get **fear** and complete the picture. Form the word twice.

r   f
a   e
e   a
f   r

workers

Trace the word.

workers

Fill in the missing letters to spell workers.

· The company is planning to hire 200 wo __ k __ r __.
· W __ r k __ r __ watered the forests.
· __ o __ k __ __ s set out to distribute products.
· Many w __ __ k __ r s were laid off at that plant.
· The poor __ o r __ e __ s began to protest.

Washington

Trace the word.

Washington

Connect the letters to spell Washington.

| w | v | s | s | n | i | t | s | n |

| d | a | h | i | h | g | t | o | n |

Greek

Trace the word.

Greek Greek

Spell the word Greek.

G

G   r

G   r   e

G   r   e   e

G   r   e   e   k

women

Trace the word.

women

How many times do you see the word women? Count and write.

women	state	slow
women	head	greek
scale	women	women

☐ times

bought

Trace the word.

bought bought

Fill in the blanks.

· She _____ a shirt for him to wear to the party.
· What was the first record you _____?
· He might have _____ it for cash.
· We _____ a lily and set it in a sunny window.
· A friend _____ me the candy.

led

Trace the word.

led led led

Color each space in the picture by sorting the right style with its color.

led	led – red
led	led – yellow
led	led – green
led	led – blue

march

Trace the word.

march march

Circle the initials to get march.

museum   apple   rattle

candle   hair

northern

Trace the word.

northern

Unscramble the word northern from the jumbled words. Color the correct letters.

r w k r
t n d o
e f s n d
p t

create

Trace the word.

create create

Rank the letters in correct order to get create.

c	r	e	a	t	e
1	4	2	5	3	6

British

Trace the word.

British British

Unscramble the word **British** from the jumbled words. Circle the right letters.

· r, s, b, d, f, r, o, i, a, l, n, t, i, m, s, h

· b, h, r, c, i, e, t, h, i, u, s, t, h, i, n, e

· s ,b, h, r, i, g, t, o, i, e, s, t, c, h, i, e, s

difficult

Trace the word.

difficult

Fill in the missing letters.

d			f	i			l
	i	f			c		l
		f	f			u	
d			f	i			t
	i			i		l	t
		f	i	c		l	

match

Trace the word.

match match

Color the letters to get match.

a	b	c	d	e	f	g
h	i	j	k	l	m	n
o	p	q	r	s	t	u
	v	w	x	y	z	

262

win

win win win

Find the word **win** 4 times in the given grid.

w	u	f	f	i	x	w	n	y	w
e	r	w	i	n	i	t	n	t	i
c	h	a	r	t	e	y	i	n	n
b	o	e	s	u	w	i	n	x	r
c	h	a	r	t	e	y	u	i	t
t	w	i	n	u	f	f	i	x	e

doesn't

Trace the word.

doesn't

Complete the sentences with **doesn't**.

· Does she eat eggs? No, she _____.
  _____ Tom like cheese?
· Does the baby walk? The baby
  _____ walk yet.
· How much time does it take? It
  _____ take very long.
· He _____ watch TV at all.

steel

Trace the word.

steel   steel

Circle the correct spelling of **steel**.

steel   stick

still   steel

stilk   silk

steel   stink

silt   steel

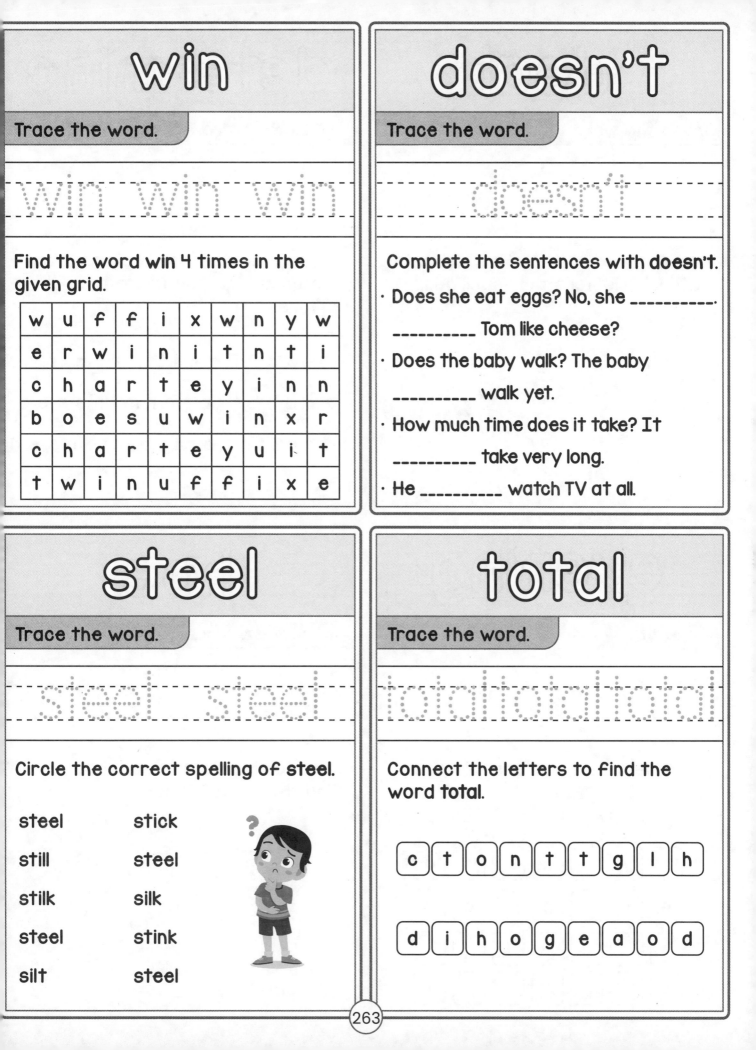

total

Trace the word.

total total total

Connect the letters to find the word **total**.

| c | t | o | n | t | t | g | l | h |

| d | i | h | o | g | e | a | o | d |

deal

Trace the word.

deal deal deal

Help Carl reach the school. Color the path with letters that spell **deal**.

determine

Trace the word.

determine

Unscramble the word column from the jumbled words. Circle the right letters.

· r, s, b, d, f, e, o, t, a, l, e, t r, i, m, i, n, h, e

· z, c, d, b, e, l, t, r, e, c, r, m, i, n, s, s, e, d

· d, r, e, l, t, r, e, o, r, l, j, m, w, m, i, n, s, e, d

evening

Trace the word.

evening

Fill in the missing letters to write the word **evening**.

e		e			n	g
	v		n			g
e			n		n	g
		e		i		
e			n		i	

hoe

Trace the word.

hoe hoe hoe

Connect the dots to spell **hoe**. Find the word 2 times.

rope

Trace the word.

rope rope rope

Color the 4 oranges that spell the word rope.

rope   saw   rope   day

rope   the   and   rope

cotton

Trace the word.

cotton cotton

Build the word cotton.

c   t   u   o   s

o   l   t   n

☐ ☐ ☐ ☐ ☐ ☐

apple

Trace the word.

apple apple

Color the shapes according to the codes of the word apple.

| a | p | p | l | e |

a					
p					
p					
l					
e					

details

Trace the word.

details details

Complete the spelling.

d			a	i	s
	e	t		i	s
d		t			s
		t	a		l
	e		a		l

entire

Trace the word.

entire entire

Complete the word pyramid.

```
      e
    e   n
  e   n   t
e   n   t   i
e   n   t   i   r
e   n   t   i   r   e
```

corn

Trace the word.

corn corn corn

How many times do you see the word corn? Count and write.

Corn corn believe corn
the office this corn
Corn office corn OFFICE Corn
office corn his corn believe

☐ times

substances

Trace the word.

substances

Complete the spelling by filling in the missing letters.

s		b		a		c		s
	u	b			a		e	s
s		s	t		n			s
	b	s			n	c		
s	u			t	a		c	s

smell

Trace the word.

smell smell

Draw a line and connect the letters to spell smell.

s   e

l   l   m

☐ ☐ ☐ ☐ ☐

tools

Trace the word.

tools   tools

Circle the initials to get **tools**.

tooth   ostrich   octopus

lemon   sandwich

conditions

Trace the word.

conditions

Join the letters to get **conditions** and write the word in the space provided.

c	n	i	i	n

o	d	t	o	s

cows

Trace the word.

cows   cows

Match the word with the one in the same style.

cows   •   •   cows

cows   •   •   cows

cows   •   •   **cows**

cows   •   •   *cows*

track

Trace the word.

track   track

Connect the dots to spell **track**. Find the word 2 times.

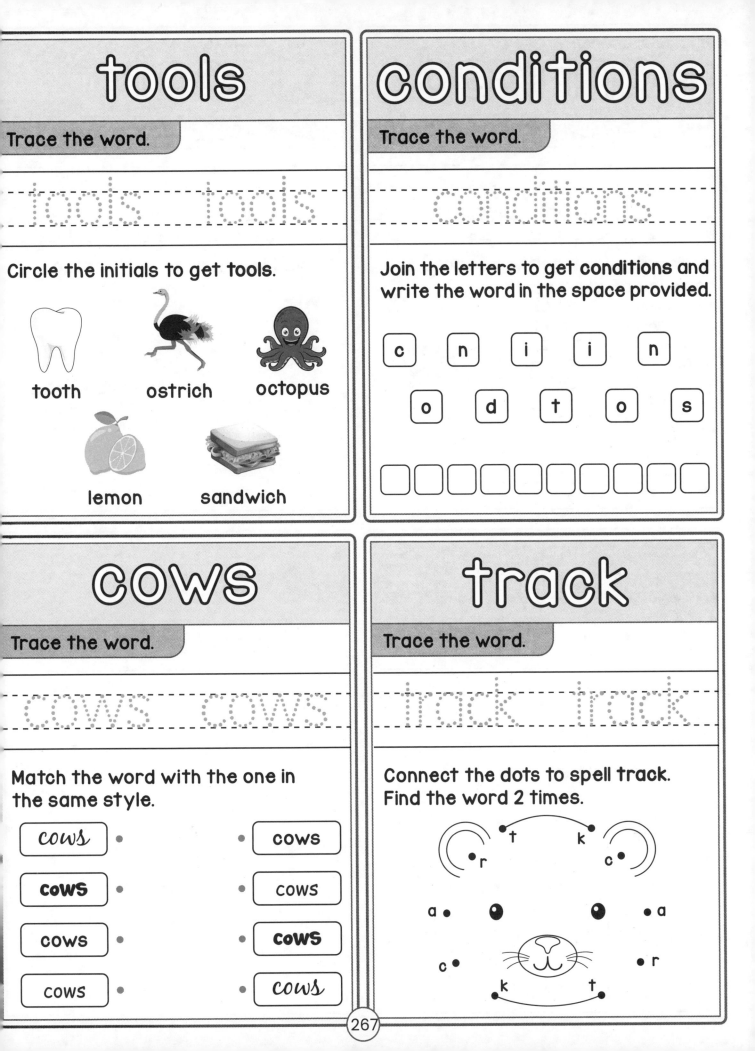

arrived

Trace the word.

arrived arrived

Color the boxes with the correct spelling of arrived.

arriveed	arived
arrived	arrived
araived	ariaved
arayved	arrived
arrived	arivved

located

Trace the word.

located

Circle the initials to get located.

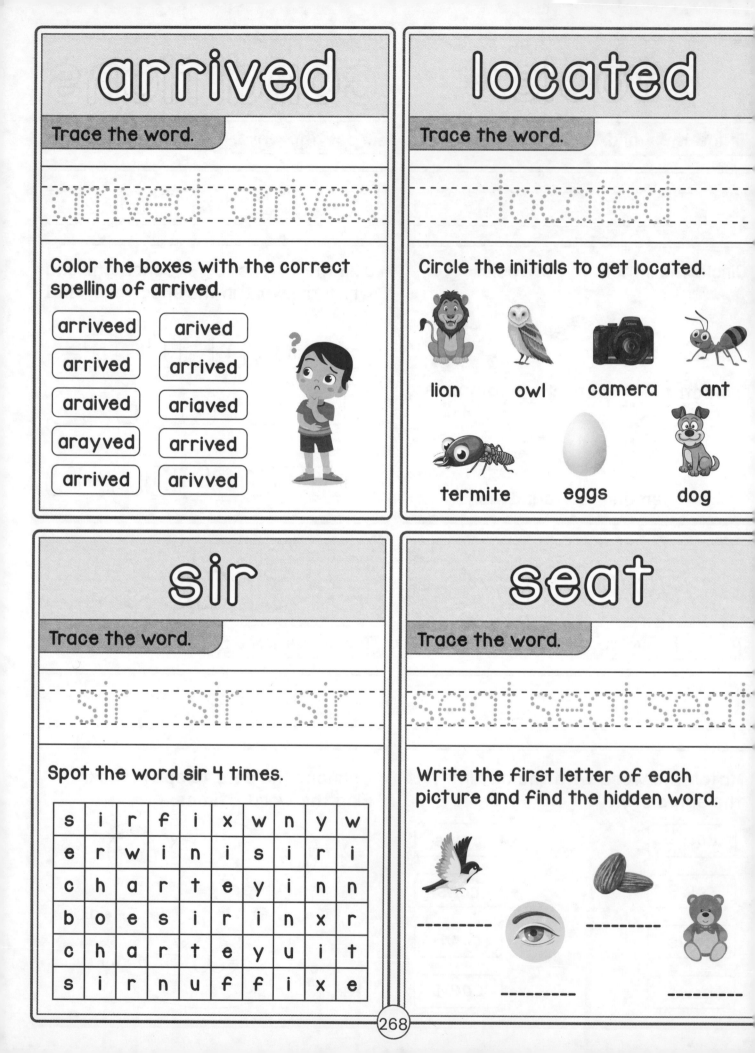

lion   owl   camera   ant

termite   eggs   dog

sir

Trace the word.

sir   sir   sir

Spot the word sir 4 times.

s	i	r	f	i	x	w	n	y	w
e	r	w	i	n	i	s	i	r	i
c	h	a	r	t	e	y	i	n	n
b	o	e	s	i	r	i	n	x	r
c	h	a	r	t	e	y	u	i	t
s	i	r	n	u	f	f	i	x	e

seat

Trace the word.

seat seat seat

Write the first letter of each picture and find the hidden word.

_____   _____

_____   _____

division

Trace the word.

division division

Underline the initials of the given words to get division.

duck   steam

iguana   interest

vendor   office

iguana   nation

effect

Trace the word.

effect effect

Spot the word effect 3 times.

s	i	r	f	i	x	w	n	y	e
e	f	f	e	c	t	s	i	r	f
c	h	a	r	t	e	y	i	n	f
b	o	e	s	i	r	i	n	x	e
c	e	f	f	e	c	t	u	i	c
s	i	r	n	u	f	f	i	x	t

underline

Trace the word.

underline

Fill in the missing letters.

	n	d	e		l		n	
		d	e			i	n	
u	n				l			e
	n			r	l			e
u			e	r	l			e

view

Trace the word.

view view

Identify the pictures and write the first letter of each to find the hidden word.

_____   _____   _____   _____

let's revise!

1. Fill in the missing form of the verbs.

base word	VI	V2	V3
arrive	arrive	_____	arrived
locate	locate	_____	located
create	_____	_____	created
buy	buy	_____	bought
stretch	stretch	_____	_____

2. Rearrange the words to form meaningful sentences.

· the/ made/ are/ of/ beams/ steel

· the/ all/ on/ the/ pillows/ couch/ match

----

3. Write the rhyming words. (win, rope, deal, fear, sir)

fur, her, _____

meal, heal, _____

hope, cope, _____

hear, dear, _____

tin, bin, _____

4. Find the words in the box. (allow, apple, cotton, create)

a	l	l	o	w	x	w	n	y	w
e	c	r	e	a	t	e	i	r	i
c	o	t	t	o	n	y	i	n	n
b	o	e	a	p	p	l	e	x	r
c	h	a	r	t	e	y	u	i	t

High-Frequency Words

1st 100 Words

the	or	will	number
of	one	up	no
and	had	other	way
a	by	about	could
to	words	out	people
in	but	many	my
is	not	then	than
you	what	them	first
that	all	these	water
it	were	so	been
he	we	some	called
was	when	her	who
for	your	would	am
on	can	make	its
are	said	like	now
as	there	him	find
with	use	into	long
his	an	time	down
they	each	has	day
I	which	look	did
at	she	two	get
be	do	more	come
this	how	write	made
have	their	go	may
from	if	see	part

2nd 100 Words

over	say	set	try
new	great	put	kind
sound	where	end	hand
take	help	does	picture
only	through	another	again
little	much	well	change
work	before	large	off
know	line	must	play
place	right	big	spell
years	too	even	air
live	means	such	away
me	old	because	animal
back	any	turn	house
give	same	here	point
most	tell	why	page
very	boy	ask	letter
after	follow	went	mother
things	came	men	answer
our	want	read	found
just	show	need	study
name	also	land	still
good	around	different	learn
sentence	form	home	should
man	three	us	America
think	small	move	world

3rd 100 Words

high	saw	important	miss
every	left	until	idea
near	don't	children	enough
add	few	side	eat
food	while	feet	face
between	along	car	watch
own	might	mile	far
below	close	night	Indian
country	something	walk	real
plant	seem	white	almost
last	next	sea	let
school	hard	began	above
father	open	grow	girl
keep	example	took	sometimes
tree	begin	river	mountains
never	life	four	cut
start	always	carry	young
city	those	state	talk
earth	both	once	soon
eyes	paper	book	list
light	together	hear	song
thought	got	stop	being
head	group	without	leave
under	often	second	family
story	run	late	it's

273

4th 100 Words

body	order	listen	farm
music	red	wind	pulled
color	door	rock	draw
stand	sure	space	voice
sun	become	covered	seen
questions	top	fast	cold
fish	ship	several	cried
area	across	hold	plan
mark	today	himself	notice
dog	during	toward	south
horse	short	five	sing
birds	better	step	war
problem	best	morning	ground
complete	however	passed	fall
room	low	vowel	king
knew	hours	TRUE	town
since	black	hundred	I'll
ever	products	against	unit
piece	happened	pattern	figure
told	whole	numeral	certain
usually	measure	table	field
didn't	remember	north	travel
friends	early	slowly	wood
easy	waves	money	fire
heard	reached	map	upon

5th 100 Words

done	decided	plane	filled
English	contain	system	heat
road	course	behind	full
half	surface	ran	hot
ten	produce	round	check
fly	building	boat	object
gave	ocean	game	am
box	class	force	rule
finally	note	brought	among
wait	nothing	understand	noun
correct	rest	warm	power
oh	carefully	common	cannot
quickly	scientists	bring	able
person	inside	explain	six
became	wheels	dry	size
shown	stay	though	dark
minutes	green	language	ball
strong	known	shape	material
verb	island	deep	special
stars	week	thousands	heavy
front	less	yes	fine
feel	machine	clear	pair
fact	base	equation	circle
inches	ago	yet	include
street	stood	government	built

6th 100 Words

can't	picked	legs	beside
matter	simple	sat	gone
square	cells	main	sky
syllables	paint	winter	grass
perhaps	mind	wide	million
bill	love	written	west
felt	cause	length	lay
suddenly	rain	reason	weather
test	exercise	kept	root
direction	eggs	interest	instruments
center	train	arms	meet
farmers	blue	brother	third
ready	wish	race	months
anything	drop	present	paragraph
divided	developed	beautiful	raised
general	window	store	represent
energy	difference	job	soft
subject	distance	edge	whether
Europe	heart	past	clothes
moon	site	sign	flowers
region	sum	record	shall
return	summer	finished	teacher
believe	wall	discovered	held
dance	forest	wild	describe
members	probably	happy	drive

7th 100 Words

cross	already	hair	rolled
speak	instead	age	bear
solve	phrase	amount	wonder
appear	soil	scale	smiled
metal	bed	pounds	angle
son	copy	although	fraction
either	free	per	Africa
ice	hope	broken	killed
sleep	spring	moment	melody
village	case	tiny	bottom
factors	laughed	possible	trip
result	nation	gold	hole
jumped	quite	milk	poor
snow	type	quiet	let's
ride	themselves	natural	fight
care	temperature	lot	surprise
floor	bright	stone	French
hill	lead	act	died
pushed	everyone	build	beat
baby	method	middle	exactly
buy	section	speed	remain
century	lake	count	dress
outside	iron	consonant	cat
everything	within	someone	couldn't
tall	dictionary	sail	fingers

8th 100 Words

row	president	yourself	caught
least	brown	control	fell
catch	trouble	practice	team
climbed	cool	report	God
wrote	cloud	straight	captain
shouted	lost	rise	direct
continued	sent	statement	ring
itself	symbols	stick	serve
else	wear	party	child
plains	bad	seeds	desert
gas	save	suppose	increase
England	experiment	woman	history
burning	engine	coast	cost
design	alone	bank	maybe
joined	drawing	period	business
foot	east	wire	separate
law	choose	pay	break
ears	single	clean	uncle
glass	touch	visit	hunting
you're	information	bit	flow
grew	express	whose	lady
skin	mouth	received	students
valley	yard	garden	human
cents	equal	please	art
key	decimal	strange	feeling

9th 100 Words

supply	guess	thick	major
corner	silent	blood	observe
electric	trade	lie	tube
insects	rather	spot	necessary
crops	compare	bell	weight
tone	crowd	fun	meat
hit	poem	loud	lifted
sand	enjoy	consider	process
doctor	elements	suggested	army
provide	indicate	thin	hat
thus	except	position	property
won't	expect	entered	particular
cook	flat	fruit	swim
bones	seven	tied	terms
mall	interesting	rich	current
board	sense	dollars	park
modern	string	send	sell
compound	blow	sight	shoulder
mine	famous	chief	industry
wasn't	value	Japanese	wash
fit	wings	stream	block
addition	movement	planets	spread
belong	pole	rhythm	cattle
safe	exciting	eight	wife
soldiers	branches	science	sharp

10th 100 Words

company	sister	gun	total
radio	oxygen	similar	deal
we'll	plural	death	determine
action	various	score	evening
capital	agreed	forward	hoe
factories	opposite	stretched	rope
settled	wrong	experience	cotton
yellow	chart	rose	apple
isn't	prepared	allow	details
southern	pretty	fear	entire
truck	solution	workers	corn
fair	fresh	Washington	substances
printed	shop	Greek	smell
wouldn't	suffix	women	tools
ahead	especially	bought	conditions
chance	shoes	led	cows
born	actually	march	track
level	nose	northern	arrived
triangle	afraid	create	located
molecules	dead	British	sir
France	sugar	difficult	seat
repeated	adjective	match	division
column	fig	win	effect
western	office	doesn't	underline
church	huge	steel	view